Green Mountain Club

The Walker's Guide to Vermont

*Rambles for Half an Hour
or Half a Day*

First Edition

Green Mountain Club
Waterbury Center, Vermont 05677

Green Mountain Club, Inc.
4711 Waterbury-Stowe Road
Waterbury Center VT 05677
802-244-7037
www.greenmountainclub.org

Information in this guide is based on the best efforts of the publisher,
using information available at the time of printing. Changes resulting
from maintenance, relocations, natural disturbance, etc. occur over time.
Use of this guide is at the sole risk of the user.

Book design by Sylvie Vidrine

Edited by Mary Lou Recor

Maps compiled by Angus McCusker

Back cover photo: Jeb Wallace-Brodeur

First Edition
2009
ISBN 978-1-888021-27-1

Contributors

Robynn Albert, Dick Andrews, Susan Gail Arey, Dave Blumenthal, Mark Bushnell, Bill Clark, Marge Fish, Cindy Gray, Dave Hardy, Phil Hazen, Lynda Hutchins, Russ Kinaman, Matt Larson, Steve Larose, Local Motion, Tim Marr, Dot Myer, Louanne Nielsen, Luke O'Brien, Rutland Area Physical Activity Coalition (RAPAC), Mary Lou Recor, Ben Rose, James Sardonis, Eric Scharnberg, Sue Shea, Sue Thomas, Sylvie Vidrine, Jeb Wallace-Brodeur, Kathy Williams, Kevin Williamson, Winooski Valley Park District.

Walking along the trails of the Missisquoi National Wildlife Refuge.

Table of Contents

Using This Guide

The Six Regions

The state of Vermont has been divided into six regions, roughly from west to east by Vt. 100 and from north to south by U.S. 4 and U.S. 2. In a few instances, trails are included in neighboring regions for geographic reasons; however, this happens rarely. The six regions are:

- Region 1: Southwest
- Region 2: Southeast
- Region 3: West Central
- Region 4: East Central
- Region 5: Northwest
- Region 6: Northeast

Region Components

Each region has three components:

1. Region Map

The region map shows trail locations. It is meant as a quick reference, not as an exact locator.

2. Map Locator Key

The map locator key lists the trails on the region maps and the page numbers where they are found in the guide.

3. Trail Descriptions and Maps

Within each region, trails are grouped north to south. Some trails are only described and not depicted on a map.

Trails are described from trailhead to destination or terminus. The one-way distance is given for most trails. Loops are indicated. The elevation gains are not given because most are minimal. Exceptions are noted.

The scales of the maps vary as shown on each map. The contour interval is 50 feet. Trails are shown as dashed lines. In Vermont, the compass points about 15 degrees west of true north.

Abbreviations

FR   Forest Road
ft.   feet
mi.   mile(s)
yds.   yards

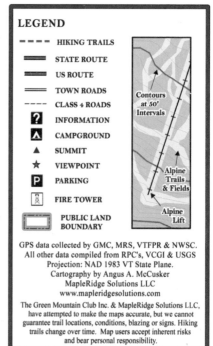

LEGEND

- - - -   HIKING TRAILS
━━━   STATE ROUTE
━━━   US ROUTE
═══   TOWN ROADS
- - - -   CLASS 4 ROADS
?   INFORMATION
△   CAMPGROUND
▲   SUMMIT
★   VIEWPOINT
P   PARKING
🗼   FIRE TOWER
▭   PUBLIC LAND BOUNDARY

Contours at 50' Intervals

Alpine Trails & Fields

Alpine Lift

GPS data collected by GMC, MRS, VTFPR & NWSC. All other data compiled from RPC's, VCGI & USGS Projection: NAD 1983 VT State Plane. Cartography by Angus A. McCusker MapleRidge Solutions LLC www.mapleridgesolutions.com

The Green Mountain Club Inc. & MapleRidge Solutions LLC, have attempted to make the maps accurate, but we cannot guarantee trail locations, conditions, blazing or signs. Hiking trails change over time. Map users accept inherent risks and bear personal responsibility.

Green Mountain Club

Membership and Volunteers

Membership in the GMC is an important way to support outdoor opportunities in Vermont and is open to anyone with an interest in the outdoors and the preservation of Vermont's backcountry. Annual membership dues support trail maintenance, trail protection, education and publications.

Anyone wishing to participate in outings and organized trail maintenance may join a GMC section. Sections provide four-season schedules of outings, including hiking, biking, cross-country skiing and canoeing. They also maintain portions of the Long Trail and its shelters. The club offers an at-large membership for anyone who wishes to support the work of the GMC but does not want to affiliate with a local section. Both section and at-large members enjoy the same benefits including a subscription to the club's quarterly newsletter, the *Long Trail News*, which provides information on trail and shelter conditions, hiking, statewide trails, club history and club activities. Members receive discounts on club publications and items carried in the GMC bookstore, reduced fees at some overnight sites served by GMC caretakers, opportunities to participate in a wide range of club activities and discounts on admission to most GMC events. Section members also receive their section's newsletter and activity schedule.

There are fourteen GMC sections. Twelve are based in Vermont: Bennington, Brattleboro, Bread Loaf (Middlebury), Burlington, Killington (Rutland), Laraway (Northwestern Vermont), Manchester, Montpelier, Northeast Kingdom, Northern Frontier (Montgomery), Ottauquechee (Woodstock), and Sterling (Stowe-Morrisville). Two sections are based out of state: Connecticut and Worcester (eastern Massachusetts).

To join the GMC, send payment for dues ($40 individual, $50 family, $22 student/volunteer/limited income) to the Green Mountain Club, 4711 Waterbury-Stowe Road, Waterbury Center, Vermont 05677 or call the GMC with your VISA or MasterCard number at (802) 244-7037. Memberships can also be purchased online at www.greenmountainclub.org.

Headquarters

The Green Mountain Club headquarters are on Vt. 100 in Waterbury Center, Vermont, midway between Waterbury and Stowe. From I-89 in Waterbury (exit 10), take Vt. 100 north four miles and turn left on Cabin Lane, which leads into the GMC parking lot. From the intersection of Vt. 108 and Vt. 100 in Stowe, the GMC is six miles south on Vt. 100.

The Visitor Center is open seven days a week (10:00 a.m. to 5:00 p.m.) from Memorial Day to Columbus Day and Monday through Friday from 10:00 a.m. to 5:00 p.m. year-round. Hikers are encouraged to stop by the center for trail information.

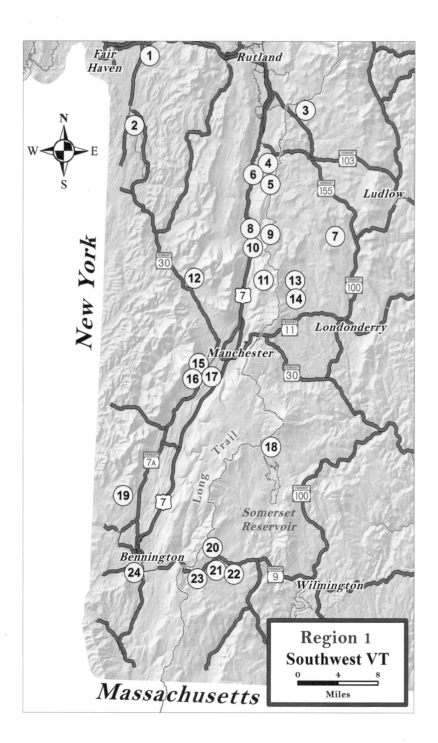

Fair Haven

Rutland

N W E S

New York

3

VERMONT 103

VERMONT 155

Ludlow

4

6 5

7

8 9

10

VERMONT 30

12

11

13

14

VERMONT 100

7

VERMONT 11

Londonderry

Manchester

15

16 17

VERMONT 30

Trail

18

VERMONT 100

Somerset Reservoir

Long

VERMONT 7A

7

19

Bennington

24

20

23 21 22

VERMONT 9

Wilmington

Massachusetts

Region 1
Southwest VT

0   4   8

Miles

1

2

7

Region 1
Southwest Vermont

❶ Delaware and Hudson Rail Trail

Comprised of two discontinuous but nearly equal lengths of converted road-bed, the Delaware and Hudson Rail Trail follows the Vermont portion of a rail route that once connected the slate-producing regions near Rutland with Albany, New York. As it passes through the dairy farms, meadows, forests, wetlands and rural communities of western Rutland and Bennington Counties, it crosses seventeen bridges and overpasses, including two railroad bridges nearly 100 ft. long in Poultney and West Pawlet. This 19.8-mi. multi-use trail is owned by the Vermont Transportation Agency and maintained by the Department of Forests, Parks and Recreation.

To the Trail: The northern segment of the trail runs from Castleton to Poultney. Parking is available at Castleton State College on Vt. 4A, and the trail can be accessed immediately west on South Street. The trail follows a southerly course and eventually reaches a southern access for the northern segment in Poultney just east of the junction of Vt. 30, Vt. 31 and Vt. 140.

The northern end of the southern segment of the trail is several miles south in the village of West Pawlet on Vt. 153. The trail continues south, at first following the Indian River, before arriving at the village of Rupert. Here the trail bears west and reaches a terminus in West Rupert on Vt. 153, where very limited parking is available.

The trail leaves Vermont to enter New York in three places. Since the New York sections of the trail have not been developed for recreational use, and in some cases ownership of the rail bed has reverted to adjacent private landowners, passage over these portions of the old roadbed is not assured.

❷ Lake St. Catherine State Park

Lake St. Catherine State Park occupies 117 acres on the east shore of Lake St. Catherine. Formerly the site of a slate quarry, the remains of old slate mills and their rubble piles are still visible. The park includes camping facilities and a day-use area with a beach. A fee is charged in season.

To the Trail: The park entrance is 3.0 mi. south of Poultney on the west side of Vt. 30.

Description: A brochure is available at the park contact station describing the 1.0-mi. Big Trees Nature Trail loop, which ascends gently to a low ridge in old pasture land. The trail passes a series of labeled trees, many rare for their exceptional size, before ending at the site of an old farmstead. From this point, a hiking trail continues west to the lake, where a spur leads to the swimming area. The hiking loop then turns east and passes the park campground before returning to the contact station.

Old Plymouth Road

Old Plymouth Road once connected the towns of Shrewsbury and Plymouth and is known as Plymsbury in the Calvin Coolidge State Forest. The wide roadbed is popular with snowmobilers.

To the Trail: At the intersection of Cold River Road and North Shrewsbury Road, turn north on CCC Road by Pierce's Store. Take the first right on Old Plymouth Road and follow it to the top of the hill where there is a parking lot and trail kiosk.

Description: The route follows the old roadbed east along Great Roaring Brook toward Plymouth Union. Numerous side trails and woods roads cross the main trail, but none are well marked.

Ice Beds Trail

The Ice Beds, which lie within a rock slide, melt slowly throughout the summer, keeping the surrounding air cool even on the warmest days.

Distance: 0.9 mi.

To the Trail: From Wallingford, follow Vt. 140 east 2.3 mi. to Sugar Hill Road and turn south for 0.1 mi. Turn right on FR 52 and follow it 0.6 mi. to the White Rocks Picnic Area and parking.

Description: The blue-blazed trail to the Ice Beds leaves the southwest corner of the parking area, crosses a stream and switchbacks to a junction at 0.2 mi.

> **Junction:** The spur trail left leads to the Parapet and a view of the White Rocks Cliff.

From the junction, the main trail continues past several viewpoints, then descends to an old woods road (0.6 mi.). Bearing left on the road, it crosses a stream, then a smaller stream, which it follows uphill to its source in the Ice Beds at the base of a rock slide (0.8 mi.). The ice often lasts late into summer.

Ice Beds Road

Distance: 1.2 mi.

To the Trail: From Wallingford, follow U.S. 7 south 1.8 mi. to Hartsboro Road. Turn left and follow Hartsboro Road 1.0 mi. to a Y-junction. Bear left on Ice Beds Road and follow it 0.4 mi. to a small parking area on the left. **Alternate trailhead:** Parking for the eastern end of Ice Beds Road is at the White Rocks Picnic Area. For directions, see "To the Trail" for the Ice Beds Trail. The route begins 0.2 mi. back down FR 52 at the unmarked eastern end of Ice Beds Road.

Description: The walk follows the route of the former Ice Beds Road, which is no longer passable by cars. The road may be used by four-wheel drive vehicles.

⑥ Wallingford Pond

Distance: 0.8 mi.

To the Trail: From the intersection of U.S. 7 and Vt. 140 in Wallingford, follow Vt. 140 east 2.3 mi. Bear right on Sugar Hill Road and follow it 1.7 mi. to FR 20 and turn right. The trailhead is 2.3 mi. down FR 20 and marked with a sign.

Description: The trail begins behind the trailhead sign and follows an old woods road 0.8 mi. to the shore of Wallingford Pond.

⑦ Greendale Trail

This 4.0-mi, loop travels through a mixed forest along gravel roads and trails.

To the Trail: In Weston, take Vt. 100 north 2.0 mi. Turn left on FR 18, also known as Greendale Road. Follow it 3.0 mi. to the campground. The road ends a half mile beyond the campground. Limited parking is available at the end of the road. The trail is straight ahead over an unused concrete bridge.

Description: The trail, which is also a cross-country ski trail, crosses Greendale Brook and follows blue blazes along the brook. It climbs a moderately steep grade for the next mile. At a junction with an old road, and now called the Jenny Coolidge Trail, the trail turns left to follow FR 17 for 2.0 mi., crossing Jenny Coolidge Brook, back to Greendale Road/FR 18. The route turns left on Greendale Road to return to the campground.

⑧ Little Rock Pond

Beautiful, chilly Little Rock Pond on the Long Trail is a popular spot for swimming, fishing and camping. The Long Trail/Appalachian Trail gains only 324 ft. in elevation from FR 10 to the south end of the pond.

Distance: 2.0 mi.

To the Trail: From U.S. 7 in Danby, follow FR 10 east 3.4 mi. to the Long Trail/Appalachian Trail crossing and a small parking area.

Description: From the parking area, the white-blazed Long Trail heads north on an old woods road and crosses an I-beam bridge over Little Black Branch (0.8 mi.). It continues on a slight uphill grade, passing a spur to Lula Tye Shelter at 1.9 mi. At 2.0 mi., the Long Trail reaches the south end of Little Rock Pond.

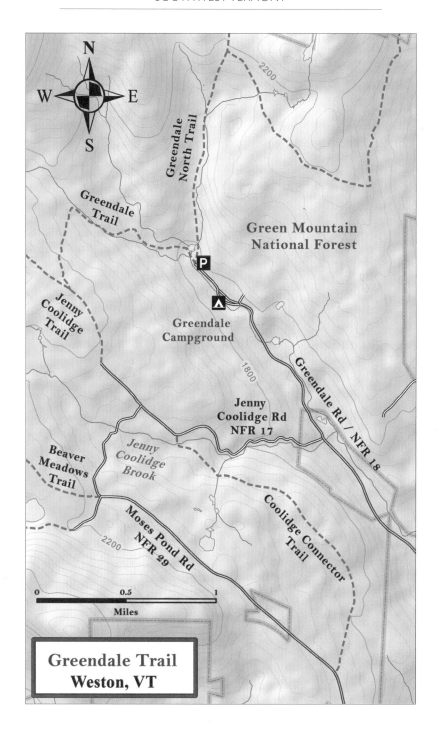

Green Mountain
National Forest

Greendale North Trail

Greendale Trail

Jenny Coolidge Trail

Greendale Campground

Greendale Rd / NFR 18

Jenny Coolidge Rd NFR 17

Jenny Coolidge Brook

Beaver Meadows Trail

Moses Pond Rd NFR 29

Coolidge Connector Trail

0   0.5   1
Miles

Greendale Trail
Weston, VT

Little Rock Pond Loop Trail

Distance: 0.8 mi. loop

To the Trail: Follow the directions to Little Rock Pond.

Description: From the south end of Little Rock Pond, the loop trail bears left and follows the west shoreline. It climbs away from the shoreline and passes above the ledges to intersect the Green Mountain Trail (0.4 mi.). Bearing right, the Green Mountain Trail leads to the Long Trail at the north end of the pond. From the junction, the Long Trail leads south 0.3 mi. back to the south end of the pond (0.8 mi.).

⑨ Big Branch Trail

This U.S. Forest Service trail descends to the Big Branch River from the Big Branch Picnic Area in the Green Mountain National Forest. Many dramatic views of the river may be seen from an adjoining trail.

To the Trail: From U.S. 7 in the village of Danby, turn on Brooklyn Street. Cross the railroad tracks and continue on the paved Mount Tabor Road/FR 10 (seasonal) through the village of Mount Tabor to the signed Big Branch parking area (2.6 mi.) on the south side of the road.

JEB WALLACE-BRODEUR

A view of Little Rock Pond.

Description: The picnic area provides a good vantage point high above the Big Branch River with a broad southwestern view of the Otter Creek Valley and Dorset's peaks. At a break near the center of a split-rail fence, the Big Branch Trail begins a steep descent via switchbacks to the boulder-filled river (0.2 mi.). At the river's edge, narrow trails proceed in both directions, giving impressive views of the rushing water and gargantuan boulders in the riverbed.

Big Branch Shelter

This stretch of the Long Trail south of FR 10 is a pleasant woods walk with little elevation gain or loss.

Distance: 1.1 mi.

To the Trail: From U.S. 7 in Danby, turn east on Brooklyn Street. Cross the railroad tracks and continue on the paved FR 10 east 3.4 mi. to the Long Trail/Appalachian Trail crossing and a small parking area.

Description: From the parking area, the Long Trail descends gradually south, entering the Big Branch Wilderness. It turns upstream at Big Branch and follows it a short distance to the shelter (1.1 mi.).

Griffith Lake Trail

Distance: 2.0 mi.

To the Trail: From Vt. 11 in Peru (0.0 mi.), turn north on Hapgood Pond Road, follow it 1.0 mi. and bear left on FR 22 (North Road). After 0.5 mi. (1.5 mi.), turn left on FR 21 (Mad Tom Notch Road) and follow it 2.0 mi. to FR 58. Turn right and continue to a gate at the end of the road where there is a parking area.

Description: The Griffith Lake Trail, which was once a carriage road, leaves the end of the parking lot and passes a beaver pond at 0.5 mi. It continues with little elevation gain and ends on the north shore of Griffith Lake at a junction with the Long Trail.

⑫ Emerald Lake State Park

The 430-acre Emerald Lake State Park encircles Emerald Lake, the headwaters of Otter Creek, which flows north through the Valley of Vermont on a 100-mi. journey to Ferrisburg and Lake Champlain. The park offers swimming, fishing, motorless boating and camping. In addition to the Vista Trail, several shorter trails are shown on a trail map of the park, available without charge at the contact station.

To the Trail: Emerald Lake State Park is on the west side of U.S. 7 in North Dorset, on the flank of Dorset Mountain.

Rainbow Pool along the Big Branch Trail

Description: The blue-blazed Vista Trail begins at a sign on the park access road, 200 ft. east of the contact station. From the trailhead, the trail heads easterly to cross the railroad tracks under the U.S. 7 highway bridge, then turns south and climbs through the woods to ledges above the highway (0.6 mi.) where there is a good view of Emerald Lake and Netop Mountain. The trail continues along the ledge, descending gradually to recross U.S. 7 and re-enter the park at the south end of Emerald Lake. Continuing near the shore through a marshy area, the Vista Trail continues around the west side of the lake and ends at the park beach (1.0 mi.), a short distance from the contact station.

⑬ Mountain Valley Trails Association

These trails in the town of Peru are maintained for cross-country skiing by a local group in the Londonderry area. During the non-winter months, they make for excellent walking through mixed hardwoods. The walks described here are just two of many possibilities.

To the Trails: From the intersection of Vt. 11 and Vt. 100 in Londonderry (0.0 mi.), follow Vt. 11 west to Reilly Road and turn right (1.7 mi.). Follow Reilly Road to its end and turn left on Landgrove Road (3.4 mi.). Follow Landgrove Road 1.5 mi. to FR 12, Little Michigan Road, (4.9 mi.) and turn left. The first parking area is on FR 10, the Danby-Mount Tabor Road, at its intersection with FR 12. **Alternate route:** From the intersection of Vt. 100 and Landgrove Road in Weston, follow Landgrove Road west 3.8 mi. to FR 12 and turn right.

The parking area for the Little Michigan Loop is further west on the south (left) side of FR 12 where road maintenance ends.

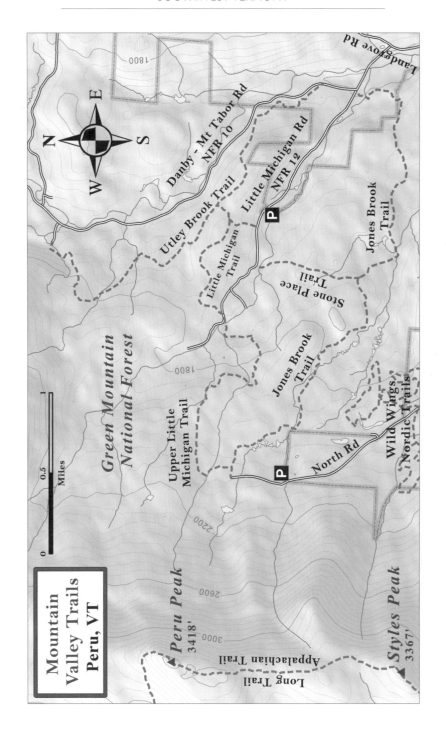

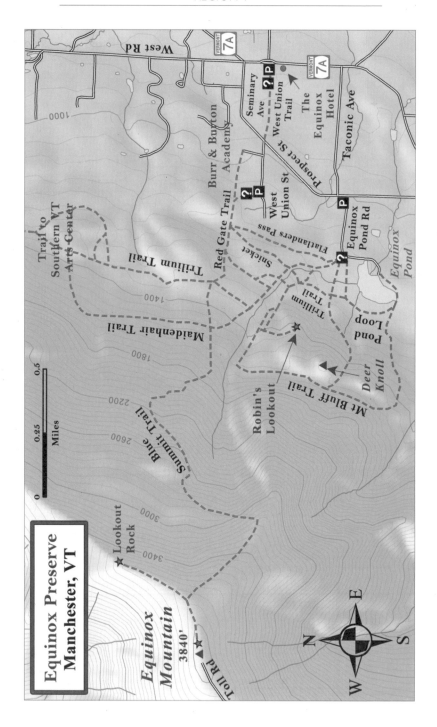

Equinox Preserve
Manchester, VT

Danby-Mount Tabor Road

Description: From the first parking area at the intersection of FR 10 and FR 12, follow FR 10 to a campsite by the river (1.1 mi.) or to the first bridge over the river (2.3 mi.). There is generally little traffic on this road, except on weekends in foliage season and during hunting season.

Little Michigan Loop

Description: From the second parking area, the loop route follows FR 12 to the first junction with the Stone Place Trail (0.2 mi.). It then turns right on the Stone Place Trail and follows it to the junction with the Little Michigan Trail (0.3 mi.). Turning left on the Little Michigan Trail, the loop continues to a logging road (the extension of FR 12), turns left and follows it back to the parking area (2.0 mi.).

⓮ Hapgood Pond Recreation Area

The U.S. Forest Service's Hapgood Pond Recreation Area, which has a picnic area, campground and swimming area, is reached from the village of Peru, located a short distance north of Vt. 11, east of the Bromley Mountain Ski Area. For information and a map, contact the Manchester Ranger District, 2538 Depot Street, Manchester Center, Vermont 05255, 802-362-2307, www.fs.fed.us.

To the Trail: From Vt. 11, turn into Peru village and bear left on Hapgood Pond Road in front of the village church. Continue 1.7 mi. to the entrance of the recreation area. The Forest Service maintains a booth in summer. Currently, no fees are charged, but there is a donation box. Parking is beyond the booth and additional parking is available about 100 yds. beyond the entrance on Hapgood Pond Road.

Description: The Land and Man Forest Trail, 0.8 mi. long, circles the pond through mature woods and across the inlet to the pond. The trail begins straight beyond the entrance booth on the eastern side of the pond. Recent beaver activity has inundated the area around the inlet, but the trail through the campground is open and returns to the parking area.

⓯ Equinox Preserve

The network of trails in the Equinox Preserve offers many possibilities for walks, both long or short, flat or hilly. The lower elevation trails generally have less than 500 ft. of elevation gain. The Equinox Preservation Trust oversees the preserve and publishes a brochure and map available from the Equinox Hotel's concierge. For information, contact the Trust at P.O. Box 46, Historic Route 7A, Manchester VT 05254, 802-362-4700, www.equinoxpreservation-trust.org. Hunting is prohibited on Trust lands.

Pond Loop

Distance: 0.7 mi.

To the Trail: From the Equinox Hotel on Vt. 7A in Manchester Village (0.0 mi.), follow Vt. 7A south 0.3 mi., turn right on Taconic Avenue and follow it to its end (0.9 mi.). Turn left on Prospect Street and park in the parking area at the beginning of Equinox Pond Road.

Description: From the parking area, follow Equinox Pond Road west up a slight grade to the trailhead where the Pond Loop begins. Continue straight from the trailhead to circle the pond in a counterclockwise direction. At 0.15 mi. the loop intersects the Trillium Trail and at 0. 4 mi. the Mount Bluff Trail. It passes the Pond Pavilion on the left at 0.55 mi. and crosses a stream before returning to the trailhead (0.75 mi.).

Both the Red Gate Trail and Flatlanders Pass leave from this trailhead and may be combined for a 1.0-mi. loop.

Robin's Lookout

Distance: 1.0 mi.

To the Trail: From the Equinox Hotel (0.0 mi.), follow Vt. 7A north 0.1 mi. and turn left on Seminary Avenue. Follow it 0.3 mi. and turn left on West Union Street (0.4 mi.). Parking for the Red Gate Trail is at the end of the street (0.6 mi.) or at the western end of the Equinox Hotel parking lot, requiring a walk on the West Union Trail to West Union Street.

Description: From the parking area, follow the Red Gate Trail 0.2 mi. to the Snicket and turn left. Follow the Snicket 0.4 mi. to the Trillium Trail (0.6 mi.) and turn right. Continue straight on the Mount Bluff Trail, then bear left on the Robin's Lookout Trail (0.7 mi.). From Robin's Lookout (1.0 mi.) there is a fine view of Equinox Pond, Manchester Village and the Green Mountains across the valley.

⑯ Prospect Rock

The view from Prospect Rock includes Manchester and Mount Equinox.

Distance: 1.8 mi.

To the Trail: From the intersection of Vt. 11/Vt. 30 and Rootville Road east of Manchester, turn east on Rootville Road and follow it 0.2 mi. to the end of the pavement where there is limited parking.

Description: From the parking area, the route climbs steadily on Old Rootville Road—passable only by high clearance vehicles—1.8 mi. to the Long Trail and a spur leading 150 ft. west to Prospect Rock.

⑰ Lye Brook Falls

Although the trail to the waterfall is a bit long, it ascends gradually on old railroad grades and woods roads for most of its length. The falls are among the highest in Vermont.

Distance: 2.3 mi.

To the Trail: From the intersection of Vt. 7A and Vt. 11/Vt. 30 in Manchester Center (0.0 mi.), follow Vt. 11/Vt. 30 east 1.9 mi. and turn right on East Manchester Road. Follow it 1.2 mi. to Glen Road (3.1 mi.) and turn left. When Glen Road bears left (3.2 mi.), continue straight 0.4 mi. to the trailhead and parking area (3.6 mi.).

Description: From the parking area, the old road heads east and enters the Lye Brook Wilderness (0.5 mi.). It continues on a steady uphill grade following the course of Lye Brook. At 2.3 mi., a spur trail right leads to Lye Brook Falls.

⑱ Grout Pond Recreation Area

A major logging site until it was purchased by the Boy Scouts of America in 1950, Grout Pond was acquired by the U.S. Forest Service in 1979. The 1,600-acre area is managed for a variety of recreational uses. Nine campsites and three lean-tos are available on a first-come, first-served basis. Some of the sites are accessible by car, others only by foot or boat. The area also offers swimming and boating (electric motors only, with a portage required for access). A U.S. Forest Service caretaker may be in residence during the summer and fall. Additional information and a trail map are available from the U.S. Forest Service's Manchester office (see Hapgood Pond Recreation Area) and at the trailhead.

More than 10.0 mi. of multi-use trails encircle the 70-acre pond along mostly flat terrain. The trails connect with the extensive trail system at nearby Somerset Reservoir. The trails are marked with blue diamond-shaped blazes and are open year-round. In winter, snowmobiles are restricted to USFS Road 262 and a portion of the trail system designated by orange diamond blazes.

To the Trail: To reach the Grout Pond Recreation Area from the east, follow Stratton Road (also known as the West Wardsboro-Arlington Road) west from Vt. 100 in West Wardsboro 6.3 mi. to Grout Pond Road (USFS Road 262). From the west, follow Kelley Stand Road (also known as the West Wardsboro-Arlington Road) east from U.S. 7 in Arlington about 12.0 mi. to Grout Pond Road. Turn south on Grout Pond Road and continue 1.3 mi. to a parking lot near the pond.

Description: From the parking lot, the Pond Loop Trail heads southeast to make a 2.5 mi. counterclockwise circuit around the pond. From a junction near the south end of the pond, about 0.75 mi. from the parking lot, the Catamount Trail leads 0.5 mi. to a junction with the East Shore Trail. This trail originates from the dam at the outlet of Somerset Reservoir, about 6.0 mi. south.

⑲ Lake Shaftsbury State Park

This 84-acre park surrounds small and picturesque Lake Shaftsbury. The park has group camping facilities and a day-use area, with a fee charged in season.

To the Trail: State Park Road leaves Vt. 7A just north of the village of Shaftsbury about 10.5 mi. north of Bennington and leads 0.5 mi. to the park contact station.

Description: A brochure is available at the contact station describing the 0.75-mi. Healing Springs Nature Trail, which nearly circles the lake. The trail begins at the western end of the dam, which forms the lake's outlet, and follows the north shore for a distance before crossing a boardwalk onto Hemlock Island. The trail follows the ridge of this glacial esker to another bridge, where it crosses to a peninsula on the south shore of the lake. The trail continues through an oak forest to a boardwalk over Warm Brook before ending at the group picnic shelter near a parking lot southeast of the lake.

⑳ Little Pond Trail

This secluded pond is reached by an unblazed and unsigned woods road. The total elevation gain is 330 feet. *(See map on p. 16.)*

Distance: 2.5 mi.

To the Trail: From the intersection of U.S. 7 and Vt. 9 in Bennington, follow Vt. 9 east 9.5 mi. to a parking area on the north side of Vt. 9. **Alternate Route:** From the intersection of Vt. 100 and Vt. 9 in Wilmington, follow Vt. 9 west 12.0 mi. to the parking area on the north side of Vt. 9.

Description: From the parking area, the trail follows FR 275 on a gradual ascent. At 0.5 mi., it crosses under the Woodford power line. After passing an old campsite (0.8 mi.), it continues to ascend to a shoulder of Hager Hill and intersects a snowmobile trail on the right. At 2.4 mi., it reaches a fork where a logging road departs left and an older road to the right leads down to the pond (2.5 mi.).

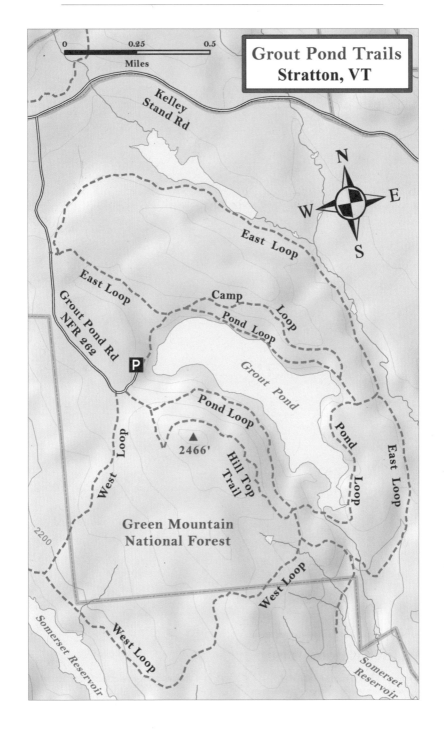

0   0.25   0.5
Miles

**Grout Pond Trails
Stratton, VT**

Kelley
Stand Rd

N
W   E
S

East Loop

East Loop

Camp
Pond Loop

Grout Pond Rd
NFR 262

P

Grout Pond

Pond Loop
Loop

East Loop

Pond Loop

▲
2466'

Hill Top
Trail

West Loop

2200

**Green Mountain
National Forest**

West Loop

West Loop

West Loop

Somerset Reservoir

Somerset
Reservoir

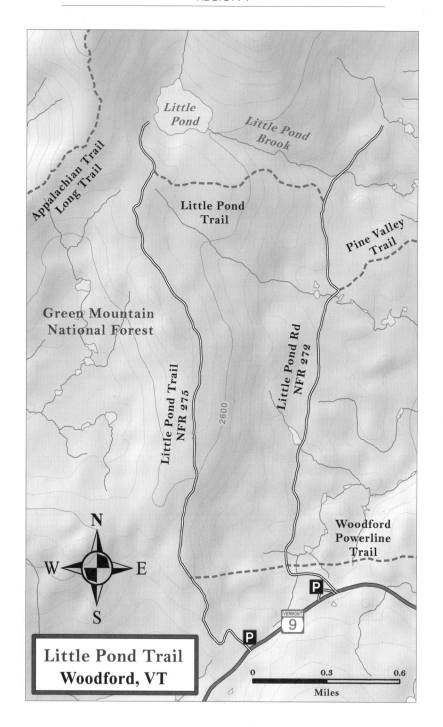

Little Pond

Little Pond Brook

Appalachian Trail
Long Trail

Little Pond
Trail

Pine Valley
Trail

Green Mountain
National Forest

Little Pond Trail
NFR 275

Little Pond Rd
NFR 272

2600

N
W   E
S

Woodford
Powerline
Trail

P

P

VERMONT
9

Little Pond Trail
Woodford, VT

0   0.3   0.6
Miles

㉑ Woodford State Park

Woodford State Park occupies 398 acres on a mountain plateau surrounding Adams Reservoir. At an elevation of 2,400 ft., it is the highest Vermont state park and is covered by a high-altitude, spruce-fir-birch forest. A number of campsites are available and a day-use fee is charged in season.

To the Trail: The park entrance is on the south side of Vt. 9, about 11.0 mi. east of Bennington and 3.2 mi. west of Vt. 8. Out-of-season, parking is available at a U.S. Forest Service parking lot on Vt. 9, north and east of the park entrance.

Description: A blue-blazed hiking trail, located mostly within the park, encircles the 23-acre reservoir, closely following its western shore. Following a clockwise loop, the trail may be found at two points along an access road that leaves the contact station to the left and continues to the park campgrounds. The first access is a left turn into the woods at the top of the hill and adjacent to a playground. The second access is on the left 100 yds. farther, just before the access road descends a hill.

The hiking trail heads south, closely following the eastern park boundary, then bears west through a small section of the George Aiken Wilderness where there are limited views of beaver ponds. The trail re-crosses state park land to enter the Green Mountain National Forest, reaching a junction at the south end of Adams Reservoir. The distance from the access road to the reservoir is about 1.0 mi.

Junction: To the right, a trail returns to the state park, reaching the campground at site 64, where the access road leads back to the contact station.

To the left, the trail follows the west side of the reservoir, re-entering state park land and eventually reaching a junction where the Atwood Trail leaves right and provides a short alternate route along the shoreline. The trails converge several hundred feet ahead and reach a parking lot at the park day-use area (1.7 mi.). The contact station lies a short distance beyond.

MARY LOU RECOR

Trail sign at Woodford State Park.

㉒ Dunville Hollow Road

Dunville Hollow Road in the Green Mountain National Forest follows Stamford Stream, a fast-flowing mountain stream with many beautiful cascades. Starting at 1450 ft., the route's elevation gain is gradual, making this walk pleasant for all ages and levels. The narrow 3.0-mile road passes two camps and receives very little motorized traffic.

To the Trail: From the four corners in Bennington (intersection of U.S. 7 and Vt. 9), follow Vt. 9 east 5.6 mi. (a quarter mile beyond the Long Trail parking lot) and turn right on Dunville Hollow Road, just before a bridge. Continue on this dirt road for 0.2 mi. to a parking lot on the left.

Description: From the parking lot, the route follows a dirt road east, crossing a bridge over Stamford Stream at 0.2 mi. It bears right along the stream and passes a house on the left. Continuing on this road, the route reaches an attractive log cabin at 1.5 mi., a good turnaround point for a 3.0-mile walk. Dunville Hollow Road joins City Stream Road at about 3.0 mi. for a longer hike.

㉓ Prospect Mountain Cross Country Ski Area

With ample parking and clear views from the former downhill ski trails, Prospect Mountain Ski Area offers several walks and rambles. In winter, this high elevation ski area tends to have abundant and early snow for recreational and competitive cross country skiers. In spring, summer and fall, walkers are welcome on the trails. Although few hunters frequent this area, due to a limited deer population, it's still best to wear orange during hunting season. For more information: Prospect Mountain Cross Country Ski Area, 204 Prospect Access, Woodford VT 05201, 802-442-2575, www.prospectmountain.com.

To the Trail: From the four corners in Bennington (intersection of U.S. 7 and Vt. 9), follow Vt. 9 east 8.0 mi., gaining 1500 ft. of elevation, and turn right into the large Prospect Mountain parking lot at a base elevation of 2150 ft.

Description: From the parking lot, the route heads straight for the ski hill, a former downhill ski area that closed in the 1980s (the T-bar still remains). The ski trails up the mountain all make good hiking, with a fairly steep ascent to the 2767 ft. summit. For more even footing and a dirt path instead of grass, an access road to the top leaves from the far left (east). The easier walks bear right on a trail in front of the base lodge and follow the Woodpecker ski trail, which ascends gradually in a westerly direction. Several trail maps are mounted on trees and they outline both short and long loops through the high elevation forest of maple, yellow birch, balsam and spruce. The trail junctions are numbered, with the lower numbers closest to the base lodge.

24 Southern Vermont College

Located on the eastern slope of Mount Anthony, Southern Vermont College has several easy trails near the former Everett Mansion, which now houses college classrooms and administrative offices. This campus features fine views of the southern Green Mountains, a historic stone mansion and a stone cascade.

To the Trail: From the four corners in Bennington (intersection of U.S. 7 and Vt. 9), follow U.S. 7 (South Street) south and turn right on Elm Street across from Friendly's Restaurant. Follow Elm Street west 0.8 mi. to the intersection with Monument Avenue. Turn left on Monument Avenue and follow it 0.3 mi., then turn right on Foothills Drive, following the signs for Southern Vermont College. Park either at the athletic complex (lower parking lot) or continue on to the upper campus (Everett Mansion). For less hill walking, park in the upper lot.

Description: From the lower parking lot, the route heads west along a path to a line of maple trees that once lined a carriage road. Bearing left at the line of trees, it climbs uphill along the path that leads to the Everett Mansion. At the stone building, the route heads toward the south end of the parking lot or up the steps along the stone cascade, which has been restored in recent years. At the south end of the parking lot to the right is a kiosk with a map of the trails on campus. The lower trails are accessible to walkers of all abilities, while the blue-blazed trail to the top of Mount Anthony is very steep.

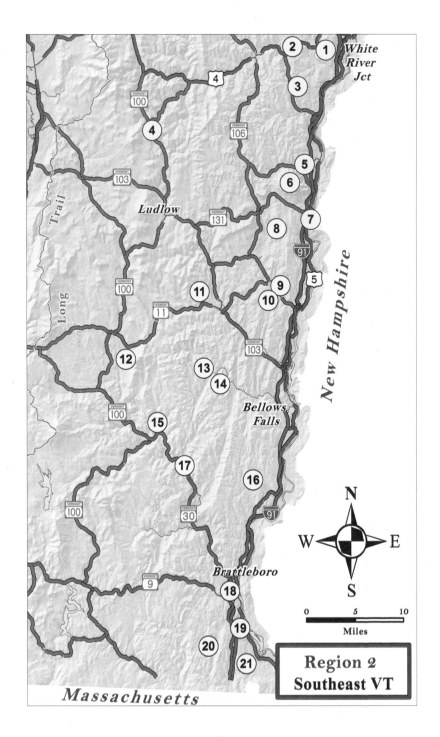

White
River
Jct

VERMONT 100

VERMONT 106

VERMONT 103

Ludlow

Trail

VERMONT 131

91

Long

VERMONT 100

VERMONT 11

VERMONT 103

5

New Hampshire

Bellows
Falls

VERMONT 100

VERMONT 100

VERMONT 30

91

N
W   E
S

0   5   10
Miles

Brattleboro

VERMONT 9

Region 2
Southeast VT

Massachusetts

Region 2
Southeast Vermont

1 Hurricane Forest Wildlife Refuge Park

The Hurricane Forest Wildlife Refuge Park in White River Junction includes 2.4 miles of foot trails laid out in multiple loops on its 142 acres. Most of the trails are on a forested hillside, but a short loop circles Wright Reservoir. Footing on the trails is good and junctions generally are well signed. Light blue blazing on the trails is haphazard, but treadways are well maintained and clear. All trails are suitable for snowshoeing, but skiing would be difficult in many spots except for strong skiers. The parking areas are usually cleared of snow in winter.

The park is managed by the Hartford Parks and Recreation Department. The trails were constructed by the Hartford Boy Scouts and the Vermont Youth Conservation Corps. Winsor and Bertha Brown donated the park land to the town of Hartford in 1973 to be kept in a natural condition, with no clear-cutting of timber and no hunting or trapping, but with provision for foot trails and picnic sites. Snowmobiles and other motorized vehicles are not permitted. Dogs must be leashed and owners must clean up after them. Fires and swimming are not permitted. The park is closed from 9 p.m. to dawn.

Because the area is close to the intersection of I-91 and I-89, the sound of traffic is audible everywhere except in the most remote or sheltered spots. However, the trails and woods are so pleasant that traffic noise fades from consciousness most of the time. On the plus side, proximity to the interstates makes the park a convenient break from driving.

The main entrance, next to Wright Reservoir on Wright Reservoir Road, has two picnic tables and a billboard with a map of the trails. The distances listed are inaccurate and should be disregarded. Trail maps are available from the Hartford Parks and Recreation Department at the Hartford Town Office, 171 Bridge Street, White River Junction VT 05001, 802-295-5036, www.hartford-vt.org.

In addition to trails within the park, the W.B. Brown Trail leads from the highest point of the park's most distant loop trail beyond the park boundary to a summit surmounted by aircraft beacons serving the Lebanon, New Hampshire Airport. The summit is 570 ft. higher than the main entrance.

Pond Loop

This 0.4-mi. loop circles Wright Reservoir, an attractive man-made pond that serves the Town of Hartford as an emergency water supply. Elevation changes are minor. Occasional benches offer rest spots.

To the Trail: From exit 11 on I-91, travel south on Vt. 5. Pass the Veterans Administration Hospital on the right (0.0 mi.), pass beneath I-89 (0.3 mi.), and immediately turn right on Wright Reservoir Road. Look for the park entrance on the left (0.5 mi.). The roadside gravel parking spot is just downhill from the entrance; park to leave as much room as possible for others. The main entrance itself has one space signed for vehicles with handicap plates.

Description: Bearing right—with the pond on the left—the trail crosses a small footbridge, enters the woods, climbs somewhat above the pond shore and passes two junctions with trails to the right, signed as connections to the Monument Trail. Crossing a larger footbridge over a stream feeding the pond, the trail passes a junction with the Creek Trail (0.2 mi.) and returns to its starting point, eventually following the grassy top of the berm that retains the pond.

Creek and Monument Loop

This 1.1 mi. loop circles halfway around Wright Reservoir, follows a deeply shaded ravine upstream, crosses the stream and returns to the pond on the other side of the stream valley. Grades are steady, but generally not steep. The total elevation change is about 200 ft.

To the Trail: Follow directions to the trailhead for the Pond Loop.

Description: The route bears right—with the pond on the left—(as described for the Pond Loop) to the junction with the Creek Trail (0.2 mi.). It then turns right onto the Creek Trail, rising to a junction with the Beacon Hill Loop Trail (0.3 mi.), where there is a bench. The loop route continues ahead on the Creek Trail, paralleling the stream, to a second junction (0.6 mi), where it meets the Beacon Hill Loop Trail for the second time and joins the Monument Trail. Turning right onto the Monument Trail, the route dips sharply 20 yds. to cross a footbridge over the stream, then climbs to the monument (0.7 mi.), a stone holding a bronze plaque memorializing the gift of the park to the Town of Hartford by Winsor and Bertha Brown. This spot is adjacent to Wright Reservoir Road, 0.25 mi. uphill from the main entrance, and it forms a second entrance to the park, with a gravel roadside parking area.

The route turns right downhill along the Monument Trail.

> **Junction:** If followed to the end, the Monument Trail ends at Wright Reservoir Road (1.1 mi.) at a one-car handicap parking spot 0.25 mi. uphill from the main park entrance.

The loop route returns to its starting point by turning right at the first junction (1.0 mi.) for a connecting trail to the Pond Loop, then left along the Pond Loop to the main park entrance (1.1 mi.).

Beacon Hill Loop

This 2.3-mi. loop rises to the highest elevation on the trail system within Hurricane Park, with a total elevation change of about 350 ft. In addition, there is an optional side trail leading a short distance beyond the park boundary to the top of Beacon Hill itself, adding 0.75 mi. to the loop and 220 ft. of elevation change, for a total of 3.1 mi. and 570 ft. The summit is open, grassy and quiet, but offers no distant views. This loop includes the Pond Loop and part of it follows the same attractive stream valley as the Creek and Monument Loop.

To the Trail: Follow directions to the trailhead for the Pond Loop.

Description: The route bears right—with the pond on the left (as described for the Pond Loop)—to the junction with the Creek Trail (0.2 mi.). It then turns right onto the Creek Trail, rising to a junction with the Beacon Hill Loop Trail (0.3 mi.), where there is a bench. It turns left onto the Beacon Hill Loop Trail, climbing steadily with some turns to a junction with the W.B. Brown Trail (0.6 mi.).

> **Junction:** The W.B. Brown Trail turns left and soon joins the route of an abandoned power line straight up Beacon Hill. The power line route is completely reforested, but some old poles remain. Footing is good, but the grade seldom relents. The trail crosses a crumbling stone wall (0.3 mi.) 130 yds. before entering the summit clearing. A grassy service road to the right descends toward Wright Reservoir Road and the aircraft beacon installation is 50 yds. ahead. The W.B. Brown trail continues beyond the clearing.

From the junction, the Beacon Hill Trail continues straight ahead, contouring along the hillside before descending to an unmarked junction (1.3 mi.), where the trail bears right toward a junction (1.6 mi.) and meets the Creek Trail and Monument Trail. The loop route turns right onto the Creek Trail, paralleling the creek downstream to the first junction with the Beacon Hill Loop Trail (1.9 mi.). The Creek Trail continues downstream to its junction with the Pond Loop Trail (2.0 mi.). The route turns right to complete the circuit of the Pond Loop Trail, returning to its starting point at the main park entrance (2.3 mi.).

② Quechee Gorge

Located in the Town of Hartford, this trail begins on a dike between Deweys Pond (or Deweys Mills Pond) and the Ottauquechee River, then parallels the river as it flows into Quechee Gorge. The land is part of 611 acres owned by the U.S. Army Corps of Engineers as part of the North Hartland Dam flood control project and is leased to the Vermont Department of Forest, Parks and Recreation, which manages it for recreation. The trail is generally easy walking. Total elevation change both ways is about 250 ft. Benches are located along the portion of the trail beyond the dike.

The trail is included on a map of the Quechee Gorge State Park Trail System, available at the Quechee Gorge Visitor Center (www.quecheegorge.com) on the south side of U.S. 4, 250 yds. east of the Quechee Gorge Bridge and at Quechee State Park (www.vtstateparks.com), also on the south side of U.S. 4, 0.4 mi. east of the bridge.

Distance: 1.1 mi.

To the Trail: From I-89 (Exit 1), proceed west on U.S. 4 about 3.0 mi. Just before the road crosses over Quechee Gorge, turn right on Deweys Mills Road and follow it to its end at a T-intersection (about 1.0 mi.). Turn left at the intersection on Quechee Main Street (also called Clubhouse Road). After 0.4 mi. turn left again, into the Deweys Pond parking area. A sign here reads "Dewey's Landing."

Description: From the end of the parking area opposite the road (0.0 mi.), a blue-blazed trail (blazes are infrequent) leads south along the dike separating the Ottauquechee River from Deweys Pond, then along the river to a hydro-electric dam and waterfall that was once the site of the Dewey Woolen Mill (0.4 mi.). The trail passes a small picnic area (0.6 mi.) with several tables.

Continuing south, the trail proceeds along the rim of the gorge (separated from the cliff by a fence) through a stand of red pines, unusual in Vermont, to an overlook with a bench on the right. Immediately after passing a short trail to the left to stores, restaurants and other businesses associated with Quechee Gorge, the trail passes under the U.S. 4 bridge (0.7 mi.), which is 165 ft. above the river. This bridge was built in 1911 for the Woodstock Railroad (1875 – 1933) to replace the original Howe Truss bridge of wood timbers and iron. With the abandonment of the railroad, the bridge and rail bed became part of U.S. 4. Edward T. Mead's book *Over the Hills to Woodstock* tells the story of this railroad, of which some structures and roadbed remain visible.

Just beyond the bridge the trail reaches a junction with a sign indicating the Quechee Gorge Visitor Center. The trail to the left leads 0.25 mi. to the visitor center, which is operated by the Hartford Chamber of Commerce and has interpretive displays, information on area tourist attractions and toilets.

Continuing ahead, the trail descends, passing a couple of footpaths to the left (1.0 mi.) that converge on a trail leading to Quechee Gorge State Park, which is open only to registered campers. The main trail then reaches the bottom of the gorge (1.1 mi.), where the rushing waters become a placid river at the upstream end of the North Hartland Reservoir. Further exploration is possible along a footpath that continues downstream, but this eventually peters out.

③ Eshqua Bog

Located in the town of Hartland, Eshqua Bog is a 40-acre sanctuary jointly owned and managed by The Nature Conservancy and the New England Wild Flower Society. The site contains a variety of cold-climate holdover plants that largely disappeared from Vermont at the end of the last glacial period some

10,000 years ago. In late spring and early summer, wildflowers bloom at the site, including several varieties of orchids and a spectacular vernal display of hundreds of lady's slippers. A 0.5-mi. white-blazed loop trail roughly circles the property, but the focal point of the preserve is a two-acre fen traversed by a boardwalk. A fen is a wetland where water comes principally from a local aquifer rather than rainfall or nearby streams or ponds.

Distance: 0.5 mi. loop

To the Trail: From its junction with Vt. 12 in Woodstock Village, follow U.S. 4 east a short distance to the edge of the village, where the main road makes a sharp left. Continue straight on Hartland Hill Road (0.0 mi.), which soon turns southeast. Turn right on the unsigned Garvin Hill Road (1.1 mi.) and follow this gravel road to a small pull-off on the right (2.3 mi.) where limited parking is available. The entrance to the preserve is a short distance beyond the pullout.

Description: After passing the entrance, the trail reaches a registration box and junction. While the boardwalk departs left and cuts across the center of the wetland, the loop trail leaves right, skirting the edge of the bog in a mature hardwood forest. The trail climbs steeply up a bank at the northern end of the bog before meeting the western end of the boardwalk. The loop trail continues straight ahead on level ground around the south end of the bog and returns to Garvin Hill Road about 40 yds. south of the entrance.

The boardwalk crosses the center of the fen, and offers an excellent view of the wealth and variety of wetland plant life. While cattails abound, more exotic species such as turtleheads, insectivorous pitcher plants, northern green orchids and tall white bog orchids are identified by small signs. Due to the fragile nature of the ecosystem, extreme care should be taken to remain on the boardwalk in the fen area. Dogs must be leashed.

Camp Plymouth State Park

Located along the east shore of Echo Lake in the town of Plymouth, the 295-acre Camp Plymouth State Park occupies the site of a former Boy Scout camp (USGS Ludlow). In 1855, gold was discovered along the banks of nearby Buffalo Brook, resulting in mining operations that continued for some 30 years. Panning for gold remains popular in the park to the present day. Camping is limited to a group camping area; obtain information at the park contact station. The park has a variety of day-use facilities, including a beach; a fee is charged in-season. A short hiking loop heads north from the park entrance to a vista overlooking the lake (www.vtstateparks.com). Note: there are no bridges at any of the stream crossings. Crossing on rocks may be tricky during high water or icy conditions.

Distance: 1.6 mi.

To the Trail: Camp Plymouth State Park is located off Vt. 100, several miles south of Coolidge State Park. From the village of Tyson on Vt. 100 at the south end of Echo Lake, 5.2 mi. south of Vt. 100A in Plymouth Union, and 5.5 mi. north of Vt. 103 in Ludlow Village, proceed east on Kingdom Road 0.5 mi. to a crossroads. Turn left on Scout Camp Road and continue 0.6 mi. to the park entrance on the left.

Description: The Echo Lake Vista Trail begins on a dirt road on the east side of Scout Camp Road, 65 yds. north of the park entrance (0.0 mi.). The trail follows the road 0.1 mi., then leaves it on the left along a footpath, which soon reaches an old cemetery. Continuing straight ahead, the trail climbs steadily, eventually reaching a vista (0.6 mi.) overlooking Echo Lake and the park. From the vista, the trail drops down the backside of the ridge and switches back, turning sharply south. It follows Buffalo Brook for a short distance before crossing the brook and rejoining the dirt road on which it began. Bearing right on the road, the route returns to the park (1.6 mi.).

⑤ Paradise Park

Some might consider the name of Windsor's Paradise Park an overstatement, but the 288-acre park, mostly forested with towering trees, is an extraordinary asset for Windsor and its visitors. The park has a pond, Lake Runnemede (sometimes known locally as Evarts Pond), brooks, streams, wetlands and waterfalls; and miles of trails, a few signed but most not. Many of the trails are suitable for snowshoeing or skiing.

The park is owned and maintained by the Town of Windsor. Beginning in the 1820s, the Evarts family acquired the land for Paradise Park. According to local lore, William Maxwell Evarts, a former U.S. Attorney General, determined to create a park in Windsor after seeing the development of Central Park in New York City, where he practiced law. The family built the dike forming Evarts Pond (later named Lake Runnemede by the family) in four years beginning in 1884, and opened it and the surrounding land to the public. Windsor bought 177 acres from Evarts descendants in 1942 and the rest in 1997, including Lake Runnemede.

The walks described here are just a sampling of many in the park. The park is large enough and the terrain varied enough so it is possible to become lost on a cloudy day. A trail map is useful. Maps are available at the Windsor Town Office on the south side of Union Street, which parallels State Street one block south.

Wildlife in the park is protected; hunting and trapping are banned. Open fires are prohibited and dogs must be leashed. Trails are closed to bicycles and motor vehicles. Swimming and boats are not permitted on Lake Runnemede. Alcohol is not permitted, and gatherings of more than 10 people require a permit from the town office. There are no toilets. For more information: Windsor

Community Recreation Center; Director: Harry Ladue, P.O. Box 47, Windsor VT 05089, 802-674-6783.

Zig-Zag Loop

This 1.1-mi. loop follows a combination of service roads and foot trails. Grades are gentle except for one steep section up the Zig-Zag Trail, which forms part of the loop. Total elevation change on the loop is minor. Part of the route is high above a swift stream and part of it follows the shore of Lake Runnemede. Benches provide pleasant stopping points.

To the Trail: Follow U.S. 5 to State Street in downtown Windsor. (Northbound on U.S. 5 from exit 8 on I-91, the intersection is the second traffic light in town; southbound from exit 9, it is the first traffic light.) Turn west on State Street to County Road (0.7 mi.) and bear right. Turn right into the small parking lot at the County Road park entrance (0.8 mi.). This parking area is cleared of snow in winter.

Description: Beyond a yellow steel gate (0.0 mi.), the route follows a gravel service road straight ahead, immediately passing another road to the left. At 70 yds. it reaches a fork, with a sign high in a tree indicating Shaggy Mane Road to the right—the route to be followed. The route continues to follow the service road, paralleling Hubbard Brook in a ravine to the left. At a grassy clearing (0.25 mi.), it passes a large three-sided log shelter with a stone fireplace on the right. (Fires are legal at this shelter with permits obtainable at the town office.) The route then re-enters the woods on the level Moosewood Trail (indicated by a sign on a tree), a wide path bearing northeast.

At a junction (0.5 mi.) the route bears slightly right down a slope, with Lake Runnemede on the right. In 100 yds. another junction is reached; the route takes a sharp right onto a narrow footpath, the Lake Trail (indicated by a sign), which follows closely the shore of the lake. The route becomes a wide graveled service road at a pump house (0.7 mi.) and reaches a second pump house 100 yds. farther. At the second pump house it turns right and ascends a steep bank on the Zig-Zag Trail, aptly named because of its many switchbacks. At the top of the bank (0.9 mi.) the route regains the clearing with the three-sided shelter and returns to the parking lot by the gravel service road.

Lake Runnemede Loop

This 1.7-mile loop traverses largely open, unforested areas, offering distant views across Lake Runnemede to Mount Ascutney. Elevation change is negligible. Benches provide places for resting or birding and a rustic gazebo at a point on Lake Runnemede provides a dry spot in wet weather and a pleasant vantage point anytime. There is no trailhead parking because the route starts in town, but on-street parking is not difficult to find. The route is suitable for snowshoeing or skiing in winter.

DICK ANDREWS

The gazebo on The Point on the Lake Runnemede Loop.

To the Trail: Follow U.S. 5 to State Street in downtown Windsor. (Northbound on U.S. 5 from exit 8 on I-91, the intersection is the second traffic light in town; southbound from exit 9, it is the first traffic light.) Turn west on State Street one block to Court Street. The loop begins at this intersection. Park on State Street or at another legal location nearby.

Description: From the intersection of State and Court Streets (0.0 mi.), the route starts north on Court Street. At the end of Court Street (0.1 mi.), it continues straight ahead down a wide gravel path, soon reaching the start of the Main Dike Trail (unsigned; 0.2 mi.). This trail heads north along the grassy crest of the main dike forming Lake Runnemede, ending at Eddie's Place, a gravel road (0.4 mi.). The route turns left and follows the road 40 yds., then turns left again onto a footpath, which reaches a fork in 60 yds. The route takes the left fork, following a mowed path along the shore of the lake with a large field to the right, eventually reaching a fork in the path (0.75 mi.). The left fork leads to the rustic gazebo at The Point on the shore of Lake Runnemede.

The right fork skirts the left side of the large field, ignoring any paths leading away to the left. It rejoins the outbound route just before the north end of the Main Dike Trail, where it turns south and returns to Court Street.

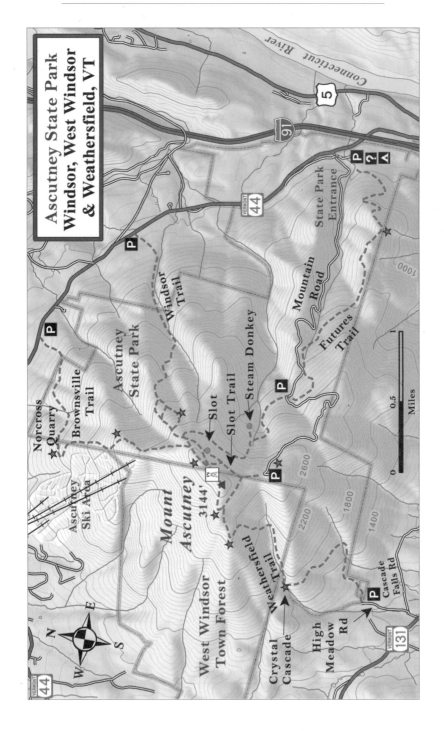

Ascutney State Park
Windsor, West Windsor
& Weathersfield, VT

Connecticut River

5

91

VERMONT 44

State Park
Entrance

Mountain
Road

Futures
Trail

1000

P
?
A

P

Windsor
Trail

Ascutney
State Park

Steam Donkey

Slot

Slot Trail

P

0.5

Miles

0

Norcross
Quarry

Brownsville
Trail

Ascutney
Ski Area

Mount
Ascutney
3144'

P

2600

2200

1800

1400

West Windsor
Town Forest

Weathersfield Trail

Crystal
Cascade

High
Meadow
Rd

P

Cascade
Falls Rd

VERMONT 131

N
E
S
W

VERMONT 44

⑥ Mount Ascutney

A monadnock, Mount Ascutney (3,150 ft.) is the dominant physical feature of southeastern Vermont and is rich in history. The mountain's quartz syenite rock has withstood the erosion and glaciation that has worn away the softer rocks of the surrounding Piedmont peneplane. Located in the towns of Windsor and West Windsor (USGS Mount Ascutney), the mountain derives its name from the Algonquin words *Cas-Cad-Nac* or *Mahps-Cad-Na*, meaning "mountain of the rocky summit," or *Ascutegnik*, meaning "meeting of the waters."

The mountain's first hiking trail was built in the 1850s. Today, four trails approach from the base of the mountain and connect near the summit. They are fairly stiff climbs; in fact, hikers often underestimate Mount Ascutney, forgetting that though the summit is not high, the base is a great deal lower. Even without going all the way to the summit, portions of these trails make interesting short walks.

Ascutney State Park occupies about 2,000 acres on the eastern slope of the mountain. The Civilian Conservation Corps (CCC) developed the park between 1935 and 1939, constructing the original stone buildings as well as a 3.8-mi. paved auto road, which ascends some 2,250 ft. to within 0.75 mi. of the summit. There are camping facilities near the base of the mountain and picnic facilities along the mountain road and near the summit. Day-use and camping fees are charged in-season. The park entrance is on the west side of Vt. 44A, which runs between U.S. 5, north of Ascutney and Vt. 44, east of Brownsville. It is marked by a large sign.

The trail system is maintained largely by the Ascutney Trails Association, established in 1967. The group has restored and improved these historic trails and publishes a fascinating guidebook, the *Mount Ascutney Guide*. Describing the trails in detail, the guide also gives historical information and natural history of the area. The guide is available from the association (see p. 237) or from the Green Mountain Club.

Mount Ascutney from Ascutney Mountain Road

Mount Ascutney offers a splendid 360-degree panorama of the Connecticut River Valley, the Green Mountains and the White Mountains of New Hampshire from its observation tower, the shortened former fire tower. The observation tower is not quite on the highest point of the mountain, which is occupied by a somewhat unsightly collection of antennas, but it offers by far the best views.

The Mount Ascutney auto road is a blessing for walkers, because it reaches within 0.7 mi. of the summit and just 350 ft. below it by the Slot Trail, the shortest route. There is also a fairly complex collection of other interesting trails that can be explored in the summit area. The road is not maintained in winter and is closed when the state park is not open.

Slot Trail

The Slot Trail begins at the top of the auto road (toll road) and climbs on moderate grades to reach the Windsor/Brownsville Trail in a saddle a short distance north of the Ascutney summit. It gets its name from a portion of the trail that passes through a high-walled slot.

Distance: 0.7 mi.

To the Trail: From U.S. 5 in Windsor, head west on Vt. 44 for 2.5 mi. to the intersection with Vt. 44A. Turn sharply left on Vt. 44A and continue south 1.7 mi. to the state park entrance and toll road. Follow the toll road 3.7 mi. to the parking lot at its end. Use care on the road, especially on the descent; it is steep, narrow and winding.

Description: From the parking area (0.0 mi.), the Slot Trail ascends gradually to a four-way intersection (0.3 mi.).

> **Junction:** To the right, the Futures Link Trail descends 0.1 mi. to reach the Futures Trail at a point 3.6 mi. above the trailhead in Ascutney State Park. To the left, the Slab Trail ascends 0.2 mi., rejoining the Slot Trail just below the ridge.

Continuing straight ahead, the Slot Trail soon reaches another junction (0.5 mi.), with the southern end of the Castle Rock Trail.

> **Junction:** The Castle Rock Trail provides a short link (0.1 mi.) connecting the Slot Trail in the south with the Windsor Trail in the north. Castle Rock lies at the midpoint of the trail and provides an excellent view east to the Connecticut River Valley.

Turning left at the junction, the Slot Trail makes a winding ascent, is rejoined by the Slab Trail and reaches the white-blazed Windsor/Brownsville Trail in a saddle 0.1 mi. north of the Ascutney summit (0.7 mi.).

Steam Donkey from Ascutney Mountain Road

Local lore says many have logged on Mount Ascutney, but none have managed to turn a profit from it. The steam donkey, the destination of this walk, was a vertical wood-burning boiler, steam engine and cable drum used in the early 1900s to pull logs up the mountain with steel cables on terrain too steep for conventional logging. The logs were used in building the road and fire tower. The steam donkey is believed to have been abandoned in the 1930s. The boiler, some cable and part of the transmission gearing for the cable drum remain. The total elevation change is 520 ft.

Distance: 0.7 mi.

To the Trail: Follow the directions to Ascutney State Park on p. 31. Continue 2.3 mi. up the road to the Futures Trail crossing (marked by an inconspicuous brown sign on the right). Park in the small parking space on the left; leave room for others.

Description: From the road crossing (0.0 mi.), the Futures Trail ascends gently, following an old logging road along the contour. Turning sharply uphill (0.4 mi.), it continues to climb steeply, still following the logging road. The skid road ends and the trail crosses three small streams just before the junction (0.6 mi.) where a spur trail, also blue-blazed, leads downhill to the right to the steam donkey (0.7 mi.).

Crystal Cascade by the Weathersfield Trail

The white-blazed Weathersfield Trail ascends the southwestern side of Mount Ascutney and is on state and town (West Windsor) forestlands. On its way to the summit, it passes the top of Crystal Cascade, which plunges over the lip of a high ledge, an excellent picnic spot with good views to the south and west. Footing is good, but there are rocky stretches. Crystal Cascade is 422 ft. above the trailhead, but total elevation gain on this trail for the round trip is about 500 ft.

Distance: 1.1 mi.

To the Trail: From Vt. 131, 3.3 mi. west of I-91 exit 8, and 3.8 mi. east of Vt. 106 at Downers Four Corners, turn north on Cascade Falls Road. Bear left at High Meadow Road and continue 0.3 mi. to a right turn leading to a parking area and the trailhead.

Description: From the parking area (0.0 mi.), the trail begins a gradual ascent through mixed hardwoods, following an old woods road and crossing a small stream. It steepens and soon crosses the brook just above Little Cascade Falls, which is dry at times. It climbs steeply by switchbacks (please stay on the trail) and re-crosses the stream feeding Little Cascade Falls in a deep rock cleft (0.4 mi.). Ascending a rock outcrop via stairs removed from the fire tower on the summit of the mountain when the tower was shortened, the trail then alternately climbs on easier grades and contours the mountain slope, passing several overlooks (0.6 mi.). Descending, the trail reaches Crystal Cascade Falls (1.1 mi.) where Ascutney Brook tumbles 84 ft. over a sheer cliff.

Norcross Quarry via the Brownsville Trail

On its way to the summit of Mount Ascutney the white-blazed Brownsville Trail passes the site of the Norcross Quarry. At 1.1 mi. from the trailhead, the quarry site is comparatively easy to reach and provides excellent views of Brownsville and many miles beyond from lookouts on the waste pile that juts away from the mountain slope. The total elevation change is 670 ft. and the trail is rocky, making this a challenging walk, but pleasant at a slow pace. The adjacent landowner asks that all dogs be leashed until well onto the trail. The trail is suitable for snowshoes, but the bottom portion is steep and snowshoes with metal creepers are usually required. The parking area is cleared of snow most winters.

The Norcross is one of four granite quarries around the 1,500-ft. level on Mount Ascutney, worked at various times in the 19th and 20th centuries. The most extensive of the four, it operated for several years until 1923 and provided stone for the polished columns on Columbia University's library in New York City and for the Bank of Montreal in Canada. Like the other three quarries, the Norcross was plagued by stone containing traces of iron, causing the stone to weather over time to an unattractive rusty brown. The owners burrowed deeper and deeper into the mountain seeking uncontaminated stone, but eventually, like the operators of the other three quarries, went bankrupt.

Forest has obscured most of what was once an extensive industrial site. At one time the quarry even included a boarding house for workers to save them the time and trouble of daily climbs up and down the mountain to the job, but it has vanished completely. Most of the iron and steel was hauled down the mountain, much of it in scrap drives during World Wars I and II. Still, some of the excavations, the remains of the massive Carolina pine booms and the webwork of steel cable that comprised parts of the hoists and rails used to tip waste stone slabs down the slope are plainly visible.

Distance: 1.1 mi.

To the Trail: The Brownsville Trail begins on the south side of Vt. 44, 4.3 mi. west of its junction with U.S. 5 in Windsor and 1.1 mi. east of the Mount Ascutney Ski Area. From the south, the trailhead is 2.8 mi. north of Ascutney State Park. Parking is available off the highway in a gravel lot with a trailhead bulletin board.

Description: From the parking lot (0.0 mi.), the trail crosses a short grassy stretch in a former pasture before entering the woods in a southerly direction. The trail bears left to cross a wooden bridge over a seasonally dry wash before ascending briefly on wooden stair treads. At the top of the stairs, the trail bears right and zigzags steeply uphill to the old road that served the quarry (0.3 mi.). Climbing on easier grades, the trail follows the road to the quarry. On bedrock on the uphill side of the road are the remains of holes drilled for black powder to blast the road out of the mountainside. Also visible at one point are the remains of an older road that proved too steep for the granite wagons.

7 Wilgus State Park

Wilgus State Park is a low-key place even as state parks go, but it has walking trails as well as camping, picnic areas, canoe rentals and a canoe launching ramp. Three walks are described here. The park also has several unmarked trails for further exploration. Trail maps are available at the park in season and online at www.vtstateparks.org.

The park is 1.1 mi. south of the junction of U.S. 5 and Vt. 131 in Ascutney village. Parking arrangements should be made with the park manager. The use fee charged when the park is open also covers the toll on the Mount Ascutney auto road. There is adequate parking outside the gate during the snow-free off-season. In winter, park at a large pulloff on the west side of U.S. 5, 0.2 mi. south of the park entrance; it is usually clear of snow. *(See map on p. 37.)*

Nature Trail

This virtually flat trail is a pleasant loop along the right bank of the Connecticut River, downstream of the park campground. Footing is good and it would be excellent for snowshoes or skis. The trail is on a narrow strip of land between U.S. 5 and the river, so traffic is audible, but it is usually light.

Distance: 0.7 mi. loop

To the Trail: Head south from the park entrance station to a large parking area. Take the first path toward the river.

Description: From the parking area, the route drops down 20 yds. to a sandy service road and turns right. Passing in front of three lean-tos, it reaches a brown sign indicating "Nature Trail" (0.1 mi.). Following along the top of the river bank, it passes a bench offering a quiet view over the river and a tributary ravine (0.3 mi.), then curves sharply right and loops back to a junction (0.5 mi.), rejoining the outbound trail.

River Walk

This walk (round trip) follows the river bank upstream along the campground. Elevation change is negligible. Farther from U.S. 5, it is quieter than the Nature Trail, but may be more sociable, since it threads between campsites and the river. Views of the river are better than from the Nature Trail and unlike on the Nature Trail, there are signs interpreting natural history as well as benches and water spigots. Footing is good and the trail is suitable for snowshoes or skis.

Distance: 0.4 mi.

To the Trail: Follow the directions for the Nature Trail.

Description: The route drops 20 yds. to a park service road, turns left, then turns toward the river bank at each opportunity. It passes a badminton court and two cabins (0.1 mi.), the canoe access ramp (0.2 mi.) and ends at the last campsite in the campground (0.4 mi.). Return is by the same route or along the road serving the campground, where toilets are available.

The Pinnacle

This low hill offers good views of the New Hampshire hills to the east. The trail is steep in places, and footing can be difficult in wet weather or in fall when slippery oak leaves have fallen. It is suitable for snowshoeing with snowshoes equipped with creepers; poles are helpful on the steep spots. It is not recommended for skiing. Total elevation change is 340 ft.

Distance: 1.2 mi. loop

To the Trail: The blue-blazed loop trail begins on U.S. 5, opposite the entrance to the park.

Description: From the highway (0.0 mi.), the trail climbs a bank and swings left, following a pleasant woods road on easy grades. Eventually turning right off the old road (0.3 mi.), the trail climbs to a lookout just below the wooded summit (0.5 mi.).

From the lookout, the trail passes over the summit (640 ft.) and makes a steep and winding descent through the woods to the highway (0.9 mi.). Following the park access road, it is 0.25 mi. south to the contact station and park entrance.

8 Springweather Nature Area

Located in the town of Weathersfield and encompassing nearly 70 acres of fields and forests, the Springweather Nature Area was developed by the Ascutney Mountain Audubon Society and the U.S. Army Corps of Engineers following construction of the North Springfield Flood Control Dam. Three blazed trails, totaling about 2.0 mi., wander through the site and offer a variety of moderate loop hikes.

To the Trails: From its intersection with Vt. 11 in Springfield (0.0 mi.), follow Vt. 106 north along the Black River. Turn right on Reservoir Road (1.9 mi.) and continue past the flood control dam to the signed nature area access road on the left (3.4 mi.). Bear right at the first intersection and continue north a short distance to the main parking lot on the right (3.6 mi.). The trailhead for the Blue Trail and Red Trail is located across the gravel road at a bulletin board, where a map of the site is posted. The access road continues north past this parking lot, ending at another parking area on the Black River, where the Green Trail may be accessed. The trail layout is intricate in places, sometimes with multiple loops and branches blazed the same color. However, the area is not large and the terrain is not complex. A trail map is available at the bulletin board.

Description: The Blue Trail leaves left from the bulletin board, crosses a small brook and climbs quickly to an open field, which it crosses southward on a mowed path. A junction in the middle of the field offers two possibilities.

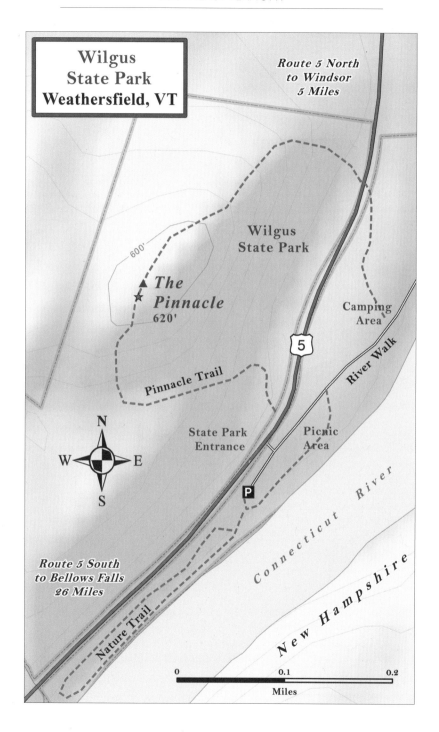

Wilgus
State Park
Weathersfield, VT

Route 5 North
to Windsor
5 Miles

Wilgus
State Park

600'

▲ The
★ Pinnacle
620'

Camping
Area

5

River Walk

Pinnacle Trail

N
W E
S

State Park
Entrance

Picnic
Area

Connecticut River

P

Route 5 South
to Bellows Falls
26 Miles

Nature Trail

New Hampshire

0   0.1   0.2

Miles

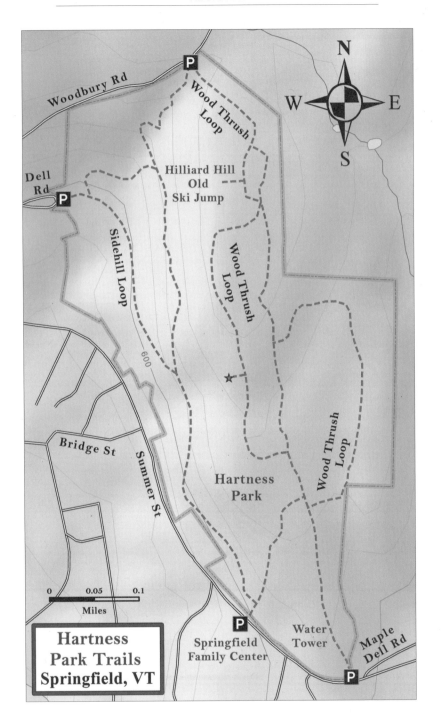

Woodbury Rd

Wood Thrush Loop

Dell Rd

Hilliard Hill Old Ski Jump

Wood Thrush Loop

Sidehill Loop

600

Wood Thrush Loop

Bridge St

Summer St

Hartness Park

Wood Thrush Loop

0   0.05   0.1
Miles

Water Tower

Maple Dell Rd

Hartness Park Trails Springfield, VT

Springfield Family Center

Continuing straight ahead, the path leads to a small pond or marshy area, then bears east to the access road, a short distance south of the trailhead. To the right, the path bears westward to another junction in the field. At this junction both paths lead to a pair of loops on a forested hill. In circling the hill and paralleling the lake on a high bank, the trail offers views west and toward Mount Ascutney in the north.

The Red Trail departs the bulletin board to the right and soon reaches a series of junctions and small trail loops. Bearing left toward the lake, this trail also reaches the high bank above the water, which it follows north. At the farthest point on the loop from the trailhead, the Red Trail reaches a junction on the left with the Green Trail. Bearing right, the Red Trail curves southward to parallel the access road and return to the head of the loop.

The Green Trail, from its junction with the Red Trail, continues along the bank overlooking the lake before turning away and also heading toward the access road. The trail quickly reaches a junction, where a spur right leads a short distance to the access road, north of the main parking lot. The more interesting route bears left and soon reaches a stream, near the site of Barretts Mill and an old bridge. The trail takes a short but steep route to cross the stream before continuing to the trailhead parking area at the north end of the access road.

⑨ Hartness Park

Gov. James Hartness donated the land for 85-acre Hartness Park to the Town of Springfield in 1934, intending it as a public picnic and recreation area within walking distance of the center of downtown. It became a town forest in 1955. At one time Hartness Park had several picnic areas with tables and fireplaces accessible by vehicle and a system of improved trails. Two ski jumps were built on steep slopes in the park and were used for several years, often under artificial light at night, the only free time for many residents. The park was the training area for the Springfield High School ski team from the 1950s until the 1980s, using both cross-country and downhill trails built by team members.

Today only traces of these earlier developments remain and the unlogged forest has grown to majestic proportions in many places. Former driveways are gated to prevent abuse by off-road vehicles. The old ski jumps are overgrown with brush and trees, but signs and some openings indicate their locations. Trails, recently cleared of debris and signed with the help of a Vermont Department of Forests, Parks and Recreation grant, community contributions and volunteer labor, are open for hiking, mountain biking, horseback riding, snowshoeing and cross-country skiing. Users are asked not to damage the trails, especially on wet or steep places.

The trail system has multiple loops, but can be generally divided into an upper and lower level, with a few short interconnections. The interconnections are steep enough to be dangerous for cross-country skiing, but the trails on the two levels generally are suitable for skis. Footing is good. The park is about 0.5 mi. long. The elevation change from the lowest point on the trails to the highest is 275 ft. The trails are not named or blazed, but signs numbering junctions correspond to numbers on trail maps and the paths are easy to follow.

Trail maps are usually available at all public entrances, where maps are also posted. These maps indicate which trails are steepest. There is also an old signboard with a less detailed map a short distance into the park from the Woodbury Road entrance.

To the Trail: Hartness Park has four entrances:

Dell Rd.: At the junction of Vt. 11 and Vt. 143 (0.0 mi.) in Springfield, turn east on Vt. 143. At Summer Hill Street (0.1 mi.) bear left. Stay on Summer Hill Street as it turns sharply right past a cemetery on its right. Turn right at Dell Road (1.2 mi.) and continue to the cul-de-sac loop at its end (1.4 mi.). There is room for three or four cars along the roadside; do not block driveways. The information board is 25 yds. up the trail.

Woodbury Rd.: Proceed as to the Dell Road entrance, but continue on Summer Hill Street past Dell Road an additional 0.3 mi. The entrance, on the right side of the road outside a yellow steel gate, has room for two cars properly parked. Snow is not cleared here.

Springfield Family Center (on weekends and after 5 p.m. on weekdays): At the junction of Vt. 11 and Vt. 143 (0.0 mi.) in Springfield, turn east on Vt. 143. Look for the Springfield Family Center entrance on the right at 1.1 mi., marked with a sign, "White Acres Springfield Family Center." The trail into the park begins across Vt. 143 from the Family Center entrance.

Water Tower: Proceed as to the Family Center entrance, but continue another 0.1 mi. beyond the Family Center to the gated gravel service road on the left at the top of a hill; it leads to a large water tank. There is room for two to three cars; please do not block the service road.

Two loops are described here; each involves some backtracking. Other loops are possible.

Wood Thrush Loop

This 1.25-mi. loop, named for a species birders frequently hear, lies generally along the ridge top that slopes down from the Woodbury Road entrance toward the Water Tower entrance to the park. It passes near the top of the precipitous former 40-meter ski jump. Footing is good and grades are generally gentle; total elevation change is about 100 ft. The loop is on old woods roads, some of which were badly damaged and eroded by illegal off-road vehicle abuse in the decades before the Town of Springfield gated the access points.

Observant walkers can see places where trespassing off-roaders detoured from woods roads to wallow through nearby wetlands. The paths and wetlands are beginning to recover from this damage and, with luck and time, they may heal completely. Use the Woodbury Road entrance.

Description: From the gate (Junction 1) the route proceeds straight ahead to Junction 2 (0.1 mi.) and turns right, reaching an unmarked junction (0.15 mi.) with a woods road on the right.

> **Junction:** The old woods road leads, with a couple of bends, 120 yds. to the top of the former 40-meter ski jump.

Continuing straight, the route leads 50 yds. to Junction 3 and bears right, then 40 yards to Junction 4, where it again bears right. Descending gently, it passes an open space on the right (0.35 mi.), a former picnic area and still a pleasant place for a snack. Reaching Junction 8 (0.5 mi.) the route turns right toward Junction 7 (0.6 mi.), continues 35 yds. straight to Junction 6, where it turns left, crosses an intermittent stream (0.65 mi.) and swings left, following the stream uphill, then re-crossing it (0.8 mi.). At Junction 5 (1.0 mi.) the route turns right, then goes straight through Junction 4, bears right at Junction 3 (1.1 mi.), right again at Junction 2 (1.15 mi.) and returns to the Woodbury Road entrance (1.25 mi.).

Sidehill Loop

This 1.35-mi. loop generally contours along the side of the ridge on which the park is located, but has enough climbs and descents—some of them steep—so the total elevation change is about 200 ft. Footing is generally good, but it can be slippery when wet on the short steep pitches.

The loop crosses the old ski jump locations several times; remnants of the wiring and fixtures for the lighting system can be spotted in some trees. Much of the loop follows cross-country ski trails built by the Springfield High School ski team in the 1950s. Use the Dell Road entrance.

Description: Ignoring an informal trail on the right 65 yds. from the start, the route contours the slope, crossing a stream just before Junction 13 (0.1 mi.), where it turns right and descends somewhat, before crossing one of the old ski jumps. It crosses another ski jump line (0.15 mi.), reaching Junction 12 (0.2 mi.), where an old trail descends right toward a residential area. (This trail is not recommended: its lower reaches are very muddy and it crosses private land with no public right of way.) At 0.3 mi. the trail makes a brief steep climb, reaching Junction 11 (0.35 mi.), where it turns right. The trail dips sharply (0.4 mi.), then contours with modest changes in elevation to Junction 10 (0.6 mi.), where it turns right, arriving at the Family Center entrance (0.65 mi.).

The Sidehill Loop may be walked from this end when parking is available at the Family Center (see above for parking restrictions there).

Backtracking along the same trail, the route turns left at Junction 10 and returns to Junction 11 (1.0 mi.), where it turns right and climbs steadily along an old cross-country ski trail to a high point (1.1 mi.), then descends gradually, crossing two ski jump lines 130 yds. apart. At Junction 14 (1.2 mi.) the route turns left, steeply downhill along a stream on the right, to Junction 13 (1.25 mi.), where it turns right and returns to the Dell Road entrance (1.35 mi.).

⑩ Toonerville Trail

The 3-mi. Toonerville Trail is a cycling and pedestrian rail trail mostly on the right of way of the former Springfield Electric Railway, which carried both passengers and freight beginning in 1897. At the peak of its activity in 1910, the railway ran a dozen trips a day to Charlestown, New Hampshire, connecting with the Boston & Maine Railroad. Re-organized as the Springfield Terminal Railway in 1921, by 1947 it carried just freight for the machine tool industry in Springfield until the end of its operation in 1984. The line began as an electric trolley line powered primarily by a generator at a log crib dam at Gould's Mills Falls on the Black River, which the trail follows. The trail gets its name from the trolley cars, which were affectionately called "Toonerville trolleys" after a newspaper cartoon strip popular in the early 20th century. The line converted to diesel power in 1956.

The Toonerville Trail is 10 ft. wide, paved smoothly enough for rollerblades and nearly level. Developed by Springfield Trails and Greenways, it is popular in snow-free seasons, especially on its upper portion, which is farther from roads and does not share space with vehicles. Total elevation change from the lower end of the trail near I-91 to the upper end is only 20 ft. The trail can be used for snowshoeing and skiing, but snow conditions are often poor for skiing, especially on portions next to Vt. 11, which pick up dirt and salt from the highway. Snowshoeing and skiing are impossible where the trail is on roadway. Except where the trail follows roads (where the railroad tracks originally shared space with cars and trucks), motorized vehicles are prohibited. Dogs must be leashed.

For more information and a pictorial trail map: www.springfieldvt.com, click on Toonerville Trail.

Distance: 3.0 mi.

To the Trail: There are two designated trailheads, a small one near exit 7 on I-91 and a large one 2.7 mi. west of exit 7 on Vt. 11.

> **To the small trailhead:** Head 0.2 mi. east of the underpass of Vt. 11 beneath I-91; parking for five cars is provided in a paved lot south of Vt. 11, marked by a sign: "Trailhead Parking."
>
> **To the large trailhead:** Travel 2.7 mi. west of the underpass of Vt. 11 beneath I-91 to a large gravel parking lot on the north side of the highway,

just after the speed limit drops to 35 miles per hour, and marked by a small sign, "To Bike Route," and a large one, "Robert S. Jones Industrial Center." The large trailhead is cleared of snow in winter; the small one may or may not be. There is a portable toilet at the large trailhead in mild weather.

Description: Beginning at the large trailhead (0.0 mi.), the Toonerville Trail first follows the Black River at some distance from the highway; this is the quietest part of the trail. It approaches more closely to the road (0.8 mi.), passes Gould's Mills Falls (1.4 mi.), where a bench provides a rest point with a view of the falls, and joins Paddock Road (1.8 mi.).

> **Junction:** Turning onto Vt. 11 and following the shoulder of the highway east (left) 0.4 mi. leads to the restored Eureka Schoolhouse, Springfield's first one-room school, built in 1785. In summer the schoolhouse is a tourist information center with toilets. Continuing east along Vt. 11 another 0.4 mi. leads to the Toonerville Trail at the other end of Paddock Rd.

At Paddock Road the trail turns left, following and sharing Paddock Road, crosses the river and continues along the left bank of the river. It leaves the road and passes beneath Vt. 11 (2.2 mi.) and crosses U.S. 5 southbound from Vt. 11 (2.5 mi.). It passes a large service station offering both food and toilets. The trail then passes beneath I-91 (2.7 mi.), and reaches the pavement of Old U.S. 5 in another 90 yds. Here, next to Young's Propane Depot, are some rails remaining from the railway. The trail follows Old U.S. 5, sharing space with an occasional vehicle, and reaches Vt. 11 (3.0 mi.) a few yards from the small trailhead. It then crosses to the north side of Vt. 11 and proceeds east a short distance to its end at U.S. 5 northbound from Vt. 11.

⑪ Lost Mine Trail

This red-blazed, 2.2-mi. loop trail takes in a historic mine, pine and hemlock groves, mature hardwood forest, a high rocky ridge, a mossy stream in a steep-sided ravine and areas of managed timber in the 550-acre Chester Town Forest. The abandoned talc diggings reached by the trail are the Gould Mine of the old Carlton Mine, which began production in 1894 and ceased in the 1930s. A rare silicate mineral with a unique crystalline structure called Chesterite was discovered at the Carlton Mine in 1977 and has been found in only two other places in the world.

Nicely laid out, the Lost Mine Trail was completed in 2007 by the Chester Conservation Committee. With its lowest point at 1,100 ft. above sea level and the highest at 1,560 ft., it spans 460 ft. of elevation. However, ups and downs between these points probably increase the total elevation change to 700 ft. There are also a few steep spots, so although it is not difficult, it is not a trail for walkers who don't like hills. Blazing is excellent and footing generally good. The trail passes through active deer habitat and wintering grounds. Dogs must be leashed.

The Lost Mine Trail is popular for snowshoeing; winter hikers are advised to use snowshoes with metal cleats and to bring poles as an aid on the steeper slopes. Skiing would be difficult in spots and demands strong intermediate skills even in good conditions.

For a map and guide, visit www.ourchester.org. Click on the "Environment" link to download the "Lost Mine Trail Map" and "Lost Mine Trail Brochure."

Distance: 2.2 mi. loop

To the Trail: From the intersection of Vt. 11 west and Vt. 103 north in Chester, follow Vt. 11 west to Balch Road (1.9 mi.) on the right just beyond the brick Army Reserve building and turn right. At Water Farm Road (2.7 mi.) turn right. Leaving room for others, park in the small lot (3.1 mi.) on the right at the trailhead. If this lot is full, drive back down the hill and use the parking area just below the reservoir dam on the right as you descend. This lower parking area is kept open for winter use.

Description: Although the loop can be walked in either direction, it is described here counter-clockwise. From the upper parking area (0.0 mi.), the trail begins on the left 25 yds. down Water Farm Road. It angles up a slope on a southerly bearing, then veers to the left, reaching the Gould Mine (0.3 mi.), evidenced by rock piles, a derrick mast, steel cables, a rusty oil drum and other mining gear, and excavations that may be water-filled. It continues generally easterly, rising along a rocky ridge, passing the end of a stone wall through the woods (0.6 mi.). After descending sharply, then rising again, it crosses a conspicuous outcrop of white quartz 90 yds. before reaching the trail's high point (0.9 mi.).

The trail then descends steadily down a ridge, eventually crossing an old stone wall, skirting a plantation of red pine on the left and crossing a woods road serving as a snowmobile trail (1.4 mi.). It follows the left side of another stone wall, then crosses a massive old stone wall (1.5 mi.) and switchbacks down a steep slope to a stream at the bottom of a ravine (1.6 mi.). After crossing yet another wall and woods road-snowmobile trail (1.7 mi.) the trail climbs higher on the left ravine slope, paralleling the stream below to a scenic overlook atop a large natural stone 25 yds. before crossing another stone wall (2.0 mi.). After a final wall crossing (2.1 mi.) the trail crosses a rivulet and climbs steeply to rejoin Water Farm Road (2.2 mi.) 35 yds. above the upper parking lot.

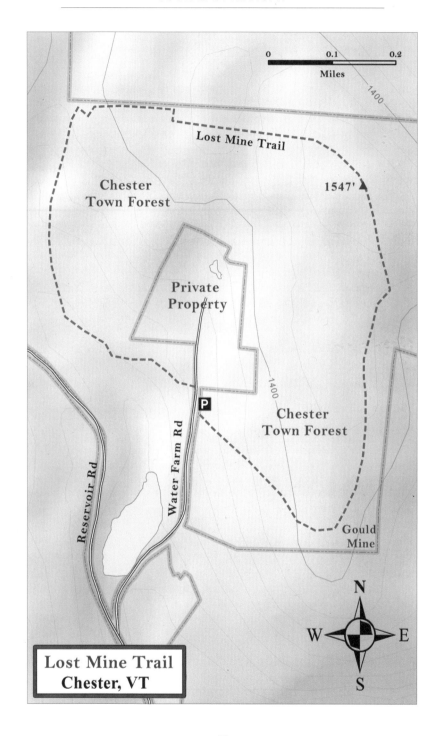

0   0.1   0.2
Miles

1400

Lost Mine Trail

Chester
Town Forest

1547'

Private
Property

1400

P

Chester
Town Forest

Reservoir Rd

Water Farm Rd

Gould
Mine

N
W   E
S

**Lost Mine Trail
Chester, VT**

⑫ Lowell Lake State Park

The blue-blazed Lowell Lake Trail is a 3.3-mi. loop circling Lowell Lake in Lowell Lake State Park, a 361-acre lightly developed, secluded and very attractive state park including most of the lake shore and all but one island. A mile of the trail follows gravel park service roads, a few yards a town road, and half a mile a snowmobile trail. Most of it is a narrow footpath through the woods, including stands of majestic white pines. The trail passes a Revolutionary War-era cemetery and features scenic views of the lake and wetlands. Trail maps are available at the park bulletin board and online.

The trail never rises very high above the lake shore, but there are a few modest rises and dips; total elevation change is about 250 ft. Footing is generally good with a few small wet spots and some moderately rough sections. Junctions are clearly signed. The park is open in winter. The trail is suitable for snowshoeing and most of it can be skied by intermediate skiers; difficult sections can be detoured if the lake is safely frozen.

A portable toilet is provided at the parking lot in the warmer months. Fires and motorized vehicles are not permitted. Pets must be kept under control. The trail crosses some private land, so it is especially important to stay on the trail.

For more information: Lowell Lake State Park, 1756 Little Pond Rd., Londonderry, VT 05148; 802-824-4035; www.vtstateparks.com.

Distance: 3.3 mi. loop

Lowell Lake in Lowell Lake State Park.

To the Trail: From the junction of Vt. 100 north and Vt. 11 east (0.0 mi.) in Londonderry, follow Vt. 11 east to the gravel Lowell Lake Road (3.1 mi.) and turn left. Where Lowell Lake Road swings sharply left (3.8 mi.), turn right on the gravel driveway into Lowell Lake State Park (small sign at entrance). Park in the graveled lot (3.9 mi.).

Description: From the park bulletin board at the parking lot (0.0 mi.), the route dips down to the lake, then turns right and follows the shore, with the lake on the left, to the dam, where a sign marks the Lowell Lake Trail. The trail crosses the lake outlet on a bridge above the dam to a junction (0.1 mi.).

> **Junction:** A side trail to the right leads 45 yds. up a slope to the Lowell Lake Cemetery.

Entering the woods and swinging away from the lake, the trail passes an informal trail to the right (0.5 mi.) that leads a short distance to the Lowell Lake Road. At a junction (0.7 mi.), it joins a snowmobile trail (VAST trail #11), which also leads right to Lowell Lake Road. Passing a cleared area visible on the right (1.1 mi.), the trail forks left off the snowmobile trail (1.2 mi.). The lake soon comes into view (1.3 mi.) and the trail climbs to a stand of conifers at the top of a knoll above the lake (1.4 mi.), descends, turns right and skirts a cove close to the shore. It passes a large beaver lodge (1.6 mi.) on the lake shore, reaches a junction (1.7 mi.)—where a trail to the right leads up the hillside to the Powder Mill housing development—and climbs again to contour the slope through a stand of towering white pine trees.

Crossing a footbridge (2.0 mi.), the trail reaches the south end of the eastern park service road (2.2 mi.) and follows it away from the lake to a junction (2.4 mi.) just before the bar closing the access road. The trail turns left, reaching a town road (2.6 mi.) and following it 80 yds. before re-entering the park and turning left at the gated north end of the western park service road. The trail follows this road south to the parking area, passing a clearing (3.0 mi.) with a barn on the right and a log lodge on the left. These buildings, and smaller structures visible through the trees, were part of a former summer camp acquired by the state in 1996. The trail passes a junction (3.1 mi.) with a service road leading right, a scenic point with picnic tables on the left (3.2 mi.) and, 50 yds. beyond, the cartop boat launch area, before returning to its starting point (3.3 mi.).

⑬ Grafton Village Park Trails

Grafton Village Trails is a 1.4-mi. network of footpaths blazed in several colors through mature forest on a hillside in the 50-acre Grafton Village Park on the west side of Grafton Village. The elevation change from the lowest to the highest points on the network is about 250 ft.

The most convenient access and parking are at The Nature Museum at Grafton, which manages the trail network for the town. The museum offers several versions of trail maps, including an interpretive map that provides information on plants and other features. The museum, open on weekends year-round (10 a.m. to 4 p.m., nominal charge) and by appointment during the week, is itself an interesting place to visit, especially for children. (The Nature Museum of Grafton, 186 Townshend Road, Grafton VT 05146, 802-843-2111; www.nature-museum.org.) It is usually open during school vacation weeks and holiday periods. Maps and trail guides are also available at The Old Tavern at the intersection of Vt. 121 and Townshend Road in Grafton Village or at the trailhead kiosk at the formal entrance of Grafton Village Park.

The trails have a few steep sections, but are generally not difficult in dry weather. They are suitable for snowshoeing in winter. Blazing and signs are clear. The network includes two gazebos, a secluded picnic spot with a fireplace and picnic table, and benches at intervals.

To the Trails: From the intersection of Vt. 121 and Townshend Road in Grafton Village, follow Townshend Road 0.1 mi. south to The Nature Museum at Grafton, which is on the west side of the road. Park in the roomy lot on the other (east) side of the road. This lot is kept clear of snow in winter. From the parking lot, walk 100 yds. south to the trailhead, marked by a white arrow indicating "To Village Park Trails" on a red barn on the west side of the road.

Alternately, walk north from the parking lot about 0.15 mi. on Townshend Road, turn left on Vt. 121 at The Old Tavern and continue about another 0.15 mi., bearing left at every opportunity (on Hinkley Brook Road, then again on Fire Pond Road), to the formal Grafton Village Park entrance on Fire Pond Road.

Parking is also available on the street in the village center.

The trail layout can be confusing, so a map from the nature museum is useful. The information kiosk and map display at the formal park entrance on Fire Pond Road are also helpful. However, the area is not large and the terrain is not complex.

Description: From the trailhead on Townshend Road, the blue-blazed Blue Access Trail follows a mowed, grassy path westward along an electric fence to a stone wall (0.1 mi.), which it crosses as it enters the woods. Just beyond the wall on the right, the white-blazed Stone Wall Trail (length 0.2 mi.) follows the wall north for some distance, contouring along the hillside, then climbs moderately to meet the red-blazed Red Trail, which forms one side of the largest of several loops in the network. From the stone wall, the more challenging Blue Access Trail continues straight, switchbacking steeply up the hillside to join the Red Trail at a higher junction farther south (stone wall to Red Trail, 0.1 mi.).

Between the two Red Trail junctions mentioned above are a rustic gazebo and a picnic spot on a broad ledge shaded by large hemlock trees, with a picnic table and fireplace.

The length of the longest loop on the network is 0.7 mi. This loop turns right from either junction on the Red Trail, which goes gently downhill to meet the blue-blazed Blue Trail. (Continuing ahead from this junction leads past a stylish gazebo to the formal entrance of Grafton Village Park, with its information kiosk, on Fire Pond Road.) The Blue Trail, a left turn, climbs steadily past two junctions with the White Trail, to meet the Red Trail at Rocky Cliff Junction, the highest point on the network. The loop continues steeply downhill on the Red Trail to the Blue Access Trail or the Stone Wall Trail and turns right to return to the nature museum.

The white-blazed White Trail (length 0.3 mi.) is enclosed within the loop described above, making it possible to walk several other loops.

Grafton Ponds Trails

About 13 miles of ski trails at the Grafton Ponds Nordic Ski and Mountain Bike Center form a popular cross-country skiing destination in winter, when the center also offers tubing, ice skating and a network of snowshoe trails. When the snow goes, the trails are open to the public for walking, with a small donation requested. A trail map on a billboard at the large parking lot indicates the many routes and loops available; a trail map may also be available at the small base lodge. There is a charge for mountain biking.

The ski trails at Grafton Ponds are wide, open and comparatively gently graded. They provide generally good footing, resembling grass-covered roads without vehicles (other than the occasional mountain bike). Most junctions are clearly signed; main junctions are designated with letters. Snowshoe trails are narrower, steeper and rougher, often without clear treadways, and brushy, requiring attention to red blazes painted high on the trees.

DICK ANDREWS

Big Bear Shelter at Grafton Ponds Trails.

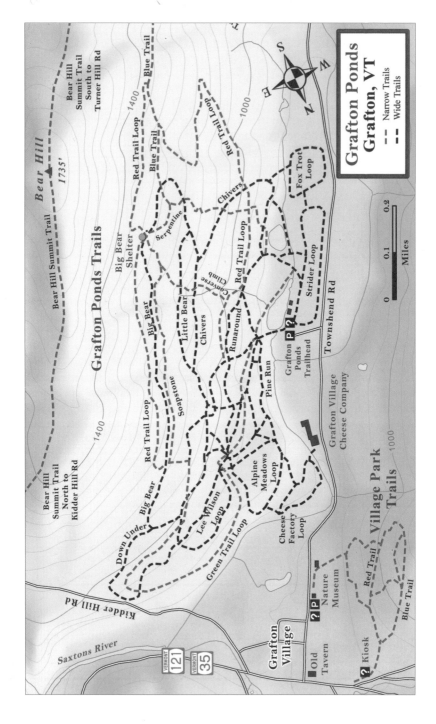

Grafton Ponds
Grafton, VT

- Narrow Trails
- Wide Trails

Bear Hill Summit Trail South to Turner Hill Rd

Bear Hill Summit Trail

Blue Trail

Bear Hill
1735'

Bear Hill Summit Trail North to Kidder Hill Rd

Grafton Ponds Trails

1400

Red Trail Loop

Blue Trail

Red Trail Loop

Red Trail Loop

1400

1000

Fox Trot Loop

Serpentine

Chivers

Big Bear Shelter

Big Bear

Red Trail Loop

Converse Climb

Strider Loop

Little Bear

Chivers

Red Trail Loop

Runaround

Grafton Ponds Trailhead

Soapstone

Red Trail Loop

Pine Run

Townshend Rd

Big Bear

Grafton Village Cheese Company

Down Under

Lee Wilson Loop

Alpine Meadows Loop

1000

Green Trail Loop

Cheese Factory Loop

Village Park Trails

Kidder Hill Rd

Nature Museum

Red Trail

Blue Trail

Saxtons River

Grafton Village

VERMONT 121

VERMONT 35

Old Tavern

Kiosk

S
E
W
N

0   0.1   0.2
Miles

The route to Big Bear Shelter is just one of many possible walks at Grafton Ponds. For more information: The Windham Foundation, P.O. Box 70, 225 Townshend Road, Grafton, VT 05146, 802-843-2211, www.windhamfoundation.org.

Big Bear Shelter

Big Bear Shelter, a cozy (8-by-12-ft.) log cabin on one of the highest points reached by a Grafton Ponds ski trail, is a pleasant destination and a dry place for a snack on a wet day. The cabin, a warming hut for skiers in winter, has a wood burning stove that should not be used in summer. The total elevation change is 400 ft.

Distance: 1.2 mi.

To the Trail: The Center is on the east side of Townshend Road, 0.9 mi. south of the junction of Vt. 121 and Townshend Road in Grafton Village. The route to the cabin starts at the billboard at the Center's parking area.

Description: The route climbs straight up the hillside above the parking area on the Main Trail, entering the woods, to Junction A (0.1 mi.). It turns sharply right along the Windham Trail, climbing gradually and passing Junction B (0.2 mi.) above the tube hill, then descends gradually to Junction D (0.5 mi.) where it takes the Chivers Trail uphill to Junction E (0.8 mi.). It turns right on the Big Bear Trail, climbing steadily past Junction U (0.9 mi.) with the Little Bear Trail. After a final climb the Big Bear Trail curves to contour the slope before reaching Big Bear Shelter (1.2 mi.). Return is by the reverse route.

⓯ West River Trail

When complete, the multi-use West River Trail will stretch 16.0 mi. from Townshend Dam, located between the villages of Townshend and West Townshend, west and north to South Londonderry. Walkers, cyclists and cross-country skiers enjoy the route, which closely follows the West River and in many places utilizes the former bed of the West River Railroad. Marked with lavender and green West River Trail markers, four sections of the trail are open. The Friends of the West River Trail (p. 237) maintain the trail. Conditions may change as sections of the trail are rerouted or improved.

All four sections of the trail, except one, require a walk of 3 mi. or less if a car is spotted at each end. The section from Ball Mountain Dam to Jamaica State Park is 4.1 mi. long, however the trail is level and easy. Sections are described in a northbound direction.

The West River Trail is suitable for snowshoeing and cross country skiing, and conditions are often good. However, access is more difficult in some places in winter. For example, the U.S. Army Corps of Engineers, Winhall Brook Campground and Jamaica State Park are closed in winter. Parking in other places may be restricted or unavailable. Local inquiry is advisable.

Conceived as a connecting link between the Connecticut River and Lake Champlain, the West River Railroad operated from 1879 to 1935 between Brattleboro and South Londonderry, first as a narrow gauge line and later as a standard gauge railroad. Much of the route from Jamaica southward remains well defined; many sections of roadbed and several bridge abutments are visible from Vt. 30. The story of the West River Railroad is told in Victor Morse's *36 Miles of Trouble* (Brattleboro, Vt.: Stephen Greene Press, 1959).

Townshend Dam to West Townshend

Following the old railroad bed and an abandoned section of Vt. 30, this 3.0-mi. section of the West River Trail (USGS Townshend) traverses the river bottomland along the east side of Townshend Reservoir and the West River. Elevation change is minor. Located entirely on U.S. Army Corps of Engineers property, much of the first half of the trail may be underwater in spring or when the Townshend Dam inundates the area for flood control. Contact the Corps office at the dam (802-365-7703) for trail information.

Townshend Dam was constructed between November 1958 and June 1961 and stretches 1,700 ft. in width and 133 ft. in height. With a drainage area of 278 square miles, the 1,010-acre lake has a maximum impoundment of 11 billion gallons.

Distance: 3.0 mi.

To the Trail: The trail starts at a large paved parking area on the southwest side of Vt. 30 at the Townshend Dam, 2.1 mi. west of the common in Townshend village or 2.4 mi. south of the post office in West Townshend.

Description: From a sign at the west end of the parking area (0.0 mi.), the trail descends steeply through young forest to a cleared area behind the concrete spillway of the dam, then turns right onto an old roadway. The trail descends more gradually to the edge of the reservoir and into open, brushy land amid broken tree limbs caused by ice damage from stored water.

With Rattlesnake Mountain lying straight ahead and the West River Railroad bed visible in the trees to the right, the trail continues north, following the blacktop roadway of a former section of Vt. 30 (0.2 mi.), abandoned when the dam was constructed.

The trail crosses a log boom and yellow gate (0.7 mi.) before arriving at a junction with a road on the right. Bearing left at the junction, the trail soon reaches the top of the reservoir where the waterway narrows and the West River veers to the far side of the valley. The trail follows a winding course past a series of small rock outcrops before meeting the river again, where both turn right (1.7 mi.). The West River Trail soon turns left off the old Vt. 30 road-bed (1.9 mi.), passes through a yellow gate and crosses Ranney Brook on a wooden bridge. (Continuing along the roadbed for an additional 0.4 mi. leads to the present Vt. 30, 0.3 mi. south of the post office in West Townshend.)

The trail, now a footpath, wends its way through a brushy area before crossing a large open field where the route is marked by West River Trail markers mounted on posts. At the far side of the field (2.2 mi.), the trail enters another brushy area, then follows the barely discernible West River Railroad bed past a row of large white pines on the right. Just beyond the trees lies the location of the former West Townshend railroad station. The trail leaves the roadbed briefly to cross a small stream, then rejoins it before coming to a washout (2.6 mi.).

The trail enters a wooded area and leaves the almost imperceptible railroad bed to parallel a channel of the West River. It makes a right-hand turn and follows an old road a short distance to a gate, where it turns left and soon ·reaches Vt. 30 at the Jamaica-Townshend town line. The trail follows the left side of Vt. 30 about 200 yds., passing a convenience store on the right side of the road, then bears left into the woods on a dirt road. This road ends in 500 yds. at the junction of Vt. 100 and Vt. 30, where parking is available.

Jamaica State Park to Ball Mountain Dam

This 2.9-mi. segment of the West River Trail follows the roadbed of the West River Railroad east and north along the West River (USGS Jamaica, Londonderry) and climbs over the U.S. Army Corps of Engineers' Ball Mountain Dam, for a total elevation change of 350 ft. The West River Trail also connects with the Overlook Trail and the Hamilton Falls Trail in Jamaica State Park. The Overlook Trail is described on p. 56.

Distance: 2.9 mi.

To the Trail: Jamaica State Park is located about 0.5 mi. north of Vt. 30, 4.5 mi. west of West Townshend village and about 9.0 mi. south and east of South Londonderry. From Jamaica village, turn north off Vt. 30 at a sign for the state park, pass the elementary school and cross a bridge over the West River to reach the park entrance on the left. The park offers a variety of camping and day-use facilities with a fee charged in-season. The park is closed in winter.

Description: From a gate at the northern end of the day-use parking area (0.0 mi.), the West River Trail follows the old railroad grade upstream and passes a series of wire cables stretched to the opposite bank of the West River (0.5 mi. to 0.8 mi.). These are used for setting kayak slalom courses. The trail then reaches a junction (1.0 mi.) where the north end of the Overlook Trail departs right to ascend Little Ball Mountain before returning to the state park campground.

The roadbed crosses several small streams, passes old foundations in thick undergrowth on the left (1.6 mi.), then skirts the posted boundary of private property for some distance before reaching a junction with an old road on the right (1.9 mi.). A sign marks the beginning of the Hamilton Falls Trail. (Reaching Hamilton Falls requires comparatively long walks from public trailheads:

either 6.0 mi. and 500 ft. elevation change from Jamaica State Park, or 4.2 mi. and 850 ft. elevation change from Ball Mountain Dam.)

The West River Trail continues on the old railroad bed to cross Cobb Brook on rocks beside the ruins of old bridge abutments (2.0 mi.). The roadbed narrows to a foot trail as it reaches the base of the Ball Mountain Dam (2.2 mi.). The trail climbs the downstream face of the dam by a series of switchbacks, surmounts the top of the dam (2.3 mi.) and descends the upstream face on a dirt road. At the dam tower (2.6 mi.), the trail follows a paved road under the bridge that connects the tower to the dam, passes a gate, then continues on the paved road to the start of the next section of the trail (2.9 mi.).

Ball Mountain Dam to Winhall Campground

This 4.1-mi. section of the West River Trail (USGS Jamaica, Londonderry) starts on the access road to the Ball Mountain Dam and follows a woodland path along the slopes above Ball Mountain Reservoir before dropping to the river's edge. The trail then follows a road along the former bed of the West River Railroad on the south and west shores of the West River to reach the U.S. Army Corps of Engineers' Winhall Campground. Elevation change is minor. This section is blazed with lavender paint as well as with West River Trail markers.

Distance: 4.1 mi.

To the Trail: The Ball Mountain Dam access road leaves the north side of Vt. 30/Vt. 100, 1.5 mi. west of the general store in the village of Jamaica or 3.4 mi. east of the junction of Vt. 100 and Vt. 30 in Rawsonville. The trailhead is located at a break in the guardrail on the west side of the access road 1.5 mi. north of Vt. 30/Vt.100, beyond a yellow gate and adjacent to a sign describing the Ball Mountain Dam. Parking is available in a lot near a building on the right 0.1 mi. south of the trailhead or just beyond the trailhead on the left.

The Ball Mountain Dam access road is closed from 3:00 p.m. to 7:00 a.m. and in winter.

Description: From the yellow gate (0.0 mi.), the route follows the narrow paved road a short distance to a sign for the West River Trail. Departing the road to the left, the trail descends gradually through a young forest to meet a junction with an old road. The trail turns left and immediately meets a gravel road on the outside of a hairpin turn (0.1 mi.). Following the left leg of the road uphill for a very short distance, the West River Trail bears right onto the broad grassy roadbed. Remaining on level grades, it narrows to a footpath to traverse a steep hillside, then crosses a rocky, washed-out area before entering an aspen-birch forest. The trail continues through rocky swales before descending to cross several small brooks on a bank overlooking Ball Mountain Reservoir.

The trail, now marked with occasional orange blazes, enters a hemlock forest (0.9 mi.) and makes a short but steady climb before dropping to cross a larger brook on a broad rock slab. Turning right onto an old woods road (1.2 mi.), the trail soon enters the open lands where the West River flows into the Ball Mountain Reservoir. The rocky slopes of Shatterack Mountain can be seen to the east across the water, while Glebe Mountain is visible upstream across the valley.

The trail crosses a brook to the right of a waterfall (1.4 mi.) and continues as a footpath through hardwood forest. After climbing a short, steep pitch, the trail takes a winding route through hemlocks atop a large rock outcrop, passes a U.S. Army Corps of Engineers' benchmark on the left, then turns onto a woods road at a point above the West River (1.9 mi.).

Soon leaving the road to the right (2.2 mi.), the West River Trail crosses a brook in a dense hemlock stand. Emerging into a white pine forest, the trail descends to a clearing and reaches a junction at the end of a dirt road (2.4 mi.). To the right, a path leads a short distance to the West River. The stone abutments of Pratt's Bridge, where the West River Railroad crossed the river, are visible on the left. Though the railroad was abandoned about 1937, the bridge remained until destroyed by ice in the 1970s.

The West River Trail turns left at the junction and follows the gravel road, which coincides with the roadbed of the West River Railroad. The road passes through a mixture of open lands and trees, with a number of views to the West River on the right, finally arriving at the southern end of the Winhall Campground (4.1 mi.).

Winhall Campground to South Londonderry

This 1.8-mi. section of the West River Trail has minor elevation change. Its start is separated from the northern end of the previous section (from Ball Mountain Dam) by a 1.5-mi. road walk through the Army Corps of Engineers' Winhall Campground.

Distance: 1.8 mi.

To the Trail: Winhall Campground, located in the town of Londonderry, is reached by turning east on the paved Winhall Station Road from Vt. 100, 2.4 mi. north of the junction of Vt. 30 and Vt. 100 in Rawsonville or 1.5 mi. south of the bridge in South Londonderry.

From a sign for the campground at the junction of Vt. 100 and Winhall Station Road (0.0 mi.), bear left almost immediately, then right at the next junction (0.2 mi.) to reach the campground gatehouse (0.9 mi.). (This is as far as the road is plowed in winter.) From the gatehouse, proceed a short distance farther to a fork.

To reach the northern trailhead for the previous section of the West River Trail, turn right at the fork to cross a bridge over the Winhall River (1.0 mi.) and continue through the open camping areas along the West and Winhall

Rivers. Parking is available at the end of the campgrounds where the road enters the woods (1.8 mi.), but vehicular traffic is permitted along the next 1.7 mi. to the site of Pratt's Bridge.

North of the Winhall Campground, the West River Trail is a dirt road extending toward the village of South Londonderry. The road is gated and follows the roadbed of the West River Railroad. To reach the trailhead, bear left at the fork beyond the gatehouse, and follow the gravel road that parallels the north side of the river. Parking is available near the amphitheater on a mowed area (1.6 mi.). The trailhead is a short distance farther down the dirt road at a yellow gate on the edge of the woods.

Description: From the yellow gate (0.0 mi.), with the West River visible to the right, the roadbed eventually passes over the abutments of a stone culvert that permitted cattle to pass beneath the railroad (1.3 mi.) and reaches a second yellow gate (1.8 mi.). The trail then becomes a dirt road and follows it, passing properties posted with no trespassing signs, ending in South Londonderry (2.7 mi.). Parking is available in South Londonderry.

Overlook Trail

This 2.0-mi. trail combined with 1.0 mi. of the West River Trail makes a pleasant 3.0 mi. loop, with 475 ft. of elevation change. One end of the trail departs from the West River Trail and the other end departs from a fence near the Hackberry Leanto.

Distance: 2.0 mi.

To the Trail: Follow directions to Jamaica State Park on p. 53. Walk 1.0 mi. north along the West River Trail.

Description: The blue-blazed Overlook Trail departs right at a signed junction, across the river from a sheer rock wall. The trail's sometimes steep initial climb over tree roots and rocks is in stark contrast to the easy, flat roadbed of the West River Trail. The Overlook Trail passes to the right of a large meadow (0.4 mi.) before skirting the left side of the remains of a pond. This area may be wet depending on the season and rainfall. The trail soon reaches a junction with a sign pointing to the right. Here a large boulder is visible near the summit ahead.

> **Junction:** A segment of trail forming a summit loop turns left, eventually rejoining the Overlook Trail below the summit.

Turning right, the Overlook Trail follows a series of switchbacks, beginning at a white birch with a triple trunk. The trail continues to climb until reaching a rock outcrop at the summit of Little Ball Mountain. (1,164 ft.), where care should be taken near the steep ledges. The trail reaches a vista with a marvelous view of the West River Valley, as well as the Green Mountains to the west.

Following blue blazes painted on both trees and rocks, the trail comes to a second vantage point (1.0 mi.), which offers a view of the town of Jamaica. From this point the trail continues along the summit ridge and passes the boulder that was visible from below. Here, the underside of the large rock is worn away, creating a small cave.

> **Junction:** A sign pointing left indicates the direction back to the first junction, below the large boulder.

Turning right, the Overlook Trail descends, steeply in places, eventually reaching a sign pointing to the right (1.4 mi.). The trail soon follows an old logging road that gently descends to an opening in the park fence near the campground. Entering the camping area at the Hackberry Leanto, the trail reaches the day-use parking lot to the right along the access road.

⑯ Windmill Hill-Putney Mountain

Located in eastern Windham County, the Windmill Hill-Putney Mountain ridge (USGS Newfane, Townshend) runs north and south, extending 16.0 mi. between Cambridgeport and Dummerston. The ridge is known as Windmill Hill or Windmill Mountain in the north, where it follows the town line between Athens and Westminster. To the south, along the town line between Putney and Brookline, it is referred to as Putney Mountain. The ridge rises steeply on the west side, then slopes gently to the east. From its highest point, in the Putney Mountain section, it drops nearly 1,000 ft. into the town of Brookline.

The Windmill Hill-Pinnacle Association (WHPA) and the Putney Mountain Association were instrumental in developing a total of 16 trails and protecting about 2,000 acres along the ridge. They depend on membership support to protect land and maintain the trails. Both organizations publish maps and brochures (p. 238).

Hiking trails ascend to high points on either end of the ridge, at the summit of Putney Mountain in the south and to the Pinnacle in the north. The following descriptions cover only a portion of the two trail systems. Display maps of the two systems are mounted at trailhead kiosks, which also provide leaflet maps. The systems use the same color coding for trail marking, with the main north-south trail using various names but always marked with white disks, and the side trails marked with yellow, blue, red or orange disks.

Dogs must be leashed. Metal detectors are prohibited and no artifacts may be removed. Groups larger than 12 and outdoor fires (allowed at the Pinnacle only with your own wood) require permits.

Ridgeline Trail to Summit Trail (Putney Mountain)

This 0.6-mi. trail, popular among area residents, follows the top of the Putney Mountain ridge before ascending a short distance to the summit, where there are good views west over the hills of the West River Valley to the Green Mountains, including Stratton Mountain, and east to New Hampshire's Mount Monadnock. The summit is an excellent place to view hawks during the fall migration. The trail is in the Putney Town Forest or on lands protected by the Putney Mountain Association. Elevation change is only 140 ft.

Distance: 0.6 mi.

To the Trail: From U.S. 5 at the general store in the center of Putney Village (0.0 mi.), follow Westminster West Road (the portion of the road in the village is also known locally as Kimball Hill Road) northwest to a junction on the left with West Hill Road (1.1 mi.). Follow West Hill Road, keeping right at a fork (2.5 mi.) and bearing left at a sharp curve where Aiken Road leaves to the right (3.0 mi.). Turn right onto the unpaved Putney Mountain Road (3.4 mi.), immediately bear right at a fork and continue past a fork on the right to the parking lot for the trail (5.6 mi.), located on the right at the crest of the mountain ridge where the road curves sharply right.

Description: The white-blazed (white disks) trail begins at the far end of the parking lot (0.0 mi.) next to a sign reading "Welcome to Putney Mountain." Here the yellow-marked West Cliff Trail leaves left.

> **Junction:** The West Cliff Trail is a slightly longer alternate route to the summit. It drops off the ridge and slabs the steep western side passing through tall hemlocks before reaching a junction (0.6 mi.). The blue-blazed Summit Trail leads right and climbs steeply 0.1 mi. to the summit of Putney Mountain (0.7 mi.).
>
> Bearing left from the same junction, the yellow-marked West Cliff Trail descends first west then north through open hemlocks and escarpments, passes a view (0.7 mi.), crosses a stream (1.3 mi.), briefly follows an old woods road (1.7 mi.) and ends at a five-way trail junction called Five Corners (2.7 mi.). From there the white-blazed Pinnacle Trail heads north 2.6 mi. to The Pinnacle (5.3 mi.).

The Ridgeline Trail immediately passes over a large outcrop of bedrock polished smooth by the continental glacier and meets a rutted road (0.1 mi.). The trail continues north through mixed forest with an occasional red pine, a tree not commonly found in Vermont. The trail splits and rejoins itself several times along its course. It passes a large ash tree, known as the Elephant Tree due to a peculiarly shaped limb (0.5 mi.), then forks. Bearing right and following white disks, the trail climbs past a stone wall to a junction (0.5 mi.). The blue-marked Putney Trail leaves left for the summit of Putney Mountain (1,660 ft.) (0.6 mi.) and continues to the junction with the West Cliff Trail (0.7 mi.).

Stratton Mountain dominates the view west, while Mount Snow and Haystack Mountain are also visible. To the east, the view encompasses much of southwestern New Hampshire, from Mount Monadnock to Mount Sunapee.

From the junction, the trail descends eastward to Banning Road (0.8 mi.), then follows white disks on Banning Road northward to the end of the town-maintained section (1.8 mi.) and continues on an old roadway northward to the five-way trail junction, Five Corners (2.6 mi.). The white-marked Pinnacle Trail leads north to The Pinnacle (5.2 mi.).

The Pinnacle

The Pinnacle is a high point on Windmill Hill located 2.0 mi. west of the village of Westminster West. Long held in private ownership, the Pinnacle was a popular destination for area residents. Purchase of lands along the ridge by the Windmill Hill-Pinnacle Association (WHPA) has secured public access. Three trails provide access to the ridge. The white-marked Jamie Latham Trail accesses the Pinnacle from the north, while the red-marked Holden Trail climbs the ridge from the east and the white-marked Pinnacle Trail accesses it from the south.

Jamie Latham Trail

This 2.1-mi. trail is a memorial to Jamie Latham, a young man from Westminster West who died in 1991. During his life he spent many hours visiting the Pinnacle. The route ascends the Pinnacle from the north and is marked with white disks. Elevation change is 430 ft.

Distance: 2.1 mi.

To the Trail: From U.S. 5 at the general store in the center of Putney Village, follow the Westminster West Road north and west 6.9 mi. to the village of Westminster West. Reaching a junction at the end of an S curve in front of a church, turn left on West Road, passing the white church on the left. From the north, the same junction may be reached by leaving Vt. 121 in the village of Saxtons River west of Bellows Falls and following the Westminster West Road south for 5.8 mi.

From the church (0.0 mi.), follow the gravel West Road to a junction and bear right on Old Athens Road (0.6 mi.). At a white wooden gate with a road leading straight ahead to a private estate (1.5 mi.), the Old Athens Road turns sharply left. At an intersection at the bottom of a short downgrade (1.9 mi.), the Old Athens Road bears left. From here, the road turns into a class 4 road with the condition of the road varying from season to season. It is generally passable by all but very low-clearance vehicles if caution is used. In winter it is recommended that cars be parked here, because the road to the trailhead is usually impassable and the parking area is unplowed. A large parking lot and kiosk are on the left (2.7 mi.).

Description: From the kiosk (0.0 mi.), the white-marked trail leads briefly south, passes a field, then turns sharply right (0.1 mi.), followed by a sharp left into young woods. The trail crosses a swale on puncheon (0.3 mi.) and climbs to where an old road comes in from the left (0.4 mi.). After descending to cross a second swale and climbing briefly in a section where several overgrown roads branch off, the Jamie Latham Trail turns right (0.7 mi.) onto an old logging road now filling in with briars.

Climbing moderately, the trail follows the logging road to its end at a small clearing with a picnic table (0.9 mi.). Continuing as a footpath, the trail almost immediately reaches and briefly follows a stone wall to the right before turning left and crossing the wall at a property corner. As the trail climbs moderately, it passes several hemlock groves before crossing another stone wall (1.3 mi.) near the top of the grade, then continues into a lovely, open hardwood forest.

The trail turns left onto a wider trail (1.5 mi.). As the forest becomes a mixture of hardwoods and softwoods, the trail reaches an intersection (1.8 mi.) with an older trail to the summit. Bearing right, the trail follows a wide, well-established path.

The footway turns to bedrock as the trail climbs toward the summit and an overgrown clearing. After passing a junction with the red-marked Holden Trail on the left, the Jamie Latham Trail continues straight to a clearing at the top of the Pinnacle (1,690 ft.) (2.1 mi.). A cabin, located here, is available for overnight camping. To reserve the cabin, contact the WHPA (p. 238). Views from the summit extend from Hedgehog Gulf at the base of the Pinnacle west to the Green Mountains.

Holden Trail

This trail climbs the Pinnacle from the east on an old woods road, with an elevation change of 458 ft.

Distance: 1.5 mi.

To the Trail: From the church in Westminster West (see directions to the Jamie Latham Trail on p. 59) (0.0 mi.), follow the gravel West Road passing the Old Athens Road on the right (0.6 mi.). Continue left on West Road to Windmill Hill Road North (1.0 mi.). Follow this road uphill until it becomes a class 4 road (1.8 mi.), then continue to a parking lot and the trailhead (2.1 mi.).

Description: This red-marked trail begins at a kiosk and an elaborate and artistically decorated gate (0.0 mi.). From the gate, the trail follows an old woods road climbing steadily to reach a trail sign (0.5 mi.). From here, the trail turns right onto another woods road. Following the road, the trail makes a gentle and variable climb, then descends slightly (0.9 mi.) to a moist area where short relocations and puncheon segments depart briefly from the road. A series of gentle switchbacks (1.2 mi.) bring the trail to the intersection (1.4 mi.) with the white-marked Jamie Latham Trail at the top of the ridge. Continuing left at this junction, the trail continues a short flat distance to the summit clearing (1.5 mi.).

⑰ Ledges Overlook Trail

Maintained by the U.S. Army Corps of Engineers, this 1.7-mi. trail loop begins and ends at a wooded picnic grove on the west shore of Townshend Reservoir (USGS Townshend). The total elevation change is 450 ft.

Distance: 1.7 mi. loop

To the Trail: From Townshend village, follow Vt. 30 north 2.1 mi. to Townshend Dam. At the dam, turn west and cross the spillway on a narrow bridge. Turn right onto an access road (0.0 mi.) and pass the beach (0.5 mi.) and picnic area (0.6 mi.) to the signed trailhead on the left. Ample parking is available on the east side of the road.

Description: The two ends of this yellow-blazed trail are separated by a short section of the paved access road. A register box at the southern trailhead contains brochures with a map outlining the clockwise loop.

From the register box (0.0 mi.), the trail enters the forest to follow a woods road, quickly crosses another woods road, then begins a steady ascent west. Reaching a stone wall, which it follows for a distance, the trail bears left off the road (0.2 mi.) on a southerly course through a mixed hardwood-softwood forest. The trail reaches and follows another road to the left on easier grades (0.3 mi.) before turning sharply west and crossing another stone wall. After resuming a steady climb, the trail turns north (0.5 mi.) and reaches the end of the woods road (0.6 mi.). Following easier grades, the trail soon reaches a rock outcrop and a picnic table (0.7 mi.), then continues to an old clearing at the top of a rock ledge (0.8 mi.). From this vantage point, there is a panorama of the West River Valley, including Townshend Reservoir and Dam and the Scott Covered Bridge. Bald Mountain lies to the southeast and the long ridge of Rattlesnake Mountain to the east.

Continuing north from the lookout, the trail climbs a short steep grade, then meanders along the top of the ridge parallel to the marked property line. In this woodland, a grassy lawn lies beneath a grove of hop-hornbeam trees. Leaving the property line (1.0 mi.), the trail gradually descends, following a well-worn footpath marked with faded yellow blazes. The trail bears right on a woods road, which it follows along a steady descent to the east, then southeast. Bearing slightly left off the woods road, the trail reaches another woods road, which it follows to the right. The trail passes some old foundations on the right (1.5 mi.) before again leaving the woods road. The trail crosses another woods road, then descends on easier grades to reach a dirt road. Bearing left on this road, the trail quickly turns right at a road junction, then reaches the paved access road (1.7 mi.) across from the Burrington Picnic Pavilion, 400 ft. north of the register box.

⑱ Retreat Trails

The more than nine miles of Retreat Trails occupy close to 500 acres owned by The Windham Foundation and the Brattleboro Retreat only a short distance from downtown Brattleboro and close to exit 2 of I-91, providing splendid walking opportunities. Most of the trails were originally constructed as either walking paths or carriage roads for patients at the Brattleboro Retreat, founded in 1834 as one of the first facilities in the United States for the humane treatment of patients with mental illness. Several reach Ice Pond, a small man-made pond that supplied as much as 96,000 pounds of ice annually in the 1800s for food preservation and ice cream at the Retreat. The trails were recently refurbished in a cooperative effort by the Retreat and the Windham Foundation, which manages the trail network, with help from the Vermont Youth Conservation Corps and support from Entergy Corporation and other donors.

Most of the trails are smooth and gently graded. While most are in forest, some traverse brushy areas and skirt the agricultural fields of the Retreat Farm, also run by the Windham Foundation. The trails are named, usually with the names applied in the early 1800s. They are not blazed, but the paths are obvious. Junctions are generally well signed. Each entry point has parking and an information kiosk with a large map. Traffic on I-91 is audible on the western portions of the network.

The network essentially consists of two sections. One is a compact network of short trails on Tower Hill, a hill next to the Retreat grounds surmounted by a Stone Tower (now closed for safety) built by Retreat patients to provide a view of the grounds and the Connecticut River Valley. Many Brattleboro residents have historically used the term "Retreat Trails" to refer to this portion of the whole network. The second section is a much larger network of longer links and loops on the slopes between the Retreat Farm on Linden Street (Vt. 30) and I-91. This area, called here the Retreat Farm section, is locally and informally called "the trails behind Solar Hill," or "the trails near the Harris Hill Ski Jump."

The Retreat Trails are open to cyclists and horseback riders as well as walkers, but are not heavily used by cyclists and show virtually no evidence of equestrian use. Pedestrians have the right of way. Motorized vehicles, alcohol, smoking, camping, fires and dumping are prohibited. Dogs must be leashed and waste must be removed. Some trails connect with private trails and access points; these are marked and walkers should stay on trails open to the public. Limiting use to daylight hours is strongly encouraged.

The Retreat Trails network is large and the topography varied, so it is wise to take a map. Trail maps and guides are available online, at all public entry points and at the following places: Brattleboro Chamber of Commerce, 180 Main St.; Guilford Welcome Center (off I-91 heading north into Vermont); Brooks Memorial Library, 224 Main St.; Burrows Specialized Sports, 105

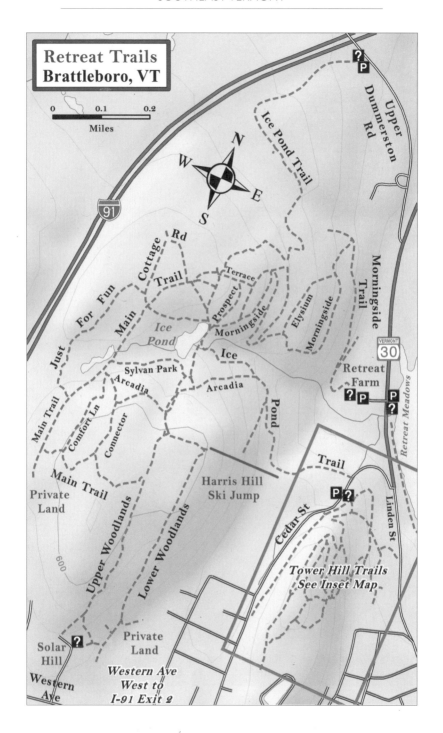

**Retreat Trails
Brattleboro, VT**

0   0.1   0.2
Miles

N
W   E
S

I-91

Ice Pond Trail

Upper Dummerston Rd

Cottage Rd

Trail

Terrace

For Fun

Main

Just

Prospect

Morningside

Elysium

Morningside

Morningside Trail

Ice Pond

Ice

Ice Pond

VERMONT 30

Retreat Farm

Retreat Meadows

Sylvan Park

Arcadia

Arcadia

Main Trail

Comfort Ln

Connector

Pond

Trail

Main Trail

Harris Hill
Ski Jump

Cedar St

Linden St

Private
Land

Upper Woodlands

Lower Woodlands

600

*Tower Hill Trails
See Inset Map*

Solar
Hill

Private
Land

Western
Ave

*Western Ave
West to
I-91 Exit 2*

DICK ANDREWS

The stone tower at Brattleboro Retreat was completed in 1887.

Main St.; Brattleboro Town Office, 230 Main St.; and Grafton Village Cheese Co., Linden St.

Children will enjoy the the chance to pet the animals at the Retreat Farm entrance (modest charge assessed; hours 10 a.m. to 4 p.m. weekdays and Saturdays, 12 p.m. to 4 p.m. on Sundays). The Windham Foundation runs the cheese factory next door, also open to visitors. There is no fee to use the trails.

For more information: www.windham-foundation.org; click on links for "Retreat Farm," then "Retreat Trails."

To the Trails: Directions are from exit 2 on I-91 (0.0 mi.).

Solar Hill: Travel east on Western Avenue (Vt. 30) to the gravel driveway up Solar Hill (0.3 mi.) on the left. Turn left, go uphill to the kiosk on the right (0.4 mi.) where the driveway bends left. There is informal parking for half a dozen cars.

Cedar St.: Travel east on Western Avenue (Vt. 30) to Cedar Street (0.8 mi.), turn left. The kiosk and entrance are on the right (1.2 mi.). Parking is on the wide shoulder of the street on the right; take care to park off the travel lane.

Retreat Farm: Travel east on Western Avenue (Vt. 30) to Cedar Street (0.8 mi.) and turn left. At Linden Street (Vt. 30) (1.3 mi.), turn left. Turn left into the entrance to the Retreat Farm (1.5 mi.). The kiosk is at the base of the tallest silo at the farm.

Retreat Meadows Boat Launch: Across Vt. 30 from the Retreat Farm (directions above). Parking is in a graveled area between the road and the water.

Upper Dummerston Rd.: Travel east on Western Avenue (Vt. 30) to Cedar Street (0.8 mi.) and turn left. At Linden Street (Vt. 30) (1.3 mi.), turn left. At Upper Dummerston Road (1.8 mi.), turn left. The kiosk and entrance are on the left just before the underpass beneath I-91. Parking (1.9 mi.) is on the right just beyond I-91. Please do not block the gated farm road.

Tower Road

This trail is an old carriage road to the stone tower built by Retreat patients. It climbs about 125 ft in a round-trip of 0.5 mi.

To the Trail: This trail begins at the Cedar Street entrance.

Description: The trail is signed from its start on Cedar Street. It winds, largely through tall conifers, in switchbacks to the base of the stone tower (0.25 mi.), an impressive construction. There are no distant views.

Tower Hill Perimeter

This series of trails circles most of Tower Hill, climbing and descending about 125 ft. over a distance of 0.8 mi. It has some steep slopes and stone steps with high rises.

To the Trail: This trail begins at the Cedar Street entrance.

Description: The route begins on the Cemetery Trail, turning left from the kiosk and descending slightly toward a residential area, then swinging right and contouring the slope on a wide footpath. At a four-way junction, it switches to the Tower Climb Trail, a narrower trail that becomes a steep climb on switchbacks, including some high stone steps, and reaches the Stone Tower. Beyond the tower, the route takes the Ledge Trail; some care is needed to avoid veering to the left on trails that lead to private land. The Ledge Trail angles downward along a steep slope affording views through tall conifers toward Cedar Street. At a junction with Tower Road, the route turns left onto Tower Road and finishes the descent to the starting point.

Ice Pond from Cedar Street

This trail follows an old carriage road to Ice Pond; the round-trip is 1.0 mi. with a total elevation change of about 175 ft.

To the Trail: This trail begins at the Cedar Street entrance.

Description: From the kiosk (0.0 mi.), the route follows Cedar Street 70 yds. downhill; the Ice Pond Trail, which the route follows, begins across the street. The trail skirts an agricultural field on the left, enters the opening at the base of the defunct Harris Hill Ski Jump (0.15 mi.) and re-enters the woods in 100 yds. It passes a woods road to the left (0.3 mi.), reaching a junction (0.35 mi.) with the Arcadia Trail, which bears left. It joins the Main Trail at Ice Pond (0.5 mi.). Return is by the reverse route.

Ice Pond from Solar Hill

This route to Ice Pond via the Lower Woodlands Trail and Main Trail is a 1.6-mi. round-trip walk through mature forest with only moderate elevation changes.

To the Trail: This trail begins at the Solar Hill entrance.

Description: The route enters the woods, reaching a junction with the Upper Woodlands Trail in 60 yds. The Lower Woodlands Trail bears slightly right, then climbs north gradually to a junction (0.5 mi.) with a short but steep gravel slope that climbs to the top of the Harris Hill Ski Jump. The view down the precipitous line of the jump will give most walkers second thoughts about taking up ski jumping. After the junction, the Lower Woodlands Trail bears west,

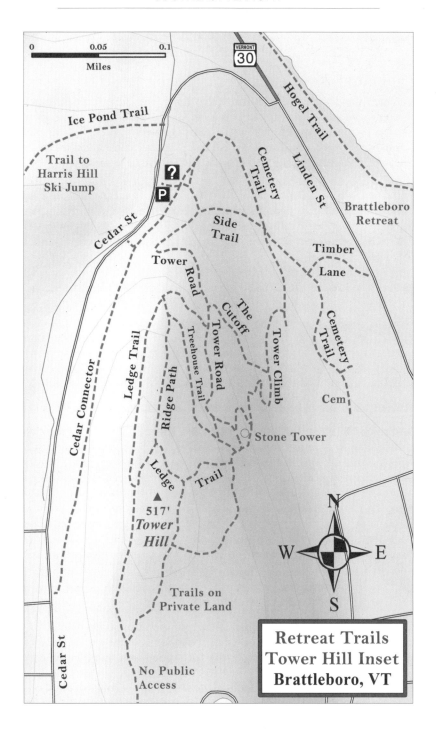

0   0.05   0.1
Miles

VERMONT
30

Hogel Trail

Ice Pond Trail

Trail to
Harris Hill
Ski Jump

?

P

Cedar St

Cemetery
Trail

Linden St

Brattleboro
Retreat

Side
Trail

Timber
Lane

Tower
Road

The
Cutoff

Cemetery
Trail

Ledge Trail

Cedar Connector

Ridge Path

Treehouse Trail

Tower Road

Tower Climb

Cem

Stone Tower

Ledge
Trail

▲
517'
Tower
Hill

N
W   E
S

Trails on
Private Land

Cedar St

No Public
Access

**Retreat Trails
Tower Hill Inset
Brattleboro, VT**

reaching its junction with the Main Trail in 140 yds. The route turns right on the Main Trail, reaching Ice Pond (0.8 mi.). Return is by the reverse route.

Ice Pond from Upper Dummerston Road

This newly established section of the Ice Pond Trail follows a farm track through agricultural fields part of the way to Ice Pond, affording an openness that can be a nice change from forested trails. The forested portion of the trail is rougher than other Retreat Trails because it is not a constructed footpath. The round-trip distance is 1.9 mi.; total elevation change is moderate.

To the Trail: This trail begins at the Upper Dummerston Road entrance.

Description: The trail follows a farm track along the edge of a field, paralleling I-91 less than 100 yds. away. It swings away from the highway and crosses the field (0.25 mi.), enters the woods (0.35 mi.) and crosses another field (0.5 mi.). Re-entering the woods, the trail reaches a junction (0.8 mi.) with the Terrace Trail in a brushy area, then a junction with the Main Trail (0.9 mi.) and arrives at Ice Pond (1.0 mi.).

Ice Pond from Retreat Farm

This 2.3-mi. round-trip walk climbs 250 ft. from Retreat Farm to Ice Pond on the Morningside Trail. The trail follows a farm track, then a former cross-country ski trail, so grades are generally not steep. Almost all of the way is forested.

To the Trail: This trail begins at the Retreat Farm entrance.

Description: Starting at the kiosk (0.0 mi.), the trail passes between two farm buildings, turns left and follows a farm track behind the buildings, then swings right, entering the woods and passing another farm road branching right (0.1 mi.). The track angles up the slope to a junction (0.35 mi.), where the Morningside Trail turns left away from the farm track. Passing junctions for the Elysium Trail (0.55 mi. and 0.7 mi.), the trail meets the Roundabout Trail the first time (0.75 mi.), makes a hairpin turn right, meets the Roundabout Trail again at a switchback to the left (0.95 mi.), meets the Roundabout Trail for the third and final time (1.05 mi.), then reaches Ice Pond (1.15 mi.).

⑲ Fort Dummer State Park

Fort Dummer State Park occupies 217 acres in the Connecticut River Valley just outside Brattleboro. Bordering the foothills of the eastern edge of the Green Mountains, the chestnut-oak hardwood forest found in the park is more typical of southern New England than Vermont. The park contains a relatively short hiking loop leading to two vistas overlooking the Connecticut River. Camping facilities are available and a day-use fee is charged in-season.

Distance: 1.25 mi.

To the Trail: Fort Dummer State Park is a short distance south of Brattleboro. From I-91 exit 1, follow U.S. 5 north 0.25 mi. to the first traffic light and turn east (right) on Fairground Road (0.0 mi.). Continue past the high school and town garage to an intersection near the bottom of a winding hill (0.5 mi.). Turn right to follow South Main Street and its continuation, Old Guilford Road, to a dead end at the park (1.6 mi.).

Description: From the park contact station, the route follows the paved road to its end at an intersection where dirt roads lead left and right to the two campgrounds. The trailhead is located a few yards north of the intersection, at a sign for the Sunrise Trail. A blue-blazed trail leads a short distance to a junction marking the head of the loop. Bearing left at the junction onto a lesser used red-blazed trail, the northern leg of the loop crosses over a small footbridge and continues an easy ascent, soon reaching another junction.

> **Junction:** To the left, a yellow-blazed lookout spur leads a short distance to an opening with views atop a granite ledge. While the original site of Fort Dummer was flooded when the Vernon Dam was constructed in 1908, its former location is visible on the western bank of the river at a point near the lumber company. From this overlook, there are also views southward to the Vermont Yankee nuclear station, and beyond to Mount Monadnock in New Hampshire and northern Massachusetts.

The main trail continues right at the junction, soon reaches another vista, then comes to a junction where a trail leaves right on a more direct route to the beginning of the loop. Continuing straight, the southernmost leg of the loop follows a marginally longer route to reach the same spot.

Another loop can be made by heading south from the park gates on an old road paralleling I-91, then bearing left up a blazed trail to overlook Algiers Village of the Town of Guilford. The trail continues from the overlook back to the park's playground.

20 Sweet Pond State Park

Once a private estate, Sweet Pond State Park (USGS Brattleboro) has a mile-long hiking trail that follows most of the undeveloped shoreline of the namesake pond. Several log benches at the ends of short spur trails offer pleasant sites for enjoying the pond and its surroundings from different angles. The park has no developed facilities, nor is there any overnight camping. There is no entrance fee.

Distance: 1.0 mi.

To the Trail: From U.S. 5 in Guilford (0.0 mi.), follow the paved Guilford Center Road west 1.7 mi. and turn left on the paved Weatherhead Hollow Road. Opposite Weatherhead Hollow Pond, turn right on Baker Cross Road (5.6 mi.). Turn right again at the next intersection (6.1 mi.) and follow the gravel Sweet Pond Road uphill, past two right-hand forks and a view of the outlet dam (7.4 mi.). At the Sweet Pond State Park sign (7.7 mi.), turn right, then quickly bear left to reach the parking area (7.8 mi.).

Description: From the parking area (0.0 mi.), the blue-blazed trail descends southwesterly for a short distance before swinging sharply left and following an easy northward route through the woods parallel to the pond. The trail enters a Norway spruce plantation and passes a spur on the right (0.1 mi.) that leads a few feet to a bench on the shore. After passing another short spur (0.2 mi.), the trail crosses two tiny inlet brooks in a wet area and continues through a clearing to yet another spur (0.4 mi.). The trail then crosses the main inlet on an old beaver dam.

From the inlet the trail soon enters an old hemlock forest and follows up and down routing above the east shore of the pond. After passing two spurs (0.8 mi. and 0.9 mi.) leading to views from the ledges, the trail reaches its terminus at the concrete outlet dam (1.0 mi.). Just beyond the dam is Sweet Pond Road, which can be followed uphill for 0.3 mi. back to the park entrance road.

㉑ Black Gum Swamp

Black Gum Swamp, located in J. Maynard Miller Municipal Forest in Vernon (USGS Bernardston), is the unlikely home of black gum trees (*Nyssa sylvatica*, also known colloquially as tupelo, pepperidge or buttonwood), some of which are more than 400 years old. Several other species of ferns and plant life that are normally found only in the southern United States flourish in this spot as well. Apparently established some 3,000 to 5,000 years ago when the region's climate was far warmer, these trees and plants have somehow managed to adapt to the present less-favorable environment.

A compact network of four color-coded trail loops provides access to two sections of the swamp, a scenic overlook and other areas within the municipal forest. There are no individual trail signs, but the generally well-defined trails are marked with diamond-shaped blazes. An interpretive bulletin board at the trailhead parking lot features a large map of the area and its color-coded trail system, regulations governing use of the forest and interesting facts about its history and features. Trail maps, supplied by the Vernon Recreation Department, are in an adjacent mailbox.

Note: Walkers are reminded to remain on the trails when viewing the environmentally sensitive High Swamp and Lower Swamp.

To the Trails: From Vt. 142 in the Central Park area of Vernon, about 7.25 mi. south of U.S. 5 in Brattleboro, turn west on Pond Road. (This junction is 1.3 mi. south of the village of Vernon and several hundred feet north of a white church and the Vernon highway garage on Vt. 142.) From the highway (0.0 mi.), follow Pond Road through the railroad underpass and past a road on the right. Turn right on Huckle Hill Road (1.2 mi.) and proceed uphill past several intersections before turning right on Basin Road (2.5 mi.). The road ends (3.2 mi.) at the trailhead parking lot and a large sign for the Black Gum Swamp and J. Maynard Miller Municipal Forest.

Description: The red-blazed High Swamp Trail (0.5 mi. long) leaves the parking area to the west and ascends a narrow gravel roadway to a dead end opposite a private dwelling. Turning sharply right, it makes a brief and fairly steep ascent to meet the west end of the Overlook Trail, then ascends westerly on easier grades. After circling three sides of High Swamp, the trail descends easterly through the woods and past a junction with the southern leg of the Lower Swamp Trail to complete its loop.

The green-blazed Overlook Trail (0.4 mi. long) leaves the parking lot along a forest road that begins a few feet east of the municipal forest sign. After a moderately steep climb on the road, the trail reaches a clearing on the right (0.2 mi.) with two picnic tables and an excellent view across the Connecticut River Valley to Mount Monadnock and its neighbors. Opposite the clearing, the trail turns left into the woods, climbs gradually for a short distance to its highest point, then descends to meet the High Swamp Trail, which leads left a short distance back to the parking lot.

The blue-blazed Mountain Laurel Trail (1.5 mi. long) shares the forest road portion of the Overlook Trail as far as the clearing. Swinging off the road to the west, the trail climbs gradually through an area of white birches and patches of mountain laurel, passes an old woods road to the right, then trends southwesterly to a woods road crossing at the edge of a large clearing. Here the trail is joined by the Lower Swamp Trail at a sharp left turn and both trails coincide over an up-and-down route through the woods to reach their end on the western side of the High Swamp Trail.

The silver-blazed Lower Swamp Trail (1.2 mi. long) begins and ends its triangular loop on the High Swamp Trail. From the southern side of High Swamp, the Lower Swamp Trail leaves westerly through the woods on easy circuitous routing to avoid wet areas. After skirting the northern edge of the Lower Swamp (and the Massachusetts State Line), the trail reaches a woods road junction. It turns sharply right and follows a woods road northerly to a junction with the Mountain Laurel Trail at the edge of a large clearing. The Lower Swamp Trail turns sharply right and follows up-and-down routing through the woods with the coinciding Mountain Laurel Trail to rejoin the High Swamp Trail on the western side of its namesake.

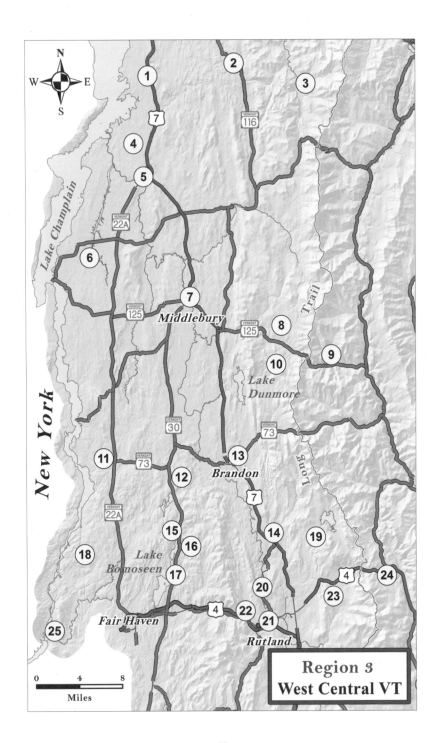

Region 3
West Central VT

0   4   8
Miles

Region 3
West Central Vermont

① Charlotte

Charlotte Park and Wildlife Refuge

This town park's 290 acres encompass active cropland, pastures, abandoned orchards, meadows in various stages of succession, woodlands and wetlands. A nature trail with 10 stations winds through the site and an interpretive brochure available at the parking area describes the flora, fauna and evidence of history that can be observed here. Dogs are not allowed.

To the Trail: From its junction with U.S. 7 (0.0 mi.), follow Ferry Road west to Charlotte and a four-way intersection (0.3 mi.). Turn north on Greenbush Road and proceed to the park entrance marked with stone pillars (1.8 mi.), just south of a railroad overpass. Ample parking is available here and a signboard describes the site and the code of conduct for visitors.

Description: From the parking area (0.0 mi.), the trail crosses a stream and reaches an overlook (0.4 mi.) before traversing pasture and woodlands to the final stop at an overlook of Lake Champlain (1.0 mi.). From here a longer loop circumnavigates another pasture or a shorter loop returns directly to the parking area.

Mount Philo State Park

Occupying 168 acres in the Town of Charlotte, Mount Philo State Park was established in 1924 and is the oldest park in the state system. A limited number of campsites are available atop the mountain and on its north side. Some very fine views of the Adirondacks and nearly the entire length of Lake Champlain can be seen from the north- and west-ledge lookouts of this 980-ft. mountain (USGS Mount Philo). A park fee is charged in season. For information: www.vtstateparks.com.

To the Trail: From the junction of U.S. 7 and Ferry Road, follow U.S. 7 south 3.0 mi. to a junction on the left with State Park Road. The same point may be reached from the south by following U.S. 7 north about 7.5 mi. from its junction with Vt. 22A near Vergennes. Turn east on State Park Road and continue 0.6 mi. to the park entrance at a four-way intersection. A paved state park road ascends to the summit area.

Description: A blue-blazed trail starts at a bulletin board next to the parking lot (0.0 mi.) and ascends the northwest side of the mountain. After crossing a park road (0.4 mi.), the trail soon reaches a junction at the base of a rocky outcrop.

> **Junction:** Here, a blue-blazed trail departs right and skirts an interesting area along the base of the cliffs, leading south and eventually ending on the park access road (0.5 mi.). From this point it is 0.7 mi. downhill along

the road back to the park entrance or about 0.3 mi. up the road to the contact station atop the mountain.

Bearing left at the junction, the main trail climbs to the top of the ledges and soon arrives at a second junction (0.5 mi.), where a blue-blazed trail departs left and leads 0.25 mi. to a camping area low on the mountain's north flank. The main trail continues straight ahead and reaches the first of several outstanding vistas atop the mountain (0.6 mi.). Near the top of the cliff, the blazes soon end and the trail skirts the summit picnic area before following an old carriage road through the woods (0.7 mi.). The trail ends on the summit access road on the western side of the mountain (1.0 mi.), a short distance below the contact station.

From 1924 to 1926, the summit of Mount Philo became a fire lookout station. From 1938 to 1940, the CCC constructed a steel tower on the mountain, which remained an active outpost until the 1950s. During the 1970s, the tower was removed.

Williams Woods

In 1996, The Nature Conservancy acquired this 63-acre wooded tract in the Town of Charlotte. It is an exceptional example of mature Vermont bottomland. Within its gently rolling terrain, unlogged stands of hemlock and oak closely resemble the forest seen by the first settlers of the Champlain Valley. The nature preserve is open to the public for foot travel over a 1.6-mi. trail loop marked by green-and-yellow plastic diamonds, wooden arrow signs and white blazes.

To the Trail: From its junction with U.S. 7 (0.0 mi.), follow Ferry Road west to Charlotte and a four-way intersection (0.3 mi.). Turn south on Greenbush Road and proceed straight through a staggered intersection (2.3 mi.) where roads leave right, then left. The trailhead is soon reached on the right at a sign (3.2 mi.). Limited parking is available on the shoulder of the road and care should be taken to park vehicles off the traveled surface.

Description: From the entrance sign (0.0 mi.), an access trail leads west a few hundred feet to a register box usually containing copies of an interpretive brochure. The access trail then winds along and crosses two wooden bridges to reach a junction with the trail loop (0.4 mi.). Following an arrow to the right, this trail makes a counterclockwise circuit around the preserve, returning to the junction with the access trail (1.2 mi.). From here, the entrance is to the right (1.6 mi.).

A conspicuous feature of the preserve's forest is the profusion of downed trees, many blown down because only a shallow layer of topsoil covers the impermeable clay. The trail is challenging due to many protruding roots and occasional wet areas.

② Hinesburg

Geprags Park

A map of Geprags Park trails can be found at www.hinesburg.org/hart.html and will be helpful as the trails in the park are not marked. The 1.1-mi. Perimeter Trail is described here.

Distance: 1.1 mi.

To the Trail: From the Hinesburg Town Hall, follow Vt. 116 north 0.8 mi. At the traffic light, turn left on Shelburne Falls Road and follow it 0.5 mi. to a parking area for Geprags Community Park on the right.

SYLVIE VIDRINE

Resting on a bench at Geprags Park.

Description: From the parking area, the route leads through a metal gate, up a small hill—passing a wooden shed on the right—and into a larger field. Bearing right along the edge of the field, it reaches a trail junction, where the loop begins. For the counterclockwise loop, the trail continues straight across a small wooden bridge. It leads to a smaller field, bears slightly right and uphill along the edge of the field to the South Bench at the top of a rise (0.2 mi.). A short distance past the bench, the Perimeter Trail turns right at a junction, while the Figure Eight Trail continues straight ahead.

> **Junction:** The Figure Eight Trail has two parallel branches starting from the Perimeter Trail. They both meet in 0.1 mi. at the North Bench. They split again, continuing to meet the Perimeter Trail farther north around its loop. The trail goes on easy grades through open areas on the hillside providing nice views of the surrounding country.

At a second junction with the Figure Eight Trail, the Perimeter Trail turns right and begins to contour the hillside at an easy grade. At 0.5 mi., two narrow connector paths leave left. The Perimeter Trail enters a field near the top of the ridge at 0.6 mi., then turns left at an arrow in the field. (A right turn leads toward Vt. 116 and a lupine garden.) Continuing along the edge of the field, the trail bears left at a fork, then heads uphill to a windmill. Passing the two connector paths and bending slightly right, it then continues straight ahead while the Figure Eight Trail enters on the left. Bearing right at the next junction with the Figure Eight Trail, the Perimeter Trail descends the hillside moderately steeply, passes along another field and heads toward a brown barn (0.9 mi.). This was part of the Geprags family homestead and has been saved and restored in recent years. From the barn, the trail turns left across the field toward the edge of the woods. At the woods, it turns right on a mowed path. At the end of the field, it closes the loop and retraces its route back to the parking area (1.1 mi.).

Russell Family Trails

The Russell Family Farm has a network of trails on a working farm. The 2.0-mi. Perimeter Trail is described here. For a shorter walk, there are a number of inner trails and roads. A map is available at www.hinesburg.org/hart.html. The Russells ask that you close all gates after passing through them.

Distance: 2.0 mi.

To the Trail: From the Hinesburg Town Hall, follow Vt. 116 south 0.3 mi. Turn left on Lyman Meadows Road, follow it 100 yds. to Lyman Park Road and turn left. Follow Lyman Park Road 100 yds. to the gravel parking area (facing the back of the Catholic Church). To access the trails, cross the Lyman Park fields in a northeasterly direction to the trailhead located just beyond the baseball diamond.

Description: The trail begins behind the backstop and is well marked with white rectangular paint blazes. It crosses the pasture road and fence and turns right along the outside of the pasture. At 0.2 mi., the Village Overlook Trail leaves left. The Perimeter Trail continues straight.

> **Junction:** The Village Overlook Trail, just under 0.2 mi. long and marked with yellow streamers, climbs steeply to the top of a hill where there are some nice views of the village of Hinesburg. From the hill top, the trail descends easily to the Perimeter Trail.

At the next junction, the trail turns left uphill in a clockwise direction. It passes the north end of the Village Overlook Trail at 0.3 mi. It then bends north, contouring a hillside. At 0.5 mi., the trail turns sharply right uphill, then sharply left before the crest of the hill, still following white blazes. It tops the ridge, then gently descends along it, bearing slightly right at blue blazes (0.7 mi.), to a pasture. Descending into a vale, it comes to a brook and wooden bridge at 0.9 mi. Continuing along the edge of an overgrown pasture, the trail re-enters the woods and crosses another bridge at 1.0 mi. It climbs a low ridge —a tepee is on the right—before turning left to descend and cross a pasture. The trail turns right along the fence line to follow it around the pasture for 0.3 mi. Some of the Russell's horses may be grazing in the pasture. At 1.5 mi., the trail returns to the woods, soon turning left at a T-intersection with a farm road from the pasture. It follows this wide road on easy grades. At 1.6 mi., it stays left at a fork and at 1.8 mi., a trail from the village condos enters from the left. At 1.9 mi., the trail crosses a pasture fence, turns left and soon reaches the end of the Perimeter Loop. It continues straight ahead to return to the Lyman Park ball field and the parking area.

Hinesburg Town Forest

The 18 miles of trails in the 850-acre Hinesburg Town Forest were developed by The Fellowship of the Wheel and are open for both walking and mountain biking. The short loop described here follows the Maiden Trail from the trailhead on Hayden Hill Road West to the trailhead on Hayden Hill Road East, then returns via an old road that is open to ATV and horse riders. An excellent trail map is posted at all trailheads and is also available at www.fotwheel.org. Please be courteous and yield the trail to bikers.

Distance: 1.8 mi. loop

To the Trail: From the intersection of North Road and Hayden Hill Road West in Hinesburg, follow Hayden Hill Road West 1.5 mi. to the parking area on the right where there is a signboard and posted map. The road continues to Hayden Hill Road East, but is narrow and not maintained. **Alternate Trailhead:** For the trailhead on Economou Road: at the intersection of Huntington Road and Texas Hill Road in Huntington (0.0 mi.), follow Texas Hill Road 0.3 mi. and bear slightly left on Texas Hill Circle. Follow Texas Hill Circle 1.3 mi., turn left on Economou Road (1.6 mi.) and follow it 1.4 mi. to its end (2.9 mi.) at a gate. The parking area is on the right and marked with a signboard. The last 0.1 mi. on Economou Road is only wide enough for one vehicle. **Alternate Trailhead:** For the trailhead on Hayden Hill Road East, continue straight past Economou Road on Texas Hill Circle to Texas Hill Road. Continue a short distance on Texas Hill Road, then turn left on Hayden Hill Road East. The trailhead is 0.3 mi. farther on the left. The entrance is marked with a large "The Eagles Trail" sign.

Description: The route to the Maiden Trail passes around the gate on an old woods road and drops briefly to a junction. The Maiden Trail, marked "more difficult," leaves left on a narrow path. It follows a small stream a short distance, then crosses it on a wooden bridge (0.1 mi.). The trail recrosses the stream, then crosses a wider old woods road. At 0.3 mi., it zig-zags uphill, traversing the hillside before beginning a long switchback (0.8 mi.) down to the Hayden Hill East parking area (1.0 mi.), crossing a steeper, more direct path several times. Across the parking area, the route back to Hayden Hill Road West turns left onto the gravel road and begins a steady climb over a single-lane, unmaintained road back to the beginning.

③ Huntington

Green Mountain Audubon Nature Center

Owned by the Green Mountain Audubon Society, the Green Mountain Audubon Nature Center is a 255-acre sanctuary that includes a great diversity of natural habitats, a working sugarbush and a butterfly garden. There is no admission fee, but contributions are accepted. Green Mountain Audubon also offers a variety of natural history programs for adults and children. For information: Green Mountain Audubon Nature Center, 255 Sherman Hollow Road, Huntington VT 05462, 802-434-3068, www.vt.audubon. org/centers.html.

To the Trail: The nature center is on the Richmond-Huntington Road, about 5.0 mi. south of Richmond village and 1.5 mi. north of Huntington village. There is a visitors center with parking on Sherman Hollow Road 0.25 mi. west of the highway and a parking lot near the sugarhouse on the main highway 0.1 mi. north of Sherman Hollow Road.

A 5.0-mi. network of trails, open every day from dawn to dusk, crisscrosses the property. These trails

During sugaring season sap buckets can be seen along the sides of the trails.

lead to a variety of wildlife habitats and offer views of the neighboring mountains, with Camel's Hump the most spectacular. A map, available at the nature center, is recommended for locating and identifying the trails on both sides of Sherman Hollow Road.

Huntington River Path

This short path along the Huntington River is maintained by the Huntington Historical and Community Trust.

Distance: 0.4 mi.

To the Trail: From Main Road in Huntington Center, turn west onto the gravel drive near the fire station and follow it 0.1 mi. to the parking lot for the picnic area.

Description: The route crosses the mowed picnic area along a line of cedars to a path marked with a small sign for the Historical and Community Trust. Bearing right, the path enters a field where there is a spectacular view of Camel's Hump to the right. It follows the course of the Huntington River downstream along the edge of the field. At 0.2 mi., it crosses a small wooden bridge into a second field and follows its edge to a path that bears left down to the river (0.3 mi.). Bearing right, the route leads east and ends at Main Road. (0.4 mi.).

Ferrisburgh

The Rokeby Museum

The Rokeby Museum features a 150-year-old homestead and was one of the most prosperous farms in the Champlain Valley in the mid-19th century. Settled in Vermont's early years of statehood by the Robinsons from Rhode Island, it is said to be the best-documented stop of the Underground Railroad in Vermont. Rowland Thomas Robinson provided fugitive slaves with the employment and education they needed to start new lives.

The 90-acre Rokeby site includes a 1.5-mi. trail, which incorporates natural and cultural history. In addition, eight agricultural outbuildings, several foundations, wells, stone walls, apple trees and a sheep dip may all be viewed by the public at no charge. A map and informational brochure are available at the museum, which is open from mid-May to mid-October. For more information, contact the The Rokeby Museum, 4334 Route 7, Ferrisburgh VT 05456, 802-877-3406, www.rokeby.org.

To the Trail: The Rokeby Museum is on U.S. 7, 3.0 mi. north of Vergennes and 2.0 mi. south of North Ferrisburgh village.

MARY LOU RECOR

Late afternoon at The Rokeby Museum.

Kingsland Bay State Park

Located in the Town of Ferrisburgh, Kingsland Bay State Park occupies 264 acres along the shores of Lake Champlain and was formerly the site of an exclusive girls camp. This striking area was also home to one of the earliest settlements in Ferrisburgh.

To the Trail: From its junction with Vt. 22A near Vergennes, proceed north on U.S. 7 about 0.5 mi. and turn west on Tuppers Crossing Road (0.0 mi.), just past a sign for Kingsland Bay State Park. Turn right on Botsford Road as indicated by a second state park sign and continue straight through a crossroads (1.1 mi.) on Hawkins Road. Follow this road along Little Otter Creek to Kingsland Bay State Park Road and the entrance to the state park on the right (4.5 mi.).

Description: A level trail, about 1.0 mi. long, leaves the northern end of the parking area and parallels the shoreline around the peninsula. The trail follows a wooded route before breaking onto the shoreline, offering intimate lake views of sailboats on Kingsland Bay and more sweeping vistas across the lake to the Adirondacks.

 Vergennes

Button Bay State Park

Located in Vergennes, Button Bay State Park occupies a 253-acre former farm site on a bluff overlooking Lake Champlain. The park is named for the button-like concretions formed by clay deposits that are found along the shoreline. Overnight camping and day-use facilities are available, with a fee charged in season. Button Point Natural Area, a 13-acre peninsula forming the western end of the park, contains fossils, old-growth forest and several rare or endangered plant species. A fee is charged in season. For information on daily nature programs for adults and children: 802-475-2377.

To the Trail: From the traffic light in the city of Vergennes, continue south 0.5 mi. on Vt. 22A, then turn west on Panton Road. Follow the state park signs 6.5 mi. northwest, then south over local roads to the state park entrance.

Description: A 0.5-mi. gated gravel road (no motor vehicles) leads west from the park picnic area to the natural area and the nature center, where a guide and pamphlet describing the interesting geology are available. From the center, the 0.5-mi. Champlain Nature Trail explores the hardwood forest and bluffs above the lake.

Vergennes Falls Park Trail

Vergennes Falls Park, with its six and one-half acres, offers walking, picnicking and bank-fishing along beautiful Otter Creek, Vermont's longest river. The creek flows quietly for over a mile and a half through Vergennes, before plummeting thirty-seven feet down natural rock ledge and continuing to Lake Champlain, about seven miles away.

This footpath offers a spectacular view of Vergennes Falls and an interesting nature walk along Otter Creek below the falls, ending at the BF Goodrich property. In spring, the parking area and parts of the trail may be flooded.

Distance: 0.75 mi.

To the Trail: From downtown Vergennes, head south on Main Street. After crossing the bridge, take the first right on Canal Street, then turn right on Mechanic Street to Falls Park. The trail begins at the far end of the parking lot, below Vergennes Falls.

⑥ Dead Creek Wildlife Management Area

The Dead Creek Wildlife Management Area (WMA), owned by the state and managed by the Vermont Fish and Wildlife Department, consists of 2,858 acres within the towns of Addison, Panton and Bridport. Over 200 species of birds have been sighted in the WMA, including marsh wrens, soras, common moorhens, pied-billed grebes, American and least bitterns, black terns, great egrets, snowy and cattle egrets, many species of songbirds, woodpeckers, ospreys, bald eagles, northern harriers, short-eared owls, American woodcocks, ruffed grouse, wild turkeys and grasshopper sparrows. Mammals include white-tailed deer, cottontail rabbits, gray squirrels, bobcats, beavers, minks, muskrats, otters, red and gray foxes, coyotes, raccoons, chipmunks, mice, voles, moles, shrews and weasels.

The WMA is a fine viewpoint for the annual migration of Canada and snow geese. The viewing area, with bird viewing shelter, provides information on migratory birds. Water levels of the WMA are actively controlled. Hunting, fishing and trapping are allowed on some portions. Access to other portions is restricted as the area is mainly a waterfowl refuge. There is a small boat access on Vt. 17 where it crosses Dead Creek. Two one-mile walks along Dead Creek and adjoining marshes offer opportunities to observe waterfowl and wildlife. A map is available at the Vermont Fish and Wildlife website, www.vtfishandwildlife.com, under the Dead Creek Wildlife Management Area link.

To the Trail: From the intersection of Vt. 22A and Vt. 17 in Addison, follow Vt. 17 west 1.0 mi. to where it crosses Dead Creek. The main viewing area is on the south side of Vt. 17, a second parking area and canoe launch is on the north side about 0.1 mi. farther west.

A view of Snake Mountain from Dead Creek Wildlife Management Area.

7 Trail Around Middlebury

Managed by the Middlebury Area Land Trust (MALT), the Trail Around Middlebury (TAM) is a 16-mi. footpath around the town, linking several hundred acres of town land, conserved properties, local schools and landmarks. Much of the TAM crosses private property, so users are asked to stay on the trail and respect the rights of landowners. The nine sections of trail include parking at most trailheads. A brochure with a map and detailed descriptions of the trail sections is available from MALT (P.O. Box 804, Middlebury, Vermont 05753, 802-388-1007, www.maltvt.org), the Middlebury Recreation Department Office, the Addison County Chamber of Commerce or the Ilsley Library in Middlebury.

Middlebury College Trails

Distance: 4.6 mi.

Description: This segment begins on South Street, west of the Middlebury College baseball fields, north of Porter Hospital. Heading west, it follows TAM signs around the southern end of the Middlebury College golf course. After crossing Vt. 30, it enters the Colin O'Neil Class of '97 Trail. The final leg, from Vt. 125 north to Vt. 23, passes through open and wooded lands, with a view of the Adirondacks. This segment ends at the Jackson Trailhead on Vt. 23 in Weybridge.

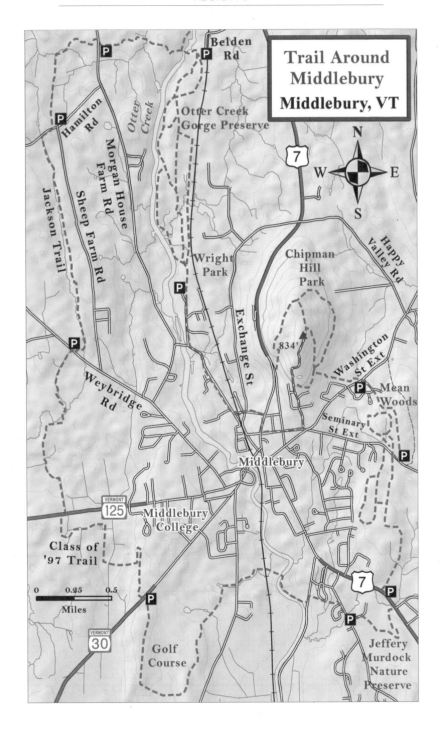

Trail Around
Middlebury
Middlebury, VT

N
W — E
S

Belden Rd

Otter Creek
Gorge Preserve

Otter Creek

Hamilton Rd

Morgan House Farm Rd

Sheep Farm Rd

Jackson Trail

Wright Park

Chipman Hill Park

Happy Valley Rd

834'

Exchange St

Washington St Ext

Mean Woods

Seminary St Ext

Weybridge Rd

Middlebury

VERMONT 125

Middlebury College

Class of '97 Trail

0   0.25   0.5
Miles

VERMONT 30

Golf Course

7

Jeffery Murdock Nature Preserve

Jackson Trail
Distance: 1.9 mi.

Description: This segment begins at the TAM parking area on the south side of Vt. 23, 1.5 mi. north of the junction with Vt. 125 in Middlebury. After crossing Vt. 23, the trail climbs over a stile near the north side of the road (caution: there may be cows in the pasture). It continues to follow the TAM signs to the lower end of a small gorge with a seasonal stream. Following the streambed for 1.0 mi., the trail enters a meadow before approaching Hamilton Road. Turning right on Hamilton Road, it continues 200 yds. east to the Johnson Trailhead and parking area on the left.

Johnson Trail
Distance: 0.8 mi.

Description: This easy stroll encompasses a pond and restored wetland, which provide habitat for a variety of waterfowl and muskrats. From the TAM parking area at the junction of Hamilton Road and Sheep Farm Road in Weybridge, the trail heads north along a fence line toward a pond and follows the perimeter to the right, entering the nearby woods. It turns east through deer habitat to the Otter Creek Gorge trailhead on Horse Farm Road.

Otter Creek Gorge
Distance: 1.7 mi.

Description: This segment, which is wheelchair and stroller accessible, begins at the parking area on Horse Farm Road, 0.2 mi. north of the junction with Hamilton Road. It follows a meadow fence line, then enters the woods passing various other trails. It follows the TAM markers toward Otter Creek and after crossing the Dan and Peggy Arnold Bridge, continues south into the New Haven section of the Otter Creek Gorge Preserve and Wright Park. A few hundred feet north of the main entrance, a short spur (only open for walkers and jog strollers) leads to a beautiful pool and protected shore of the creek. Walkers may continue to Belden Falls. Spectacular views of the Otter Creek Gorge may be seen upstream. (In the spring, water may be heard thundering in the gorge.) The Preserve highlights ecosystems of the Champlain Valley, including Valley Clayplain Forest, Transition Hardwoods, Limestone Forest and Limestone Bluff Cedar Pine Forest.

Wright Park Trails
Distance: 3.8 mi. network

Description: For easy access to the TAM, with bike and jog stroller options, the route begins either at the Belden Dam area north of the park or at the southern entrance off Seymour Street in Middlebury. Encompassing 150 acres, Wright Park has three main trails, running north/south. The White Circle Trail runs along Otter Creek, a small bay, a thirty-foot cliff and a marsh. The White Triangle Trail passes along the eastern boundary of the property near the railroad tracks. The TAM/White Square Trail passes through the central part of the park. Various cross trails connect to the main trails, forming loops. Reference maps posted at the north and south entrances of the park provide detailed information.

Chipman Hill

Distance: 2.5 mi.

Description: Chipman Hill, at 360 ft. above the town center, is the highest point in Middlebury, providing interesting views of the surrounding area. The hill was the site of Middlebury College's downhill ski area in the 1940s and 1950s, which featured a ski jump (remains of this can still be seen). The re-generation of the forest offers opportunities for walking, hiking and mountain biking. Trailheads are located at Springside Street, High Street or the TAM trailhead off Seminary Street Extension (east of the Co-operative Insurance Building).

Battell and Means Woods

Distance: 1.1 mi. in Battell Woods, 0.7 mi. in Means Woods

Description: This wheelchair- and stroller-accessible segment begins at the parking area on Seminary Street Extension, east of the village of Middlebury. From the Battell/Means parking area, the trail heads south through the Battell Woods into farmland. It follows TAM markers past the old Sabourin farm and homestead along U.S. 7 to Boardman Street near G. Stone Motors. The route crosses U.S. 7 to enter the Jeffrey Murdock Nature Preserve.

To access Means Woods, from the Battell/Means Woods parking area, the route begins 100 yds. east on the north side of Seminary Street Extension. It follows an old town road, then a wooded trail north, to a paved road (Peterson Heights). The route continues on this road 200 yds. to a junction with Washington Street Extension and follows TAM markers through a field to the base of Chipman Hill to join that trail network.

Jeffrey Murdock Nature Preserve

Distance: 0.6 mi.

Description: This segment begins on U.S. 7 across from G. Stone Motors or from Middlebury Union Middle School (MUMS) and follows TAM signs through the 16 acres of the Jeffrey Murdock Nature Preserve. There is a small cave at the north end of the preserve and huge oak and hickory trees throughout. Emerging from the woods onto the fields of the Middle School, the route follows TAM signs out of the MUMS driveway and heads right (north) on Middle Road.

Boathouse Bridge

Distance: 1.1 mi.

Description: From Middlebury Union Middle School (MUMS) or Middle Road, the route heads north on Middle Road, turns left across a field, then left again (south) on Creek Road. It turns right along the edge of Otter Creek behind the MUMS playing fields and crosses the creek on the "boathouse" footbridge (near the site of the former Middlebury College boathouse). Following TAM markers along the dirt road, the trail crosses railroad tracks—still in use—and turns left behind the playing fields to emerge on South Street, which it crosses to join the Middlebury College Trails.

⑧ Ripton

Robert Frost Interpretive Trail

The first part of this loop trail is wheelchair accessible, while the remainder uses boardwalks, gravel paths and an unimproved dirt footbed. Several of Robert Frost's poems are posted along the trail, where they may be enjoyed in an outdoor setting.

Distance: 1.0 mi.

To the Trail: This USFS trail loop begins at a parking area on the south side of Vt. 125, 2.0 mi. east of Ripton and 3.8 mi. west of Middlebury Gap (USGS East Middlebury).

Description: From the parking area, the loop trail passes through woods and old clearings. A spur trail connects to the Water Tower Trails. To preserve the scenic, open appearance, the U.S. Forest Service maintains all the old fields along this trail with prescribed fire.

Robert Frost Interpretive Trail.

SYLVIE VIDRINE

Water Tower Trails

The Water Tower Trails form a loop around a small wooded hill, with two shortcuts offering steeper options bisecting the loop. The namesake water tower, which can't be seen from the trails, stands off USFS Road 32 near the former site of a Job Corps center run by the Forest Service in the 1960s. The tower lent its name to a timber sale in the area and subsequently to the trail system established on the skid roads that remained.

The description below follows a counterclockwise circuit of the hill on wide, fairly smooth trails.

Distance: 2.3 mi. loop

To the Trail: A short spur trail leads from the Robert Frost Interpretive Trail to the start of this well-signed USFS loop.

Description: From the point where the spur trail leaves the Robert Frost Trail (0.0), the path climbs slightly to a T-intersection marked with the number 5. This is the start of the loop. Turning right onto the Crosswalk Trail, the route climbs gently through mixed woods to a junction on the left with the Afternoon Delight Trail.

> **Junction:** To the left, the Afternoon Delight Trail cuts across the hillside on steeper grades for 0.5 mi. and rejoins the loop.

Continuing straight, the trail descends slightly and crosses a narrow stream. In a small clearing immediately beyond the stream, it turns sharply left on the Sundown Trail (0.4 mi.), which climbs steadily as it winds toward the south slope of the hill and a junction with the other end of the Afternoon Delight Trail and a trail called Trepidation (0.8 mi.).

> **Junction:** Bearing slightly left, the Trepidation Trail climbs steeply a short distance to the south end of the wooded summit plateau. From here, there are winter views through the trees before the trail drops more gently to rejoin the loop after 0.3 mi.

About 75 yds. beyond this multi-way intersection, the route joins the Widow's Clearing Trail, which comes in from the right.

> **Junction:** To the right, the Widow's Clearing Trail rolls and dips gently through open understory westward to a parking area on USFS Road 32, 1.9 mi. south of Vt. 125, across the road from the Wilkinson Trails network.

The loop continues straight ahead, following the base of the hill until the Widow's Clearing Trail departs again right (1.2 mi.). Bearing left, the main trail almost immediately passes the end of the Trepidation Trail on the left and begins a gentle descent, on what's now called the North Star Trail, where there may be glimpses through the trees of the Breadloaf Range north of Vt. 125.

Soon the trail bends slightly right and begins a steadier descent. Rocks and numerous rivulets make this next section the roughest portion of the trail. At the end of the loop (2.2 mi.), the trail turns right onto the spur trail to return to the Robert Frost Interpretive Trail. The most direct route back to the parking area is to the left.

Spirit in Nature Path Center

MARY LOU RECOR

Located on 70 acres behind the Robert Frost Trail, a short distance from Ripton, the Spirit in Nature Path Center offers numerous pathways for quiet walking, in addition to nature study. With 9,000 feet of river and brook frontage in mixed forest and open areas, the center has space for reflection, with posted sayings along the paths that provide insight into spiritual beliefs. Spirit in Nature is a non-profit group of environmentalists and naturalists whose mission is to educate and remind us of our connection to, and responsibility for, the environment. The center is open to the public year-round, dawn to dusk. There is a donation box placed at the entrance. The trails are open in winter for snowshoeing and cross-country

Kiosk at Spirit in Nature Path Center

skiing. For more information, contact Spirit in Nature, P.O. Box 255, East Middlebury, Vermont 05740, 802-388-3694, www.spiritinnature.com.

Distance: 10 paths, from 0.5 to 2.0 mi. long

To the Trail: From Middlebury, follow U.S. 7 south to Vt. 125. Turn east on Vt. 125 and follow it 5.5 mi. through Ripton. Turn right on Goshen Road and look for a signpost for The Spirit in Nature Path Center on the left side of the road.

From Vt. 100 in Hancock, follow Vt. 125 west 10.3 mi. to Goshen Road on the left.

Wilkinson Trails

This network of short interconnected USFS trails totaling 5.2 mi. offers many possible routes and a maximum elevation change of 400 ft. Some of the trails follow a brook where the beavers are active.

To the Trail: The trail system begins across from the Widow's Clearing parking area on USFS Road 32, 1.9 mi. south of its intersection with Vt. 125, just east of Ripton village.

Texas Falls Nature Trail

Texas Falls lies in a dramatic ravine; several observation points and a bridge overlook the ravine.

Distance: 1.2 mi. loop

To the Trail: From Vt. 125, 3.2 mi. east of Middlebury Gap and 3.1 mi. west of Vt. 100 in Hancock, a paved road leads north 0.5 mi. to a parking area on the left.

Description: From the parking area, a self-guided nature trail (descriptive brochure available at the site) crosses a rustic bridge over Texas Falls and follows Hancock Brook upstream 0.3 mi. toward the Texas Falls Picnic Area. Bearing right just before the paved road at the picnic area, it reaches the upper section of the nature trail, which leads 0.9 mi. back to the falls.

⑩ Moosalamoo Area

The 20,000-acre Moosalamoo region includes a large network of hiking, biking, cross-country skiing and snowmobile trails on Green Mountain National Forest and Branbury State Park lands. Silver Lake, the cliffs at Rattlesnake Point and the Falls of Lana are natural highlights in this area (USGS East Middlebury), which is bounded on the north by Vt. 125, on the west by Lake Dunmore, on the south by Vt. 73 and on the east by the Long Trail. The name "Moosalamoo" is derived from an Abenaki word meaning moose call.

Moosalamoo is roughly bisected by USFS Road 32 (also known as the Goshen-Ripton Road or the North Goshen Road). The majority of the summertime day-use destinations lie west of this road. A free map printed by the Moosalamoo Partnership is widely available and is useful for year-round exploration. Contact the Green Mountain National Forest, Branbury State Park or the Green Mountain Club for a copy of the brochure. For information: Moosalamoo Association, P.O. Box 108, Forest Dale VT 05745-0108, 802-747-7900, www.moosalamoo.org.

Branbury State Park is on the eastern shore of Lake Dunmore and is transected by Vt. 53. The park site at the foot of Mount Moosalamoo was formerly a farm, then a summer camp for boys before becoming the 69-acre Branbury

State Park in 1945. Named for its location in Brandon and Salisbury, the park offers a variety of camping accommodations. Day-use facilities include a large sandy beach on Lake Dunmore. A park access fee is charged in season.

On the eastern shore of Silver Lake, in the northwest corner of Leicester, is the U.S. Forest Service Silver Lake Campground. The area is accessible only by two non-motorized, multi-use trails and a foot trail. Primitive camping without charge at 15 established sites is available on a first-come, first-served basis.

The USFS Moosalamoo Campground is in the northeast corner of the town of Goshen, west of USFS Road 32. The campground lies on USFS Road 24B and is accessible to motor vehicles during the summer camping season, when a fee is charged.

Branbury State Park Nature Trail

To the Trail: Follow Vt. 53 north 6.0 mi. from Vt. 73 at Forest Dale, or from the junction of U.S. 7 and Vt. 53 south of Middlebury, follow Vt. 53 south 3.5 mi. Branbury State Park is on the east side of Lake Dunmore.

Description: About 0.3 mi. long, the nature trail begins and ends on the east side of Vt. 53 about 0.1 mi. north of the park entrance. It climbs the hillside and makes a short loop before returning by the same route. A nature trail guide is available at the park, where naturalists are on duty during the camping season.

Falls of Lana Trail

This trail provides access to the Falls of Lana picnic area, an important way point for reaching other trails in the western portion of the Moosalamoo area. Walkers not staying in Branbury State Park, where the trail starts, will find ample free parking a short distance south at the head of the Silver Lake Trail, which also ascends to the picnic area. Used in combination, these two trails provide interesting loop possibilities.

Distance: 0.7 mi.

To the Trail: The Falls of Lana Trail starts in the Branbury State Park camping area on the east side of Vt. 53, opposite the main state park entrance.

SYLVIE VIDRINE

The Falls of Lana

Description: The blue-blazed trail departs the paved road in the rear of the campground between sites 22 and 23 (0.0 mi.) and zig-zags up the ridge to a softwood plateau. Bearing right to scramble up the rocks, the trail reaches a spur on the right (0.3 mi.) that leads to a pool below the falls. After again ascending steeply and trending left, the trail reaches an overlook with views of Lake Dunmore (0.4 mi.). Bearing right and descending slightly, the trail soon reaches a junction with another blue-blazed trail on the left, which descends over rocky and sometimes steep terrain to the nature trail. The Falls of Lana Trail climbs moderately to the right to pass through the Falls of Lana Picnic Area (0.5 mi.) to a signed trail junction.

Junction: To the left, the Rattlesnake Cliffs Trail provides access to Rattlesnake Point, other trails leading to Mount Moosalamoo and the USFS Moosalamoo Campground. Doubling back to the right, the Falls of Lana Trail crosses Sucker Brook on a bridge and follows a woods road downstream to its terminus at the Silver Lake Trail (0.7 mi.).

Junction: From this junction, it is a 0.5 mi. descent along the Silver Lake Trail to Vt. 53, from which point it is 0.4 mi. north via the highway to the park. The Falls of Lana are located a short distance downhill and can be viewed from above via unmarked spurs off the Silver Lake Trail.

In this area Sucker Brook has carved a deep gorge in the solid rock. When U.S. Army General Wool visited the site in 1850, his fellow travelers decided that Sucker Brook Falls was too prosaic a name. During his tour of duty in Mexico, the general had become known as General Llana, the Spanish word for wool. In tribute to the general, the party christened the site the Falls of Lana.

Goshen Trail

Distance: 0.6 mi.

To the Trail: Marked with blue blazes, this USFS trail begins at a parking area at the end of USFS Road 27. From Vt. 73, 1.6 mi. east of Forest Dale, follow the Goshen-Ripton Road (USFS Road 32) north 2.3 mi. to a crossroads. Turn left on USFS Road 27 and continue north to the end of the road (4.3 mi.) and the parking area.

Description: From the parking area (0.0 mi.), the trail crests a low ridge and crosses a power line (0.1 mi.). Descending through the woods, it reaches a junction on the left with the Ridge Trail (0.2 mi.), crosses a small stream in a hollow (0.3 mi.) and rises to join an old road (0.4 mi.). The trail then descends to its terminus near the northern end of the Leicester Hollow Trail (0.6 mi.).

⑪ Mount Independence

Occupying a peninsula on the east shore of Lake Champlain in the Town of Orwell, this low hill (306 ft.) has a commanding view of the narrow lake and nearby Fort Ticonderoga (USGS Ticonderoga). For this reason, the site was fortified by the Americans to bolster the weak defenses of Fort Ticonderoga after the fort's capture by the Green Mountain Boys in 1775.

A strong show of force at Independence and Ticonderoga, plus the lateness of the season, prompted the British to give up their plans for recapturing the fort in late 1776. The following spring, however, they made the American positions untenable by laboriously hauling their heavy artillery to the summit of Mount Defiance, a craggy hill on the west shore, which the Americans had thought inaccessible. The hasty retreat from Fort Ticonderoga and Mount Independence gave the British control of the lake again and set the stage for the battles of Hubbardton, Bennington and Saratoga.

Most of Mount Independence is owned by the Fort Ticonderoga Association and the state of Vermont and is open to the public between Memorial Day and mid-October. An admission fee is charged to walk the foot trails leading past the marked sites of the remains of the fortifications. Respect these sites in particular, and the area in general, by leaving them undisturbed. Collecting artifacts is prohibited by law. For more information: Site Administrator, 7305 Vt. Route 125, Addison VT 05491, 802-759-2412, www.historicvermont.org/mountindependence.

To the Trail: From Vt. 22A near downtown Orwell, turn west on Vt. 73 (0.0 mi.). At 0.3 mi., bear left at a road junction onto Mount Independence Road, which changes to gravel (4.8 mi.). At the junction with the Catfish Bay Road (5.2 mi.), turn left up the steep, narrow road to the parking area at the top of the hill on the left (5.3 mi.). The bateau-shaped museum and visitor center is on the right and is open from late May to mid-October, 9:30 a.m. to 5:00 p.m.) A brochure and map are available at the center and are recommended. The trails are open year-round.

Description: All trails begin at a trailhead kiosk near the museum and pass a signboard with a map. They climb northerly through a meadow for 0.3 mi. to the trail information outpost, where the trails diverge. The trails pass various archaeological remains (i.e., batteries, blockhouses, general hospital, barracks, soldiers' huts), and include scenic views of Lake Champlain and the surrounding area. Follow directional signs or colored trail markers for the Blue and Orange Trails.

The Baldwin Trail (1.6 mi.), which covers the southern half of the Mount with its two spur trails, has compacted surfaces, gentle grades and is compatible with outdoor wheelchair use. Along with interpretive signs and outstanding views of Lake Champlain, Fort Ticonderoga and Mount Defiance, the trail features two brigade encampments, the foundations of the general hospital, two soldier huts, two blockhouses, a storehouse, southern battery defenses and a likely powder magazine.

The Southern Defenses Trail (0.2 mi.) loops near the parking lot. Composed of compacted surfaces, stairs and stone steps (not wheelchair accessible), it passes the remains of a blockhouse, providing views of rugged rock formations and a vantage of Lake Champlain to the south. A short spur trail leads to the dock for the M/V Carillon tour boat.

The Orange Trail (2.5 mi.) crosses the highest point of the mountain and continues to a junction at the northern tip of the peninsula, where a short loop leads to the shore and back. Continuing straight ahead, the trail descends to the water along the slope of an old road, reaching the spot where a floating bridge led across the lake to Fort Ticonderoga. The trail makes a counter-clockwise loop around the end of the peninsula, past a rock outcrop and a junction with the Blue Trail on the right. Continuing, the Orange Trail then returns toward the starting point via parallel routing along the eastern side of the peninsula, at one point passing through a large area of black chert, a tool-making stone.

The slightly more difficult Blue Trail (2.2 mi.) leaves the information outpost to follow the route of a Revolutionary War supply road along the west side of the peninsula and ends at the Orange Trail near its tip. Some of the original stonework, built by American troops, remains visible along the roadbed. A quarry site along this trail was used by the French for stone that was hauled across the ice to build Fort Carillon, later renamed Ticonderoga by the British.

⑫ High Pond

Despite its name, the hike to this deep, pristine pond in Sudbury is almost entirely downhill. The pond is part of a roughly 2,800-acre preserve owned by The Nature Conservancy and notable for having one of the state's finest virgin stands of eastern hemlock. The land also once supported cross-country trails connected to a ski area called High Pond Mountain that operated from around 1940 until the early 1980s. Remnants of the trails and directional signs can still be found.

Distance: 1.6 mi.

To the Trail: From Vt. 30 about 6 mi. south of Sudbury village or 7.5 mi. north of U.S. 4, turn east on Monument Hill Road. Follow it uphill 3.4 mi. and turn north on Ganson Hill Road, where a large house stands on the corner. Alternatively, from U.S. 4 at exit 5, travel north on the unmarked East Hubbardton Road (which becomes Monument Hill Road) about 10.0 mi. to Ganson Hill Road. The parking lot is 0.6 mi. up Ganson Hill Road on the left, surrounded by "No trespassing" signs and 0.2 mi. below a house at the end of the road. The trail begins across the road about 75 ft. farther.

Description: From the road (0.0 mi.), the trail follows a small stream uphill and crosses a low ridge before turning right onto an old road at the end of a clearing (0.3 mi.). After descending briefly, it again turns right, leaving this woods road for another one (0.4 mi.), and enters an older hemlock forest. The trail reaches an intersection where there is a weathered wooden sign that once pointed the way on cross-country ski trails (1.1 mi.). Following the modern green-and-yellow markers to the left, it resumes its descent. At the bottom of the hill, it bears left onto another old road, then another that soon reaches one end of the narrow pond (1.6 mi.).

Hawk Hill

This route on Old Brandon Road passes cellar holes and stone walls from the original 18th-century settlement.

Distance: 1.5 mi.

To the Trail: From the intersection of U.S. 7 and Vt. 73 in Brandon, follow U.S. 7, 1.0 mi. south to Nickerson Road and turn right. Follow Nickerson Road 0.3 mi. to Old Brandon Road. Turn left and follow Old Brandon Road 0.8 mi. to a red barn on the right and a sign for the Vermont Land Trust. Parking is limited to the roadside. Please do not park in the barnyard.

Description: The route follows Old Brandon Road southwest 1.0 mi. to the ridge of Hawk Hill. It continues another 0.5 mi. and ends at the high school soccer field.

Pittsford

Pittsford Recreation Area

This system of trails is in the town-owned Pittsford Recreation Area and consists of a half-dozen interconnecting paths, blazed in different colors and totaling about 3.0 mi. The 200-acre recreation area lies north and east of U.S. 7 and is roughly bounded on the northwest by Plains Road, which leaves U.S. 7 about 0.25 mi. north of the Pittsford village green, and on the southeast by Furnace Road, which leaves U.S. 7 about 0.75 mi. south of the village green.

The trail network, designated for foot travel only, is open to the public year-round without charge and leads through abandoned pastures, woodlands and wetlands. A flyer with a map of the trails, as well as brief descriptions, is available at the town offices on Plains Road, about 0.75 mi. from the junction with U.S. 7.

To the Trail: The main entrance to the recreation area is on Furnace Road, about 0.5 mi. from U.S. 7 and adjacent to the Vermont Police Academy. This entrance is near the day-use facilities, which include picnic areas and a swimming pond (a fee is charged in season). Other trailheads are behind the Pittsford Congregational Church on the village green and behind the municipal offices on Plains Road.

Description: The six trails within the Pittsford Recreation Area cut through woodlands, meadows, and pine groves. Convenient access to the network may be gained from two of the trails. The Blue Trail traverses most of the recreation area and starts behind the Pittsford Town offices. The trail leads south and east to the main entrance of the Pittsford Recreation Area on Furnace Road. The White Trail starts behind the Pittsford Congregational Church near the village green and leads into the recreation area and a junction with the Blue Trail. Sections of the Orange and Green Trails follow Sugar Hollow Brook. Short sections of the White, Blue and Orange Trails are rated moderately steep. A loop can be made between the Red and White trails by walking along the Telemark Ski Club property, onto the sidewalk along U.S. Route 7, then through the village green to the Congregational Church.

Pittsford Trail Network

The Pittsford Trail Network was developed and is maintained by volunteers, with the support of the Town of Pittsford, private landowners and by grant funding from the state. The network has more than 12 miles of year-round easy-to-moderate recreation trails open to the public free of charge. They provide opportunities for walking, hiking, bird watching, jogging, showshoeing and cross country skiing. Trail maps are available in boxes at the trailheads. As the network encompasses a sensitive ecological environment, please respect plant and animal life and nearby brook waters.

Meadow Loop

Distance: 1.6 mi. loop

To the Trail: The trailhead is on the south side of Arch Street, near the fire station; parking is off Arch Street west of the fire station. A link to the Cadwell Trail is possible by crossing a bridge over Sugar Hollow Brook and following a short moderately steep connecting trail.

Description: Cutting through open fields and woods, this trail follows Furnace Brook as it merges with Sugar Hollow Brook. With panoramic views, the trail is easy with one moderate uphill.

Cadwell Trail

Distance: 2.4 mi.

To the Trail: One access point for both east and west sections is a farm road approximately 0.6 mi. south on Elm Street from its intersection with U.S. 7. Another access point is 1.0 mi. from U.S. 7 south on Elm Street at the Cooley

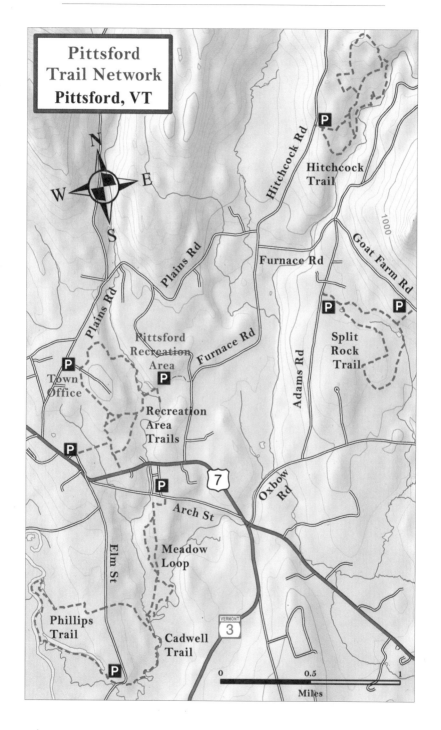

Pittsford
Trail Network
Pittsford, VT

N
E
W
S

Hitchcock Rd

Hitchcock
Trail

Goat Farm Rd

1000

Plains Rd

Furnace Rd

Plains Rd

Plains Rd

Pittsford
Recreation
Area

Furnace Rd

Split
Rock
Trail

Town
Office

Recreation
Area
Trails

Adams Rd

7

Oxbow Rd

Arch St

Elm St

Meadow
Loop

Phillips
Trail

VERMONT
3

Cadwell
Trail

0   0.5   1

Miles

Covered Bridge. A link with the Meadow Loop Trail is possible by following the connecting trail and bridge, indicated by a sign at the intersection with the east loop of the Cadwell Trail. Walkers at either access point can shorten the walk by selecting only the east or west loop and returning to their vehicle by following Elm Street.

Description: Consisting of a west section (1.5 mi.) and an east section (0.9 mi.), this trail is easy walking with two short uphills. It passes through fields and meadows, following Otter Creek, Furnace Brook and a lagoon. Varied habitats provide homes to beavers, otters, turtles, fish, ducks and other birds. Wildflowers can be seen during certain times of the year.

Split Rock Trail

Distance: 1.9 mi. loop

To the Trail: Parking is available at trailheads on both Adams Road and Goat Farm Road (the 300-yd. access from Goat Farm Road is moderately steep).

Description: This trail, between Adams and Goat Farm Roads, covers mostly level ground or rolling hills. It passes through wooded areas, a meadow surrounded by pines and open fields. Two ponds offer opportunities to view waterfowl.

Hitchcock Trail

Distance: 1.7 mi. loop

To the Trail: This trail is located off Hitchcock Road, approximately 0.7 mi. north of its intersection with Plains Road, on the north side of Pittsford. The trailhead and parking area are 100 yds. off the east side of Hitchcock Road at a sign: Pittsford Trails-Chaffee Falls Trail. The trail is marked with white markers with green arrows. In addition to the main loop, the Ridge Loop and Crossover Trails offer other options for portions of the Chaffee Falls Trail.

Description: Meandering mostly through woods and along Furnace Brook, this trail provides beautiful views of Chaffee Falls and rapids. A few relatively steep areas may make it difficult to navigate on cross country skis or when the trail is wet or icy.

⑮ Hubbardton Battlefield

In the summer of 1777, after a British force captured Mount Independence and Fort Ticonderoga, the American army hastily retreated through Hubbardton. The only Revolutionary War battle fought in Vermont occurred here on July 7, 1777 when Seth Warner's Green Mountain Boys staged a rear-guard action against General Burgoyne, checking the British advance and allowing the main American force time to escape. A small visitors center, with a diorama and period artifacts, gives a good overview of the battle and the terrain. An easy path encircles Monument Hill, the site of the Battle of Hubbardton.

To the Trail: Leave U.S. 4 at exit 5 near Castleton and turn north on the paved East Hubbardton Road. The visitor center is on the left, about 7.0 mi. north of U.S. 4.

Description: The trail begins at the visitors center parking lot (0.0 mi.) and follows a mowed strip through open fields. Turning right at a fork (0.1 mi.), then left, the trail follows the northern edge of the field and reaches a small hill. Passing west of a small slate house, it descends easterly to a junction at a small bridge (0.4 mi.). The trail follows the right fork to a small loop around the Selleck Cabin Site (0.5 mi.), before recrossing the bridge and gently ascending Monument Hill. Passing south of the visitors center, the trail reaches the monument dedicated to the battle before returning to the parking lot (0.7 mi.).

16 Taconic Mountains Trails

This network of trails links some highly varied terrain in a relatively small area—sheer rock cliffs, waterfalls, deep forests, rolling meadows, high peaks with wide mountain views and the most extensive oriental garden in Vermont, if not New England. The trails are on private property surrounding the owners' home, and walkers may share the land on the understanding that there will be no smoking and no fires—ever.

To the Trail: From U.S. 4 west of Rutland, take exit 5 (0.0 mi.) north on the unmarked East Hubbardton Road (which becomes Monument Hill Road) toward the Hubbardton Battlefield. Just before reaching the battlefield, turn left on the unpaved St. John Road (6.0 mi.). Turn left (6.3 mi.) into a private drive—the first possible left turn from St. John Road. Continue to a parking area on the left (6.8 mi.), just beyond the second cattle guard and a short distance uphill from a mobile home.

Trails are blazed in red except for two in yellow. Triple blazes indicate the beginning or end of a trail; double blazes mean a sharp change in direction.

Japanese Garden, Mount Zion Minor and Moot Point

Distance: 1.2 mi. loop

Description: From the parking area (0.0 mi.), the trail heads downhill and passes near the end of the mobile home (where trail maps are available at no charge). From the field below the home, there are views southwest to the cliffs of Mount Zion Minor, south to Bird Mountain and the Herrick Mountains and east to the central range of the Taconic Mountains. The trail continues downhill to an arched bridge and the Japanese Garden (0.2 mi.), with pools, waterfalls, stone lanterns, an island reached by another arched bridge and views of the cliffs above.

At the north end of the garden is a large boulder with a ladder partway up it. Around the right side of this rock is the start of the red-blazed trail leading uphill. This trail weaves among massive boulders as it climbs to a junction (0.25 mi.) with the yellow-blazed Cave Trail.

Taking a sharp left, the trail ascends to a switchback, passes under a 20-ft. rock overhang and climbs a short steep section leading to the top of the Mount Zion Minor ridge. Farther south along this ridge is the best viewpoint from Mount Zion Minor (0.3 mi.), overlooking the Japanese Garden 115 ft. below. There are also wide views of the Taconics from north to southeast.

At this point the trail turns sharply west, crossing the ridge and reaching the red-blazed Moot Point Trail (0.4 mi.). It turns left to follow mossy ledges, crosses a small marsh on steppingstones, passes a woods road and ascends to a ledgy ridge overlooking valleys on both sides. At Moot Point (0.6 mi.), there are fine views of the distant northeast to southeast, including Bird Mountain, and of the nearer southwest. Like the garden, this is a wonderful "carry in, carry out" picnic spot.

Returning to the junction with the Cave Trail on the right, the route continues past it on the red-blazed trail. It descends by two switchbacks to reach the yellow-blazed Cave Trail once again (1.0 mi.). Turning left on the Cave Trail, the route crosses a bridge, ascends among hardwoods along a ravine and intercepts the red-blazed Springs Trail. This left continues up to Mount Zion Major (see the following description). The trail turns right and crosses the stream to the parking area.

Mount Zion Major and Boulder Maze

Distance: 0.8 mi. loop

Description: From the parking area (0.0 mi.) the route leads downhill toward the right-hand end of the mobile home, turning right just before reaching a tool shed. The red-blazed Springs Trail starts at a blazed post in the field west of the shed. It enters the woods, crosses a stream and passes the yellow-blazed Cave Trail on the left, as previously described (0.1 mi.). The trail ascends toward Mount Zion Major through mixed hardwoods and conifers, with one switchback. At the second switchback, the yellow-blazed Cliff Trail branches right (0.3 mi.).

Junction: The Cliff Trail presents an alternate route to Mount Zion Major and offers many panoramic views. It is spectacular but challenging, for it follows the base of the cliffs through several steep ups and downs. It could be dangerous for children or inexperienced hikers and is impossible for dogs.

The red-blazed Springs Trail continues past this switchback and another above it, attaining a fairly level plateau. It soon emerges onto an open rocky ridge with sweeping views from northeast to southeast. The trail then dips slightly, traveling closer to the cliff edge, finally ending at the 1,220-ft. peak of Mount Zion Major (0.5 mi.). This rock outcropping is an impressive lookout, with views northwest of the distant Adirondacks. Nearer are the Hubbardton Battlefield and the Taconic Mountains to the north, east and southeast.

The return trip is on the Mickie Trail, also blazed in red, which starts near the edge of the peak plateau opposite the ending of the Springs Trail. It descends steeply through four switchbacks and reaches the base of the cliffs, soon passing the north end of the yellow-blazed Cliff Trail on the right. Continuing down, it winds through a maze of boulders (0.6 mi.) and enters the forest, where grazing cows are occasionally seen. The trail crosses a stream on steppingstones and shortly enters a field just north of the cattle guard beside the parking area (0.8 mi.).

North Woods Trail

This short red-blazed trail is almost entirely level. In conjunction with various much longer loops through fields on both sides of Monument Hill Road, it makes a relaxed and scenic ski trail in winter, and in summer, a quiet, undemanding amble. The trail starts near the point where the access road leaves the large field north of the house and enters the woods (0.0 mi.). The trail meanders in a roughly M-shaped course through an open, almost park-like stand of pines interspersed with small meadows and ends at the North Lookout (0.5 mi.), which is just left (east) of a lone pine. This spot offers perhaps the most panoramic mountain vistas on the property.

Meadows Path

This path offers a leisurely stroll through gently rolling fields, with benches along the way. It also takes in some fairly spectacular distant views, as well as the Japanese Garden. (A special map is available for the Meadows Path.)

From the parking area, the route passes through a gate in the fence, then heads north to the start of the North Woods Trail, which it follows to the North Lookout before heading downhill (south) through another gate. Continuing down, past a bench in the meadow (a possible turnoff to the Japanese Garden) between two groups of trees, it crosses at the low point of Monument Hill Road.

Across the road in another large field, the trail continues east and slightly north to a small opening in the tree line. Passing through, it heads gradually uphill and north, making a large loop through the upper meadow, then south to the high point. From here, it leads south again and west, to the same road crossing.

Instead of following the previous route on the other side, another path heads west and slightly north through a field, crosses a stream and ascends northwest to the highest part of the field. From there a short woods road leads to the area below the Japanese Garden.

Leaving the garden and crossing the arched bridge to the north, avoiding the straight uphill, the path turns right to angle up the next ridge to the east. It passes through a grove of pines and joins the previously taken path at a bench in the field where the parking area is to the left.

Falls and Canyon Trails

Distance: 2.3 mi. loop

Note: To shorten the walk to the waterfalls, use the alternate parking area. From the main parking area, drive out the access road, turn right on St. John Road and right again on Monument Hill Road. Pass several houses along a straight stretch, then one more house on the right. Turn right, then left. Just beyond is a low point in the road, with a turnoff into the alternate parking area on the right.

Description: From the main parking area (0.0 mi.), the trail leads downhill to the southeast, past the left end of the mobile home. Descending between occasional pines to a brook crossing by a white birch on the opposite bank, it turns uphill a short distance, then continues southeast down an open field with wide mountain views. Passing between two groups of trees growing from old foundations, the trail reaches a crossing at the low point of Monument Hill Road (0.4 mi.).

Heading east across the paved road and entering another large field, it climbs uphill to the northeast, following a sometimes-discernible farm track through an opening in the tree line (0.6 mi.). It continues in roughly the same direction to the high point of this field (360-degree view). The trail heads northeast to the tallest pine on the eastern edge of the field, roughly 175 ft. south of the northeast corner. The red-blazed Falls Trail starts beside this tree (0.7 mi.).

The Falls Trail crosses two small brooks, ascends a grassy hill and descends to the first of the waterfalls (1.0 mi.). It climbs upstream along the left bank, past several other falls and a narrow gorge, finally crossing the stream above the highest cascade (1.1 mi.). It then heads downhill to the southwest and joins a woods road, at which point the red blazes end. Descending by the more-worn left fork, at 1.5 mi., it crosses a stream and reaches the Canyon Trail on the left.

This lengthy red trail turns several times before descending to the bottom of a deep canyon. Blazing ends at this point, but walking can continue, often on the rock floor of the stream. (This surface may be extremely slippery and, without waterproof boots, wet feet are almost inevitable.) The route passes numerous waterfalls interspersed with level stretches to a long deep canyon with two high falls dropping into it at the far end, one from each side. Some distance farther, it ends at a series of low falls from very wide rock shelves stretching across the stream. At this point, the route turns left (north) to an unblazed woods road leading downhill to the start of the Canyon Trail.

The Canyon Trail follows the edge of a small field southwest beside a brook, crossing it (1.6 mi.) and continuing west across a larger field to the Monument Hill Road crossing (1.8 mi.). The route leads west through a field, crosses a stream and ascends northwest to the highest point of land, entering a woods road on the narrow north edge of this field. Emerging below the Japanese Garden (2.1 mi.), it passes through the garden and continues uphill to the parking area.

Lake Bomoseen Area

Situated at the northern end of the Taconic Mountain Range, Lake Bomoseen is the largest lake lying entirely within the boundaries of Vermont. The terrain is characterized by a series of north-south ridges heavily wooded with hemlock-white pine forest. Numerous smaller ponds are located throughout the area, but 202-acre Glen Lake, with its nearly undeveloped shoreline, offers the most spectacular scenery.

Within the 2,940-acre Bomoseen State Forest lie two state parks. Bomoseen State Park, in the southern part of the forest, offers picnicking, swimming and boating, as well as extensive camping accommodations and access to a pair of short trails. In the north, Half Moon State Park offers more secluded campsites and two short trails. Although it has no day-use area, walkers will not be turned away.

Half Moon State Park

Part of Bomoseen State Forest, Half Moon State Park is in the Town of Hubbardton and occupies a small sheltered basin surrounding Half Moon Pond.

To the Trail: From the south, follow the unpaved Moscow Road north from Bomoseen State Park 3.0 mi. Alternatively, from exit 4 of U.S. 4 in Castleton, follow Vt. 30 north 7.5 mi. and turn west on the paved Hortonville Road. Continue west 2.0 mi. then turn left on Black Pond Road. Follow this road south 1.5 mi. to the state park entrance.

Daniel Coffey Memorial Trail

This blue-blazed trail leaves the north side of the park access road about halfway between the contact station and the camping area, roughly 0.1 mi. from each. The trail ascends easily 0.5 mi. on a winding woods road through open forest. The final 0.25 mi. of trail scrambles over a rocky ridge and descends to secluded High Pond, a small body of water rimmed by thick brush and sphagnum moss.

Half Moon Pond Trail

This path, marked with blue blazes and a sign reading "Nature Trail," is an easy 0.4-mi. lakeside walk around the eastern side of Half Moon Pond connecting the campgrounds on the north and south shores. Near the southwest end of the trail is a junction with the Glen Lake Trail, which crosses Moscow Road and proceeds south to Bomoseen State Park.

Distance: 0.4 mi.

Bomoseen State Park

To the Trail: Located along the western shore of Lake Bomoseen in the Town of Castleton, Bomoseen State Park is easily reached from exit 3 of U.S. 4 in Fair Haven by following the paved Scotch Hill Road (which becomes Glen Lake Drive at its northern end) north 4.5 mi. through the hamlet of West Castleton. Alternatively, from Vt. 4A in the village of Hydeville, follow the paved Creek Road north 4.0 mi., roughly following the west shore of Lake Bomoseen. Fees are charged in season.

Bomoseen Loop Trail

Distance: 1.5 mi.

Description: This blue-blazed trail starts in a meadow behind the contact station and soon crosses Cedar Mountain Road. Proceeding through an old hayfield and past scattered rock walls, foundations and apple trees at an old farm site, the trail crests a low hill where there is a good view of Glen Lake to the west. The trail continues through a mixed pine and hardwood forest with an open understory and returns to the starting point.

Slate History Trail

The story of the rise and fall of the local slate industry is told on a self-guided trail passing through the now-abandoned village of the West Castleton Slate Company. Sixty to seventy buildings once stood between Lake Bomoseen and Glen Lake where the West Castleton Mill operated between 1850 and 1929. A pamphlet describing the trail and its observation points is available at the park contact station and is recommended.

Distance: 0.75 mi.

To the Trail: Leaving the Bomoseen State Park entrance, walk a short distance south on the public Creek Road, then turn right onto a mowed path. One of the three slate houses the route passes lies within the park and is open to the public on a limited basis.

Glen Lake Overlook

Distance: 1.5 mi.

To the Trail: From the entrance to Bomoseen State Park, continue around a curve to the left onto Moscow Road (gravel) and follow it north 0.8 mi. to a sign for "Bomoseen State Park-Glen Lake Block" on the left. Turn left into the driveway and park in the large grassy field.

Description: The route follows the roadway south from the southwest corner of the field, turns right, then right again before following a blue-blazed trail to the left. It skirts the east shore of Glen Lake, then crosses the northern neck over a bridge. The trail turns left and climbs steeply to a viewpoint over the lake.

Shaw Mountain

Owned by The Nature Conservancy and located in the southwest corner of Benson, the Shaw Mountain Natural Area is notable for a great diversity of plant and animal life. The area is recognized for its ecological significance by the Vermont Non-Game and Natural Heritage Program and includes twenty-five rare plant species and seven distinct natural communities. A flyer available at the site identifies many plants found near the single trail, which leads from the road access to a loop atop a limestone uplift north summit (715 ft., USGS Benson). *(See map on next page.)*

Distance: 2.4 mi. loop

To the Trail: From Vt. 22A in the Town of Benson, 7.0 mi. north of its junction with U.S. 4 in Fair Haven, turn west on Mill Pond Road (also known as Lake Road) (0.0 mi.), following signs for the villages of Benson and Benson Landing. Continue straight through a crossroads in the village of Benson (0.7 mi.) and proceed west along Benson Landing Road to a second four-way intersection (1.7 mi.). Turn left on Park Hill Road and proceed south to a junction on the right (2.1 mi.) with Money Hole Road. Bear right and proceed past a road entering left (2.6 mi.). The trailhead, near a wooden sign on the left (3.7 mi.), is easy to miss. Parking is available for three cars.

Description: From the parking lot, the lightly used trail ascends steeply to a sign and register. Following white markings, it then descends to cross a marshy area on a footbridge before ascending moderately to reach a signed junction at the head of the summit trail loop. Turning right at the junction to make a counterclockwise circuit, the trail ascends gently west and passes through an open oak-hickory forest near the heavily forested, viewless north summit. Continuing around the south side of the ridge, the trail returns to the start of the summit loop.

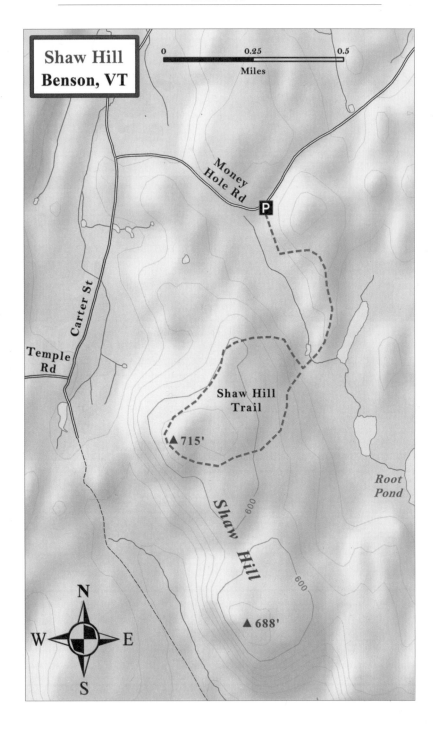

Shaw Hill
Benson, VT

0   0.25   0.5
Miles

Money
Hole Rd

P

Carter St

Temple
Rd

Shaw Hill
Trail

▲ 715'

Shaw Hill

600

Root
Pond

600

N
W   E
S

▲ 688'

⑲ Chittenden

Chittenden Brook Trail

The Chittenden Brook Recreation Area is a popular destination for cross-country skiers and snowshoers. In addition to the Chittenden Brook Trail, other trails in or near the campground provide options for loops and short walks.

Distance: 1.9 mi.

To the Trail: From the intersection of U.S. 7 and Vt. 73 in Brandon, follow Vt. 73 east 12.1 mi., over Brandon Gap, to FR 45. Turn right and follow FR 45, 0.6 mi. to the trailhead parking area on the right. Alternatively, from Vt. 100 near Rochester, follow Vt. 73 west 5.5 mi. to FR 45. FR 45 is not plowed in winter.

Description: The trail leaves the south end of the parking area and parallels FR 45 and Chittenden Brook on old woods roads 1.7 mi. to the Beaver Pond Spur, which leads to a wetland and the possibility of seeing beaver or moose. After crossing a branch of Chittenden Brook, the trail passes a short spur to the campground and FR 45 (1.9 mi.). The Chittenden Brook Trail continues uphill, at times steeply, to intersect the Long Trail (3.7 mi.).

Lefferts Pond

Distance: 0.5 mi.

To the Trail: From the intersection of U.S. 4 and U.S. 7 in Rutland (0.0 mi.), follow U.S. 4 east 4.0 mi. and turn left on Meadow Lake Drive. Follow Meadow Lake Drive to its end and turn right on Chittenden Road (5.7 mi.). Follow Chittenden Road—it will become Dam Road (8.6 mi.)—1.4 mi. to Wildcat Road and bear right (10.0 mi.). Follow Wildcat Road 0.9 mi. to a gate on the left. Turn left through the gate and follow the access road 0.5 mi. to a parking lot.

Description: The trail heads east from the parking lot, passing the picnic area on the right. It crosses a stone bridge, then reaches a T-junction with a V.A.S.T. trail (0.5 mi.). The trail beyond this point has been impassable for many years due to beaver flooding.

⑳ Clarendon and Pittsford Railroad

The Vermont Marble Company built the Clarendon and Pittsford Railroad in 1902 to connect the quarry in Florence with the marble works in Proctor. The quarry was not productive and was abandoned in the early 1900s. Huge blocks of marble may still be seen from the railbed.

Distance: 2.2 mi.

To the Trail: From Main Street in Proctor, turn right on North Street, then bear right on Florence Road and follow it to its intersection with Beaver Pond Road; the pond is on the left. Continue on Florence Road 0.7 mi.; the abandoned railbed is visible on the left. Park on the wide shoulder or continue 0.3 mi. farther to a one-car pull-off on the left at a sharp right curve.

Description: Heading north, the old railbed passes through woods to open fields with sweeping views of pastures and distant mountains. The path continues over flat terrain to a point where the old railroad tracks are visible (2.2 mi.).

 Rutland

Patch Pond Loop

This short, level trail in a Rutland neighborhood is maintained on private land by the Rutland Area Physical Activity Coalition (RAPAC) through the generosity of the landowner. Since the path borders a farmed field, walkers are asked to stay on the path and keep dogs leashed and out of the field.

Distance: 0.5 mi.

To the Trail: From U.S. 7 north of its intersection with U.S. 4 east in Rutland, turn west on Field Avenue, near Godnick Furniture and the Green Mountain National Forest office. Just beyond the Church Street intersection, the trailhead and a signboard are on a short dead-end street to the right. Parking is limited at the trailhead, but vehicles may be parked on nearby side streets.

Description: From the trailhead, paths lead in either direction halfway around the field to Patch Pond where ducks and geese are often seen.

Pine Hill Park

Pine Hill Park offers a variety of trails and woods roads, remote ponds and scenic views, all easily accessible from Rutland. Some of the trails are open to mountain biking and signs indicate which are pedestrian–only. There are several view points, including some with benches as at Tim's Vista and Rocky Pond. Because the sheer number of trails can be confusing, walkers are encouraged to pick up a trail map at the trailhead kiosk. All intersections are clearly marked with signs and most are numbered, making it easy to pinpoint the location on the map. While not many of the trails are flat, the hills are mostly gentle and the high point (marked on the map) is only 999 ft. The Giorgetti Park loops are the flattest and easiest. Dogs must be leashed and cleaned up after.

To the Trail: From U.S. 7 in Rutland, turn west at the traffic light on Crescent Street. After several blocks, turn right after the bridge over East Creek on Preville Avenue. Parking is at Giorgetti Park and the trails begin at the west end of the lot. Bathrooms may be available when the building is unlocked.

Diamond Run Trails

This trail system behind the Diamond Run Shopping mall lies on a 28-acre natural area, rich in varied wildlife habitat including old farm fields, mixed forest and a wetland. The grass pathways are mowed and brochures explaining the history and ecology of the site are available at the trailhead or at the mall office. Signs along the way provide information. Dogs must be leashed.

Distance: 2.0 mi.

To the Trail: The Diamond Run Mall is at the intersection of U.S. 7 and U.S. 4 just south of Rutland. There are 2 trailheads, one behind Sears, which requires climbing a short, steep hill, and another near the Rutland Regional Fieldhouse.

 West Rutland

West Rutland Marsh

This is an easy walk on dirt and paved roads around the perimeter of an 800-acre wetland, home to many species of birds, turtles, frogs and marsh plants. Rutland County Audubon, a local chapter of the national organization, reports that 134 different species of birds have been sighted here. The local Audubon deserves credit for rescuing and restoring this important habitat. The group built a boardwalk into the middle of the marsh for an up-close look at life in the reeds and it hosts regular monitoring walks to record visiting species. The public is welcome to join the free, weekly walks. For information and a schedule: www.rutlandcountyaudabon.org. Brochures are available at a kiosk and the trail is dotted with interpretive stations. Also at the kiosk is an up to date listing of species sighted in the marsh. Visitors are encouraged to record their observations in the logbook located in the mailbox.

Distance: 3.7 mi. loop

To the Trail: From Vt. 4A in West Rutland, turn north at the flashing light on Marble Street. The pavement ends just past the old Marbleworks, now a carving and sculpture studio. Continue straight to Water Street and turn left. Station 1 on the interpretive trail is 0.25 mi. west on Water Street where there is room to park on the side of the road. Parking is also available at the kiosk and boardwalk, a short distance farther north on Marble Street.

West Rutland Recreation Trail

This trail is a work in progress. While in 2008 it was blazed and walkable, construction of stone steps and puncheon is scheduled to continue and signs are planned. The Vermont Youth Conservation Corps did much of the trail work and an official opening was held in September 2008. Dogs must be leashed.

Distance: 1.0 mi. loop

To the Trail: From Vt. 4A in West Rutland, turn south on Vt. 133 (Clarendon Road). The trail may be accessed in two ways: from the bike path parking lot on the left just beyond the highway overpass; or by driving into the West Rutland Recreation Area a little farther on. Watch for the brown sign and turn left on Fairview Avenue.

Description: The trail follows a road behind the building at the West Rutland Recreational Area, through a gate and crosses the Clarendon River on a bridge. The next section is messy, as beavers have tried to re-design the trail system. Reconstruction continues. Crossing the field, the trail enters the woods on an old road and is marked with yellow and red blazes. Shortly it comes to a junction where the loop begins. The left branch follows yellow blazes clockwise; the right branch follows red blazes counterclockwise. Either direction ascends steeply to the ridge top. More construction is needed here and a future extension will lead to a nice view.

㉓ Bucklin Trail

The Bucklin Trail is maintained by the Green Mountain Club as a side trail to the Long Trail/Appalachian Trail on Killington Peak. The lower section offers a pleasant and easy walk alongside Brewers Brook.

Distance: 1.2 mi.

To the Trail: Take U.S. 4 east 6.5 mi. to Wheelerville Road (gravel) and turn right. Follow Wheelerville Road 4.0 mi. south to the trailhead on the left at Brewers Corner. Wheelerville Road is 4.3 mi. west of Sherburne Pass. From Rutland, turn east on Killington Avenue, then right on Notch Road. Beyond the end of the pavement, turn left on Wheelerville Road and follow it 3.1 mi. to the trailhead on the right.

Description: The blue-blazed trail begins at Brewers Corner and follows a logging road east through pine forest. At 0.2 mi., it crosses Brewers Brook on a bridge. The trail continues on the logging road to the base of a short hill (1.0 mi.), where it then climbs to a second bridge (1.2 mi.). The trail continues along the south side of the brook another 0.8 mi. before climbing steeply to Cooper Lodge (3.3 mi.) on the Long Trail, 0.2 mi. from the summit of Killington Peak.

㉔ Killington

Gifford Woods State Park

The Appalachian Trail passes through Gifford Woods State Park 2.0 mi. east of its departure from the Long Trail at Maine Junction in Willard Gap. These trail systems are described in the GMC's *Long Trail Guide* and in a brochure available at the park contact station. Camping facilities are available and a day-use fee is charged in season.

Across Vt. 100 from the park gate lies Gifford Woods Natural Area, a seven-acre, old-growth virgin hardwood stand containing many grand trees with an understory of native wildflowers. The area has no formal trails nor development of any kind and is designated both as a National Natural Landmark and a State Fragile Area.

To the Trail: Gifford Woods State Park is on Vt. 100, 0.6 mi. north of its junction with U.S. 4 in Killington.

Description: Within the park, the Kent Brook Trail follows fairly gentle terrain to make a counterclockwise loop of the camping area through a northern hardwood forest. Starting just inside the park entrance, the yellow-blazed trail follows a well-defined footpath north through the day-use area. The trail crosses a cross-country ski trail and climbs the hillside before descending slightly to cross the Appalachian Trail west of the campground. It crosses a woods road and briefly follows Kent Brook before doubling back left and ending on a road at the south end of the park (0.7 mi.). The park entrance is to the right on this road.

Kent Pond via the Appalachian Trail

Distance: 0.6 mi.

To the Trail: From the intersection of U.S. 4 and Vt. 100 in Killington, turn north on Vt. 100. The parking area for Kent Pond is on the right a short distance past Telemark Village. Please do not block the boat access. **Alternate trailhead:** For the other end of this walk, continue east on U.S. 4, past the Killington Peak access road and turn left on Thundering Brook Road. Pass Mountain Meadows Lodge to the causeway beside Kent Pond. A small parking area is on the right.

Description: This route follows the white-blazed Appalachian Trail. Leaving the south end of the parking area, the trail crosses a bridge and bears left downhill to a waterfall and pool. It follows the shoreline until emerging from the woods into a clearing below Mountain Meadows Lodge. Continuing straight toward Thundering Brook Road, the route ends at the parking area on the left.

㉕ Helen W. Buckner Memorial Preserve

The Buckner Preserve in West Haven is one of a very few places in Vermont where walkers have a chance—albeit slim—of seeing an Eastern timber rattlesnake. Two varieties of the reptile live among the rocky outcrops on the south face of Bald Mountain. They are among the 11 rare animal species, 18 rare plants and 10 rare natural community types on this 3,500-acre property owned by The Nature Conservancy. The preserve is an outpost of Vermont nearly surrounded by New York State, occupying most of a peninsula bounded by the Poultney River and Lake Champlain. Its heights present sweeping views up the headwaters of the lake.

Because the area is home to rattlesnakes, visitors are cautioned to look before sitting down and to use a walking stick to part tall grass and brush. Rattlers will strike only if they are stepped on or harassed. Visitors are as likely to see a rattler stretched out on the sun-warmed gravel access road as on the trails.

Two paths wind through this site. Tim's Trail is a 2.8-mi. walk through fields and forests. The Susan Bacher Memorial Trail is a 2.5-mi. route that traverses a wooded ridge and skirts open fields near the former Galick farmstead whose lands are at the heart of the preserve. Each hike has an out-and-back portion that leads to a loop; a mile-long connector trail on private land links them. Brochures describing both hikes are available at the site.

To the Trail: From U.S. 4, 5.5 mi. west of the Vermont-New York border and about 0.3 mi. west of a railroad crossing, turn north on NY 9A (0.0 mi.). At a T-intersection (0.9 mi.), turn left on NY 9, then immediately right (1.1 mi.) on NY 10 (Doig Street), just after cresting a small hill. Turn left onto a dirt road (1.6 mi.) where the paved road curves right. Cross the bridge and bear left. Parking for Tim's Trail is down this dirt road on the right (2.3 mi.). Parking for the Susan Bacher Trail is a mile farther. This road is often flooded in spring.

Tim's Trail

Distance: 2.8 mi. loop

Description: From the parking pullout (0.0 mi.), the well-marked trail follows the base of a cliff and talus slope eastward to an informational kiosk (0.2 mi.), passes a pond and views of Ward Marsh, then joins an old woods road at the second of two fence openings. It soon turns left to begin the loop (0.4 mi.) and ascends the ledges, from the top of which are views south and east (0.9 mi.). The trail descends quickly along rocky outcrops, crosses a small brook and climbs again, eventually reaching a bench on the left (1.3 mi.) with expansive views. The path meets an old stonewall (1.5 mi.) at a junction, where Tim's Trail turns sharply right. This intersection is easily missed from this direction, but a sign where the connector trail passes through an opening in the wall draws attention to the junction.

Junction: The connector trail passes two small pools and ascends Austin Hill (elev. 641 ft.). It then bends west and drops steeply to the Susan Bacher Trail (1.0 mi.)

From the junction, Tim's Trail doubles back to the right and follows the stonewall on a gentle descent, crossing several streams. It winds back uphill and joins an old woods road. Just before this road crosses onto private property, the trail leaves it to the right and follows another stonewall. It joins and leaves a series of woods roads on the descent back to the fields along Ward Marsh. It bears right at the edge of the field (2.4 mi.) to return to the start of the loop.

Susan Bacher Memorial Trail

Distance: 2.5 mi. loop

Description: This well-marked trail climbs steeply from the parking area (0.0 mi.) past a view of the Galick farmstead, where the family once raised mink and sheep to supplement their dairy operation. Turning sharply left and crossing an old field, the trail soon reaches the start of the loop (0.5 mi.). The left fork emerges into an open field and follows the fence line to a short spur leading to an information kiosk (0.65 mi.). Bald Mountain is visible ahead as the main route continues north along the perimeter of the hayfield, then turns right into the woods on an old logging road near a renovated barn. The trail leaves this road to the right (1.2 mi.) and climbs steeply to a hemlock grove before turning southward on more gentle terrain. After descending to cross a stream, it rises again and turns left along a ridge with winter views to the west. On descending from the ridge, the trail soon returns to the start of the loop (2.0 mi.).

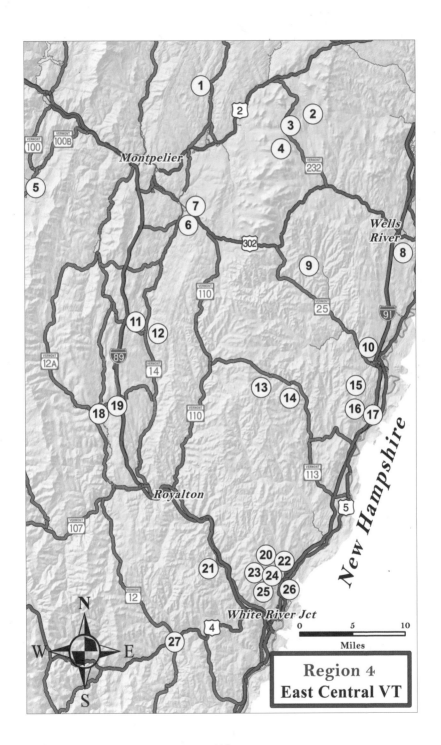

Region 4
East Central VT

Miles

New Hampshire

Region 4
East Central Vermont

① Chickering Bog Natural Area, Calais

Located in Calais and East Montpelier, Chickering Bog is owned and managed by The Nature Conservancy. Because the bog-like area is fed by a source of alkaline groundwater, it is actually an example of a fen. A wide variety of unusual plants grow here, some of which are unique to this environment. Please stay on the designated trails and leave pets home. Use caution when crossing bog bridges, as they tend to be slippery. Waterproof footwear and a bug net are recommended.

Distance: 2.2 mi.

To the Trail: From the junction of U.S. 2 and Vt. 14 in East Montpelier, follow Vt. 14 north 4.1 mi. to an intersection. Turn left on Lightening Ridge Road and follow it 1.5 mi. to the trailhead—marked by a post with the letters "TNC"—on the left. Parking is limited to the very narrow shoulder of this road. Please do not block the nearby driveway.

Description: From the trailhead (0.0 mi.) the trail leads uphill, paralleling a long driveway for several hundred feet. After leveling off, the trail winds through a wet area before turning left onto a roadbed (0.25 mi.). This road eventually swings right as it gains elevation, makes a short descent and passes through another soggy section (0.5 mi.). It then swings left, passing another woods road on the right at a triangular junction (0.6 mi.). A footpath, marked by a small sign, passes through an opening in an old stone wall on the right. After climbing away from the roadbed, this pathway soon crosses a brook and reaches the signed entrance to the natural area.

The trail comes to a junction where the bog loop is formed (0.8 mi.). Continuing straight through this junction and after passing by a small kiosk, the trail zig-zags to a second junction (0.9 mi.) where there is a registration box and a side trail on the right. The first segment of this side trail reaches a bench, where a short spur path leads to the edge of the bog (1.0 mi.). The trail beyond the bench leads to private property.

After returning from this side trail (1.1 mi.), the bog loop continues for 150 ft. to another spur path on the right. This short pathway leads to a boardwalk, which extends 100 ft. into the bog where open water can still be seen. Back at its junction with the boardwalk path, the main trail follows the edge of the bog until it crosses another wet area on some puncheons. From here the trail climbs uphill, away from the bog on drier ground. Returning to the loop junction (1.4 mi.), the trail to the right leads back to the parking area (2.2 mi.).

② Devils Hill

Just a half-mile walk and a 300 ft. elevation change brings you to a rock outcrop with a sweeping view of the Green Mountains, including Camel's Hump and the Worcester Range.

Distance: 0.5 mi.

To the Trail: From U.S. 2 in Danville (0.0 mi.), take Peacham Road, which becomes Bayley-Hazen Road. At Peacham Village (6.7 mi.), turn right at the Peacham Store on Church Street. At a fork (6.9 mi.), bear left on Academy Hill Road. Continue straight through a four-way intersection (7.4 mi.) on Green Bay Loop. Turn right just beyond Pussy Willow Farm (8.7 mi.) on Devils Hill Road and continue to a parking area on the right (9.6 mi.).

Description: From the parking area, the route follows the road to a red gate marked GSF18. It continues on the road past the gate and is marked with blue blazes. When the dirt road reaches a grassy area, several trails depart from it, including some marked with signs for snowmachine riders. The left trail, marked by a blue blaze, follows an ATV track to the west-facing Devils Hill rock outcrop (elev. 2,053 ft.). It then continues through the woods to a more limited view east to the White Mountains.

③ Groton State Forest

Groton State Forest, at 25,000 acres, is the second-largest contiguous block of land owned by the state of Vermont. Located in the towns of Groton, Peacham, Marshfield, Orange and Topsham (USGS Groton, Barnet, Marshfield), the forest is generally bounded on the north by U.S. 2, north of Marshfield, and on the south by U.S. 302, west of Groton. Vt. 232 bisects it. Along this road lie five state park campgrounds; from south to north they are Ricker, Stillwater, Big Deer, Kettle Pond and New Discovery. Day-use facilities are available on Lake Groton.

The campgrounds and many of the area's waterbodies and mountains are linked by a network of hiking and multi-use trails, which are shown in the Department of Forests, Parks and Recreation's "Groton State Forest Guide," available free at various contact stations. A second department pamphlet, the "Groton State Forest History Guide," may be obtained in-season at the Groton Nature Center, located near the north end of Lake Groton on the Boulder Beach access road. Groton's geology is more similar to the White Mountains of New Hampshire than Vermont's Green Mountains. The exposed granite bedrock makes for a rocky, rough topography.

Logging is common in Groton State Forest and may disrupt portions of the trail system, so hikers should obtain current trail information from park personnel. In some cases, trees have been marked for cutting with blue paint.

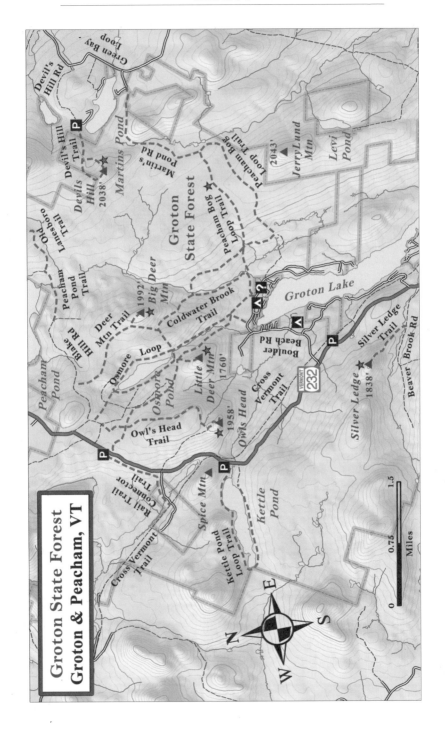

Groton State Forest
Groton & Peacham, VT

Devils Hill Rd

Green Bay Loop

Martins Pond

Devil's Hill Trail

Devils Hill Trail

2038'

Old Lanesboro Trail

Peacham Pond Trail

Martin's Pond Rd

Peacham Bog Loop Trail

2043'

Jerry Lund Mtn

Levi Pond

Groton State Forest

Peacham Bog Loop Trail

Coldwater Brook Trail

Groton Lake

Big Deer Mtn

1992'

Deer Mtn Trail

Blake Hill Rd

Peacham Pond Trail

Peacham Pond

Osmore Loop

Osmore Pond

1760'

Little Deer Mtn

Cross Vermont Trail

Boulder Beach Rd

VERMONT 232

Silver Ledge Trail

1838'

Silver Ledge Trail

Beaver Brook Rd

1958'

Owls Head

Owl's Head Trail

Rail Trail Connector Trail

Spice Mtn

Kettle Pond

Kettle Pond Loop Trail

Cross Vermont Trail

0   0.75   1.5

Miles

N   E   S   W

Be especially careful to follow the trail in these areas. Primitive camping is allowed within designated areas of the forest, including many backcountry lean-tos. Check with park personnel before camping away from the established campgrounds.

Osmore Pond Hiking Loop

Distance: 1.8 mi.

To the Trail: This blue-blazed trail begins at the Osmore Pond picnic shelter, accessed through the New Discovery Campground off Vt. 232.

Description: From the shelter (0.0 mi.), the trail descends to the shore and continues southerly through the picnic area. After following the shore for some distance and passing views across the pond to Big Deer Mountain, the trail bears away from the pond and reaches a junction on the right (0.4 mi.) with the Little Deer Trail. Continuing straight ahead, the trail first crosses the outlet of Osmore Pond on a plank bridge, passing a spur path left that leads to a shoreline lean-to. The trail then passes through a wet area on puncheon built by the Vermont Youth Conservation Corps in 1997, before reaching a four-way junction (0.5 mi.).

> **Junction:** From this junction, the Osmore Pond/Big Deer Mountain Trail leads straight ahead 1.0 mi. to a vista near the summit of Big Deer Mountain. The Hosmer Brook Trail departs right, leading about 1.3 mi. south to the Boulder Beach access road at the north end of Lake Groton.

Turning left at the junction, the Osmore Pond Loop passes through open forest for some distance before entering deep woods and passing two lean-tos (1.0 mi., 1.4 mi.). At the north end of the pond, the trail reaches a junction on the right (1.5 mi.) with the New Discovery Campground/Osmore Pond Trail before following the shoreline back to the picnic shelter (1.8 mi.).

Owl's Head Mountain

Although not high, this mountain with its rocky summit offers outstanding panoramic views. A 1.9-mi. foot trail leads to the summit, while a 1.0-mi. auto road, open to cars only in summer, leads to a parking area and summit trail 0.25 mi. from the top. A drive up the road and short walk to the summit make a perfect hike for children. Alternatively, a loop a little longer than 4.5 mi. may be hiked using the trail described, the auto road, a 1.5-mi. walk on Vt. 232 and the trailhead access road.

Distance: 1.9 mi.

To the Trail: This blue-blazed trail begins on the road to the Osmore Pond picnic shelter. From the entrance to the New Discovery Campground on

SYLVIE VIDRINE

View from the top of Owl's Head.

Vt. 232, continue south a short distance to the second left turn. Follow the dirt road east, bearing right at a fork after 0.25 mi., before reaching the trailhead on the right, about 0.5 mi. from Vt. 232. Limited roadside parking is available.

Description: From the access road (0.0 mi.), the trail follows an old road that links the picnic shelter with the maintenance area to the north and turns left (0.1 mi.) into the woods just before the maintenance area. The trail then follows a level path under a power line (0.3 mi.) before starting a gentle ascent. Climbing steadily, then more steeply to attain the ridgeline (1.2 mi.), the trail passes over a rock ledge, descends west into a small dip, then ascends to the Owl's Head picnic area parking lot (1.6 mi.). The trail climbs rock stairs on steep terrain to the open summit (1,958 ft.)(1.9 mi.) with its airy stone shelter. From the summit, there are good views of Lake Groton, Kettle Pond, the White Mountains and the Green Mountains. No camping is allowed on Owl's Head.

Kettle Pond Hiking Loop

Distance: 3.2 mi.

To the Trail: This trail begins at the large Kettle Pond parking area on the west side of Vt. 232, 7.1 mi. north of U.S. 302 and 4.0 mi. south of U.S. 2. Although there is a sign for the parking area, no sign indicates the trailhead.

Description: This blue-blazed trail begins at the northwest corner of the parking lot (0.0 mi.). Following a level grade, it divides (0.2 mi.) a short distance before reaching the pond. At the junction, a spur left leads to the pond's edge. Bearing right at the junction, the trail follows the north side of the pond, passes two lean-tos and continues through the woods to a left turn (0.5 mi.). It then passes through a wet area to the shore where it continues along the shoreline, traversing an area with large boulders at the site of an old camp (0.8 mi.) and former lean-to (1.2 mi.).

The trail then bears right and shortly passes another lean-to (1.7 mi.). Circling the west end of Kettle Pond, it traverses some wet and rocky areas.

After passing a private camp, the trail climbs over and around some large boulders to another lean-to. The trail remains near the shoreline for a distance, before reaching its terminus at the Kettle Pond Group Camping Area (3.0 mi.). Straight ahead via the access road, it is a short distance back to Vt. 232, then a short distance north to the Kettle Pond parking area.

Cross Vermont Trail

The Cross Vermont Trail (CVT) is Vermont's first west-to-east, long-distance, multi-use trail—spanning 85 mi. from Lake Champlain in Burlington to the Connecticut River in Wells River. The trail was created to provide a safe, scenic link between villages, public places, schools, playgrounds and state parks.

West of Montpelier, the trail follows existing bike and recreation paths as well as on-road routes. East of Montpelier, the trail utilizes some rail-trail paths (portions of the former Montpelier-Wells River Railroad bed) as well as some state and town roads, both paved and unpaved. The CVTA is currently working with public and private landowners to establish additional off-road trail sections.

In the spring of 2009, just in time for its tenth birthday, the Cross Vermont Trail Association, a grassroots non-profit organization founded in 1999, has designated a complete, statewide route for the CVT. The three best sections for walking are outlined here. For more information: Cross Vermont Trail Association, c/o CVRPC, 29 Main St., Suite 4, Montpelier VT 05602, www.crossvermont.org.

East Montpelier and Plainfield: Route 14 to Country Club Road

This signed and designated 2-mi. section of the CVT passes along what was once the Montpelier-Wells River Railroad bed. Walkers, cyclists, horseback riders, nordic skiers, snowshoers and snowmobilers enjoy the trail. Trail users should yield to snowmobiles and horseback riders. The trailhead is on the east side of Vt. 14, 0.8 mi. south of its junction with U.S. 2 in East Montpelier. The off-road section of trail currently ends at Country Club Road in Plainfield. From there, the on-road bicycle route follows Country Club Road north to U.S. 2, then follows U.S. 2 east to the village center of Marshfield, where it eventually rejoins the railroad bed (see maps on CVTA's website).

Groton State Forest

This 9.2-mi. section of the CVT can be accessed from several places in Groton State Forest. Parking areas are at Ricker Pond and Kettle Pond, found on the east and west sides of Vt. 232, respectively.

The trail is shown as a class IV road on USGS quads and in *DeLorme's Vermont Atlas & Gazetteer*. The signed and designated segment of the trail borders private property at either end of the state forest, where the boundaries are clearly marked. Walkers, cyclists, horseback riders, nordic skiers, snowshoers and snowmobilers enjoy the trail. During winter, trail users should yield to snowmobiles; during summer, trail users should yield to horseback riders.

As it travels through the state forest, the trail passes historic railroad markers, through a boreal-transitional forest and along glacial ponds and lakes, including Marshfield Pond, Kettle Pond, Lake Groton and Ricker Pond. The Lake Groton Nature Center can be accessed via a side road. One of the highlights of the trail is a view of Big Deer Mountain with its sheer granite cliffs.

Southeast of the state forest boundary, the trail continues as a bicycling route south on Vt. 232, then east on U.S. 302. After passing the Upper Valley Grill, the trail leaves the highway at Little Italy Road, where the route rejoins the old rail bed. For the next 3.0 mi., the CVT passes through a mixed spruce, birch and beech forest, with views of farms, ponds and bogs. The route ends at the Mills Memorial Ballfield in South Ryegate, where there is ample parking. Maps of the bicycling portions of the CVT are available at the CVTA's website.

Newbury and Wells River

Two points on U.S. 302 provide access to the trail. A western trailhead (recommended) with ample parking is on the Ryegate-Newbury town line on the north side of U.S. 302, near the Boltonville Road, and behind a now-closed gift shop. Eastern access is just west of the state fishing access, where Wells River comes closest to U.S. 302.

The Wells River CVT is remarkably diverse along its short 1.75-mi. length, passing through a large white pine and eastern hemlock stand, as well as wetlands and bogs with viewing benches and wildlife habitat boxes. At its mid-point, the trail segment passes under the I-91 bridge over the Wells River.

Two trails intersect the CVT. West of the I-91 bridge is the Boltonville Nature Trail, approximately 1.0 mi. long (see p.124). It explores the upland slopes and riparian floodplain of the Wells River and intersects the CVT at two points from the north. East of the I-91 bridge is the Blue Mountain Nature Trail, which is also approximately 1.0 mi. long and joins the CVT from the north. This trail passes through upland hemlock and spruce-fir forest and offers views of the Wells River from cliffs and ledges.

⑤ Mad River Greenway

The Mad River Path Association (www.madriverpath.com) created and maintains walking trails on both sides of the Mad River. Along the trails are many views of farms and mountains on both sides of the valley. In several places walkways have been cut through the brush to the riverbank, giving visitors easy access to the water.

To the Trail: From I-89, exit 9 (0.0 mi.), follow U.S. 2 east and turn right (south) on Vt. 100B (0.7 mi.) toward Waitsfield. Turn left on Meadow Road (10.1 mi.). There is a parking area immediately on the right, before the bridge.

Description: From the signboard at the end of the parking area, the trail begins along a chain link fence. It soon becomes a mowed path between the river and a farm field. Passing a picnic pavilion, the route then parallels Vt. 100 for a short distance before crossing the field and looping back to the parking lot. There are similar paths on the other side of the river, with entrance points just across the one-lane bridge on Meadow Road. The total length of the Greenway is 3.0 mi.

⑥ Millstone Trails Association

A non-profit organization maintains a network of trails on 1,500 acres of privately owned land around Millstone Hill in Barre. The trails are used for mountain biking and walking in summer, cross-country skiing and snowshoeing in winter. A seasonal walking pass is available, as well as day passes. For more information: www.millstonetrails.com or 802-479-1000.

⑦ Barre Bike Path

This paved bike path connects Graniteville and the Barre Town Elementary School, running past the Rock of Ages granite manufacturing facility.

Distance: 1.4 mi.

To the Trail: From the junction of Vt. 14 and Vt. 63 in South Barre, take Middle Road uphill 1.5 mi. to a parking area at the Lower Graniteville Picnic Area on the right.

Description: At the bike path's terminus with a soccer field behind the elementary school, a woods trail loops back to the bike path. The trail enters the woods at a sign on a tree identifying a nature trail. Immediately on the left, there is a sign for the Beaver Pond Trail. The trail crosses a wet area and continues on easy grades until reaching a V.A.S.T. trail. It turns right down a hill, crosses a bridge and rejoins the bike path.

8 Boltonville Nature Trail

The Boltonville Nature Trail is a cooperative effort of the Newbury Conservation Commission, the Blue Mountain Union School, the Blue Mountain Grange and the Al-lens Farm. The Nature Trail is located off U.S. 302, 3.6 mi. west of Wells River.

To the Trail: From I-91, exit 17, take U.S. 302 west 1.4 mi. to the junction with Boltonville Town Road. Park in the designated trailhead parking area. From Boltonville Road, the CVT runs along the old Montpelier and Wells River railbed, parallel to U.S. 302, behind the gift shop. Follow the trail east for 0.1 mi. to the Allen Farm property line and the beginning of the Boltonville Nature Trail, which is marked with blue rectangles.

9 Galusha Hill

The Upper Valley Land Trust has created a trail that climbs to the top of Galusha Hill in Topsham. Most of the hilltop was cleared for pasture and it still offers extensive views for very little effort.

To the Trail: Follow Galusha Hill Road north from East Topsham village (0.0 mi.). Ignore the "Road Closed" sign near the junction for Clark's Crossroad (3.1 mi.)—presumably this sign is intended for through traffic—and continue straight on Galusha Hill Road for a short distance to the trailhead on the right (3.3 mi.).

10 Wright's Mountain/Devil's Den

Located in the northeast corner of Bradford, Wright's Mountain has good views north, west and southwest from a rock lookout west of the summit (USGS East Corinth). Because of the efforts of the Bradford Conservation Commission and local volunteers, many improvements have recently been made to the Wright's Mountain trail system, a 278-acre forest with scenic overlooks. A second trailhead was established off Chase Hollow Road. Parking lots and kiosks were built at both trailheads and the trail network was expanded to include the cave known as Devil's Den.

To the Trail: The trail begins on Wright's Mountain Road, 2.3 mi. from its junction with Vt. 25. From Vt. 25 (0.0 mi.), follow Wright's Mountain Road north. Stay on the main road past the fork intersection with Fulton Road (2.1 mi.) and park in the lot at the trailhead on the right (2.3 mi.). **Alternate trailhead:** From Vt. 25, take Chase Hollow Road north 1.3 mi. Parking and the trailhead are on the left.

Description: Wright's Mountain Trail (1.6 mi.): From the Wright's Mountain Road parking area, the distance to the summit lookout via the Wright's

Mountain Trail is 0.8 mi., about half the trail's total length. This north section of the Wright's Mountain Trail, as well as Sylvia's Trail and Ernie's Trail, are unblazed woods roads, but all the junctions have signs.

Leaving the summit to the south, the newer section of the Wright's Mountain Trail is marked with yellow blazes. It soon comes to another view of Mount Ascutney, Winslow Ledges and Smarts Mountain. The trail gradually levels out in hardwoods before meeting Ernie's Trail.

Sylvia's Trail (0.4 mi.): Climbing steeply at first, this trail gets easier and rejoins the Wright's Mountain Trail below the summit.

Chase Hollow Trail (0.6 mi. in, 0.7 mi. out): This yellow-blazed trail starts at the Chase Hollow Road parking area. It begins with a steep climb through the forest and a small stream crossing, following the "Best Way In" and "Best Way Out" signs. The trail follows an old logging road for a short distance before turning left and leading between a rock ledge and a stream. Crossing the stream, it arrives at the junction of Ernie's Trail and the Devil's Den Spur Trail.

Devil's Den Spur Trail (0.2 mi.): The Devil's Den spur is a primitive, unblazed trail over rough terrain. Anyone wanting to explore the two-room standup cave chamber should bring a flashlight.

Ernie's Trail: (0.9 mi.): Ernie's Trail switchbacks uphill from the Chase Hollow Trail, then follows an old logging road. At 0.4 mi., it meets the Wright's Mountain Trail, with a vernal pool just north of the intersection. From here, the trail is gradual until its intersection with Sylvia's Trail.

⑪ Allis State Park

STEVE LAROSE

Established in 1928, this state park is named for Wallace Allis, who willed his Bear Mountain Farm to the state for a campground and recreation area. It is located on the summit of Bear Hill, which provides sweeping views from a fire tower. The park was developed by the Civilian Conservation Corps beginning in 1932. Between Memorial Day and Labor Day, there is a $3 day-use fee.

To the Trail: From I-89, exit 5 (0.0 mi.), take Vt. 64 west to a junction with Vt. 12 (2.7 mi.). Turn left on Vt. 12 and continue south. Turn left (east) on Vt. 65 (7.1 mi.) and

The fire tower at Allis State Park.

continue uphill to the park entrance on the right (8.4 mi.). After the park ranger's cabin, bear left to the picnic area and fire tower.

Description: The trail begins at the edge of the field beyond the fire tower and picnic area. It immediately heads downhill, past old stone walls. A bench at a pond overlook offers a nice stopping point. Continuing downhill past a stone outcrop, which has an unusual cave said to be used as a bear den, the trail levels out, then climbs uphill to return to the fire tower (0.75 mi.). More than a dozen points of interest are marked on the trail, with information included on a trail map available at the park ranger's cabin at the entrance.

⑫ Cram Hill Road

This two-mile walk begins in West Brookfield, which is between Northfield and Randolph. It is on a shaded class IV road beside a brook with a couple of beautiful cascades. Hillsides rise steeply on either side of the road, which is not plowed in winter, making for a good snowshoe or cross-country ski outing.

Distance: 2.0 mi.

To the Trail: From I-89, exit 5 (Northfield exit), turn west on Vt. 64. At the bottom of the hill, take a left on Vt. 12 (south) and follow it 8.0 mi., passing Baker Pond on the right and going through Brookfield Gulf. Shortly after emerging from the gulf, take the first right on West Brookfield Road (a cemetery is on the corner). Follow it uphill 0.75 mi. to the hamlet. Park in front of the West Brookfield Community Church on the grass.

Description: The route follows Cram Hill Road next to the church and passes between two houses before crossing a brook. It bears right at a fork and begins to climb gently uphill, eventually reaching a small clearing with an iron gate on the left and a "No Trespassing" sign. Beyond this point, the route to the top of Cram Hill climbs more steeply, becomes increasingly eroded and is more difficult to walk.

⑬ Flagpole Hill

This walk on easy grades leads to an open meadow with a spectacular view of the Green Mountains to the west, including Camel's Hump, and Mount Cube to the east in New Hampshire. Flagpole Hill gets its name from the pole at the summit with a large wooden flag that also serves as a weather vane.

Distance: 1.2 mi.

To the Trail: From the town office in Vershire village (0.0 mi.) follow Vt. 113 west 0.9 mi. toward Chelsea and turn left on Brown Road. Turn right on Taylor Valley Road (2.5 mi.) and follow it to the parking area on the right

(4.6 mi.) where there is a sign for the Cross Rivendell Trail on a tree. **Alternate approach:** From the junction of Vt. 110 and Vt. 113 in Chelsea, follow Vt. 113, 5.9 mi. to Brown Road on the right.

Description: From the parking area (0.0 mi.) the trail follows a logging road for a short distance and enters the woods at a sign with the Cross Rivendell Trail logo. The blue-blazed trail is well-maintained and easy to follow, except where it crosses a logged over area (0.6 mi.). The trail does not follow the logging road downhill. Rather, it forks left and follows stone walls to a junction with an unmarked trail to the right, which leads to Reed Road. At the junction, the route turns left and follows an ATV track for 0.2 mi. to reach the summit and flagpole.

This clearing is the western terminus of the Cross Rivendell Trail, which stretches eastward to Mount Cube in Orford, N.H. There are several other opportunities for walks on portions of the Cross Rivendell Trail. For more information and maps, visit www.crossrivendelltrail.org.

⑭ Hawkins Mountain

This walk leads to the summit of Hawkins Mountain (el. 2370 ft.), the highest point on the Cross Rivendell Trail in Vermont.

Distance: 0.9 mi.

To the Trail: Follow the directions for Flagpole Hill.

Description: From the parking area for the Flagpole Hill walk, the route follows Taylor Valley Road 250 ft. south, then bears left off the road to enter a recently logged area. At Logging Road #1, it bears right through a large clearing. Continuing on Logging Road #1, the trail follows blue blazes at a fork to reach the summit.

⑮ Bradford Municipal Forest

This 584-acre forest, owned by the Town of Bradford, is managed as a backup water supply area for the town. Logging roads make a 2.8-mi. circuit through the property. The trails have been given names, but there are no trail signs. A map is recommended.

To the Trail: From I-91, exit 16 (0.0 mi.), follow Vt. 25 north toward Barre and turn left on South Road (0.6 mi.). Take an immediate left on Rowell Brook Road, then left on Brushwood Road (1.8 mi.), which eventually becomes one lane. Turn right on Knobloch Road (2.3 mi.) and follow it to a road that branches left and dips down to a wooden bridge across a stream (2.5 mi.). There is a pullout big enough for one or two cars before the bridge. The Hemlock Hill Road Trail begins at the bridge.

Description: From the parking area (0.0 mi.), the Hemlock Hill Road Trail heads uphill, reaching the junction of the Butternut Notch Trail and the Hurricane Brook/Waterbar Loop Trail (0.5 mi.). From here, the Hurricane Brook/Waterbar Loop Trail continues uphill to the left on moderately steep grades, crossing several small bridges until reaching Sand Landing and Brushwood Road (1.3 mi.). The route follows Brushwood Road until it veers left and the Beaver Meadow Road Trail begins on the right. Following the Beaver Meadow Road Trail for a few hundred feet until the Doe Orchard Road Trail enters on the right (1.5 mi.), it climbs steadily on the Doe Orchard Road Trail and reaches a large clearing (2.0 mi.). From here, the Butternut Notch Trail follows the logging road over a notch, which was once home to a healthy butternut stand, and returns to the intersection with the Hemlock Hill Road Trail (2.3 mi.) and the parking area (2.8 mi.).

16 Eagles Bluff Trail

The network of trails around Lake Morey in Fairlee is a cooperative effort of the Town of Fairlee, the Lake Morey Protective Association and the Lake Morey Foundation. One of the trails leads to Eagles Bluff, an outlook 800 ft. above the west shore of the lake, with a view of the entire lake and the mountains across the Connecticut River in New Hampshire. *(See map on next page.)*

To the Trail: From I-91, exit 15 in Fairlee, turn west on Lake Morey Westside Road. The trailhead parking is at the Lake Morey boat ramp, approximately 1.4 mi. from I-91.

Description: From the parking lot across from the boat ramp, the blue-blazed Bald Top Trail begins at the signboard (0.0 mi.). The Echo Mountain Trail begins on the right, marked by a yellow sign (0.5 mi.). The trail to Eagles Bluff continues uphill (1.0 mi.), with several perches for resting and enjoying views of the lake below. For a circuit, the Echo Mountain Trail descends to the northern end of Lake Morey and the road leads 1.0 mi. back to the boat ramp.

17 The Palisades

Rising dramatically west of the Connecticut River, the Palisades are a series of cliffs along the east side of Morey Mountain. A trail created by the Lake Morey Trails Association ascends to the edge of the precipice from the west. In recent years, the rocky outcrops have become a nesting site for peregrine falcons, which are legally protected from human disturbance during the breeding season. A clearly marked area near the cliff top is off-limits to hikers between March 15 and August 1. Since the ascent to the edge of the nesting area is fairly short, it is recommended this hike be reserved for the fall season when the cliff top is accessible.

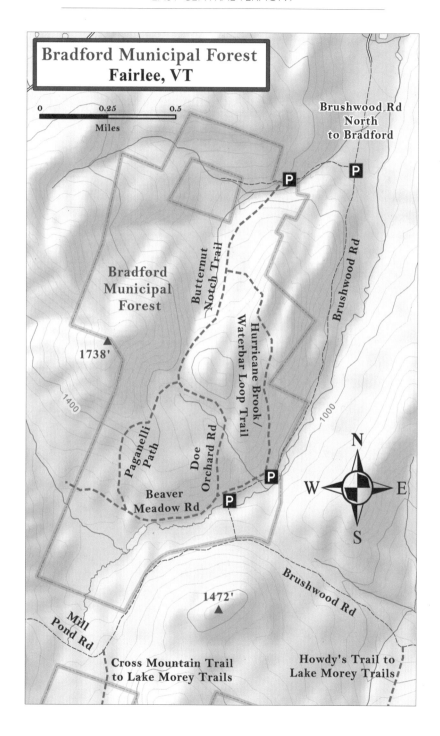

Bradford Municipal Forest
Fairlee, VT

0   0.25   0.5

Miles

Brushwood Rd
North
to Bradford

Bradford
Municipal
Forest

Butternut Notch Trail

Hurricane Brook/
Waterbar Loop Trail

Brushwood Rd

1738'

1400

1000

Paganelli
Path

Doe
Orchard Rd

Beaver
Meadow Rd

N
W   E
S

Brushwood Rd

1472'

Mill
Pond
Rd

Cross Mountain Trail
to Lake Morey Trails

Howdy's Trail to
Lake Morey Trails

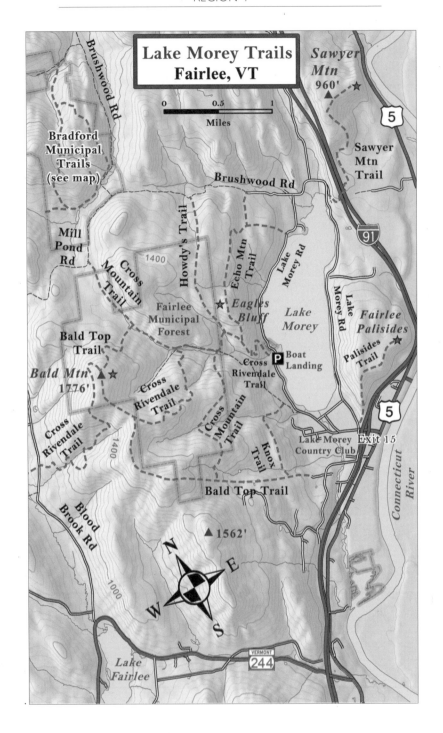

Lake Morey Trails
Fairlee, VT

Distance: 1.1 mi.

To the Trail: From I-91, exit 15, a short distance west of U.S. 5, turn west on Lake Morey Road. Turn right almost immediately at a four-way intersection, then turn right again into the parking lot of the Fairlee Fire Department across from the Lake Morey Country Club. Ample parking is available, but care should be taken to park on the right side of the lot as far from the fire station entrance as possible.

Description: Although there are a few remaining yellow "Lake Morey Trails" metal squares, the trail is marked with white blazes, the first one being on one of the I-91 signposts. From the south end of the parking lot at the corner nearest the interstate (0.0 mi.), the trail passes between the chain-link fence and the I-91 exit ramp to the right of several old crab apple trees before making abrupt turns left then right. Now an obvious path in the woods, the trail winds steeply for a few hundred feet, still heading north, parallel to the interstate. Passing through a mixed hardwood-softwood forest, the trail follows a fence on the left and soon arrives at a sign warning of the peregrine falcon nesting area ahead.

The trail levels off briefly (0.1 mi.), then resumes its climb, but less steeply. It passes through an opening in the fence, levels off, then ascends gradually before making jogs left, then right (0.2 mi.). Passing another trail on the left, the path crosses a seasonal stream and reaches a power line. There is no trespassing past this point during the peregrine falcon nesting season from March 15 to August 1. From this cut there are views south to Fairlee, the Connecticut River and Mount Ascutney. The trail continues straight across the swath cut by the power line and reenters the woods, winding along ledges to a level ridge that leads to the open area above the Palisades (0.7 mi.). To the east, the view encompasses farms, church steeples, the white clapboard houses on the river at Orford, New Hampshire, Mount Cube and Smarts Mountain. The trail continues north and ends (1.1 mi.) at another partially open area with views south and east.

⑱ Randolph Floodplain Forest Conservation Area

This short loop trail traces a branch of the White River in downtown Randolph. The 18-acre tract is one of Vermont's largest remaining sugar maple-ostrich fern floodplain forests. The Randolph Area Community Development Corporation and Randolph Technical Career Center are partnering to conserve, manage and maintain the forest.

To the Trail: On Vt. 12 southbound in Randolph, cross a bridge and turn right on Prince Street. The road curves under the bridge. Park on the left at

SYLVIE VIDRINE

The fire tower on top of Gile Mountain.

the Valley Bowl, a long metal building with a Pepsi sign. A kiosk at the far end of the parking lot marks the trailhead.

 Mari Castle Trails

On the hillside above the historic Mari Castle in Randolph, multi-use trails criss-cross conserved land. This short walk leads to a view of Randolph village.

Distance: 0.5 mi.

To the Trail: From Vt. 12, across from Gifford Medical Center, turn right at the sign for Mari Castle. Park in the gravel lot before reaching the Singer Eye Center.

Description: The route starts at a gate on the left across from the Eye Center (0.0 mi.) and follows a woods road uphill. At the first clearing, it takes a sharp right to continue uphill. A clearing with a view of Randolph is on the right (0.5 mi.). Beyond the viewpoint, there is a network of woods roads and V.A.S.T. trails to explore.

Gile Mountain

Located in a municipal forest in the northwest corner of the town of Norwich, the summit of Gile Mountain (USGS South Strafford) has a well-maintained fire tower (1,873 ft.) from which there are panoramic views. An easy ascent along an obvious, well-trodden trail makes this a good hike for young children.

Distance: 0.7 mi.

To the Trail: From the junction in the village of Norwich where U.S. 5 turns east off Main Street (0.0 mi.), continue north along Main Street a short distance before turning left on Turnpike Road (0.6 mi.). Continue past the end of the pavement (2.5 mi.) and ascend through a sheltered valley to the signed parking area on the left (5.2 mi.), just before a farmhouse on the right.

Description: From the back of the parking lot (0.0 mi.), the trail follows the tower trail sign to a logging road (0.1 mi.) on the left, which it follows along blue blazes. The trail soon leaves the road right (0.2 mi.), crosses a log bridge and ascends to cross an open swath beneath a power line (0.3 mi.), where there is a fine view of the neighboring New Hampshire hills. Entering the woods again at a stand of old birches, the trail follows easy switchbacks to ascend to a cabin (0.7 mi.), just below the fire tower. From the observation platform there are spectacular views in all directions. To the east, over the nearby Connecticut River Valley, lie the White Mountains, while Mount Ascutney's bulk dominates the southern horizon. To the west, the spine of the Green Mountains is visible in the distance.

21 White River Ledges Natural Area

This trail in Pomfret circles a 187-acre property owned and managed by The Nature Conservancy.

Distance: 1.6 mi.

To the Trail: From I-89, exit 2 (0.0 mi.), turn west on Vt. 132 for 0.1 mi. Turn left on Vt. 14 south. In West Hartford village, turn right to cross over a bridge (6.1 mi.) and take an immediate right at the end of the bridge on Pomfret Road. Turn right on White River Lane (7.0 mi.) into the parking area. The trailhead is on the corner of Pomfret Road and White River Lane. Look up the bank for the Nature Conservancy sign.

Description: The well-marked loop through a hardwood forest above the White River leads to a small clearing at the highest point (791 ft.), but with very little view.

22 Ballard Trail

This three-mile trail runs along Norwich's Charles Brown Brook in a forested ravine.

To the Trail: From Main Street in Norwich, turn on Beaver Meadow Road at the Norwich Inn. Follow it 3.9 mi. to a pull-off on the left. A sign for the trailhead is on a tree at the pull-off.

23 Griggs Mountain Loop

This loop in Norwich, which skirts Griggs Mountain (1680 ft.), follows a section of the Appalachian Trail (AT) and woods roads, passing many old stone walls.

Distance: 4.0 mi.

To the Trail: From Main Street in Norwich at the Norwich Inn (0.0 mi.), take Beaver Meadow Road and turn left on Bragg Hill Road (0.4 mi.), then left again on Happy Hill Road (1.7 mi.). Park at the end (2.3 mi.). Take care not to block landowner gates.

Description: From the end of the road (0.0 mi.), the blue-blazed Tucker Trail crosses land conserved by the Upper Valley Land Trust. The trail joins the Appalachian Trail southbound (0.5 mi.) and continues straight ahead, as the blazing becomes white for the AT At a clearing (1.4 mi.), the route departs the AT by turning right toward the Burton Woods Road. Entering the woods, it bears left at the sign for Podunk Road and, on reaching the Burton Woods Road (1.7 mi.), turns right. The route comes to a T-intersection (1.9 mi.) and turns right to continue past hunting camps on the right and then the left. At the second camp, the trail reenters the woods and shortly reaches a three-way intersection. Bearing right, it connects to another woods road and returns to the clearing and the AT, which it follows north back to the Tucker Trail.

Cossingham Road Farm Trails

The Upper Valley Land Trust (www.uvlt.org) maintains 3.5-mi. of trails on a 120-acre conserved property. While the trails were designed for cross-country skiing, most of them are open for walking during the warmer months.

Distance: 1.0 mi.

To the Trail: From Main Street in Norwich at the Norwich Inn (0.0 mi.), take the Beaver Meadow Road. Turn left on Bragg Hill Road (0.4 mi.) and left again on Cossingham Road (1.6 mi.). The parking area is 100 yds. farther on the right.

Description: The East Loop begins and ends at the parking area, crossing open fields and managed forests. The West Loop adds two more miles to the circuit.

Alternate walk: A 3-mi. circuit can be made by walking up Cossingham Road from the parking area, past the farm buildings to the intersection with the Appalachian Trail. This route turns right and follows the AT northwest 1.4 mi. to the intersection with the Tucker Trail. It follows the Tucker Trail, which becomes Happy Hill Road, turning right at the intersection with Bragg Hill Road. The route follows the paved road a short distance before reaching Cossingham Road on the right and the trail parking area.

Montshire Museum

The Montshire Museum maintains more than four miles of foot trails through its 110-acre property on the bank of the Connecticut River. The trails range in distance from the 0.1 mi. long Wildflower Trail to the 1.1-mi. long Ridge Trail and some of them are hard-packed for strollers and wheelchairs. The museum is open 10 a.m. to 5 p.m. daily. An admission fee covers both the science museum and the trails. For information: Montshire Museum of Science, One Montshire Road, Norwich VT 05055, 802-649-2200, www.montshire.org.

To the Trail: From I-91, exit 13, turn east toward Hanover. Take the first right on Montshire Road and follow the signs to the parking lot.

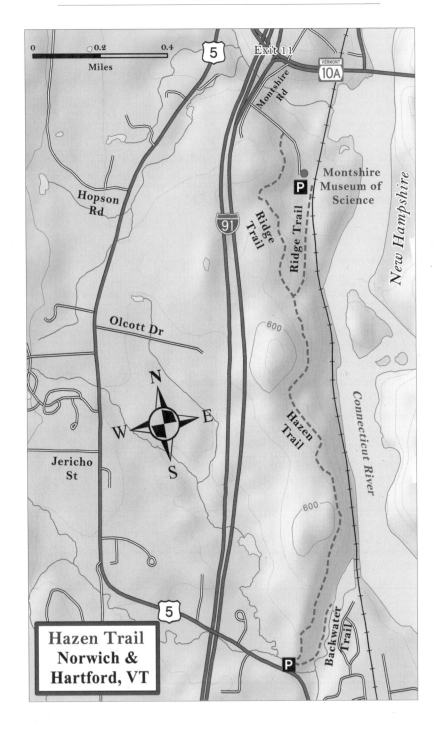

Hazen Trail
Norwich &
Hartford, VT

㉖ The Hazen Trail

The Hazen Trail was created after the Upper Valley Land Trust purchased the development rights to the Brookside Farm in Wilder from the Hazen family in 1992. The trail is maintained by community volunteers.

Distance: 1.5 mi.

To the Trail: From I-91, exit 11 (0.0 mi.), follow U.S. 5 north, turning left at the traffic light (0.8 mi.) and continuing up a hill. The trail and parking area are on the right (3.3 mi.) Park off to the side and take care not to block the gate. The trail begins on the right before the gate.

Description: This 1.5 mi. trail runs along the Connecticut River between Hartford and Norwich. It begins at U.S. 5 and links to the trails at the Montshire Museum of Science, passing cliffs and a hayfield along the way.

㉗ Woodstock

Rising above the village of Woodstock northwest of the Ottauquechee Valley, Mount Tom (USGS Woodstock North, Woodstock South) has more than 20.0 mi. of foot trails, cross-country ski trails, logging roads and carriage roads. The main natural features in the area are Mount Tom, Mount Peg, Eshqua Bog and Quechee Gorge (see Region 2).

The Billings Museum, the Rockefeller home and the Mount Tom lands were incorporated into the Marsh-Billings-Rockefeller National Historic Park in 1998. George Perkins Marsh (1801-1882), an early conservationist, first owned the farmlands, later purchased by Frederick Billings (1823-1890). Billings developed his farm as a model of wise agricultural stewardship. The property has numerous "reforestation plantation" areas, clearly identified on the official park map, available at the Prosper Road Trailhead kiosk or the Visitor Center. Especially interesting is the stand of European larch planted in 1887, found off the carriage road between the Pogue and the South Peak of Mount Tom. After his death, his wife Julia and their three daughters sustained Billing's plan. Later, his granddaughter, Mary French, and her husband, Laurence S. Rockefeller continued this commitment to stewardship of the farm, and eventually donated it to the federal government, establishing Vermont's first national park.

The park includes the Billings Farm and Museum, a working dairy farm with a museum of agricultural and rural life, as well as carriage roads, walking trails and a visitor center with displays in the Carriage House. A trail map issued by the national park is invaluable for exploring the area. During winter, the Woodstock Ski Touring Center grooms the trails for cross-country skiing; walking on the trails is not allowed. For more information, contact the national park at Marsh-Billings-Rockefeller National Historic Park,

34 Elm Street, P.O. Box 178, Woodstock, Vermont 05091; 802- 457-3368; www.nps.gov/mabi. Access to the trails is via Prosper Road, the National Park visitor's center, Faulkner Park on Mountain Avenue or the River Street Cemetery.

Unnamed High Point at 1421 feet

The elevation change to this high point is about 400 ft.

To the Trail: From the Billings Farm and Museum parking area, travel 2.7 mi. north on Vt. 12. Turn left on Prosper Road for 0.7 mi. to the trailhead parking area on the left.

Description: From the Prosper Road trailhead of the Marsh-Billings-Rockefeller National Historic Park, the route follows a woods path to the carriage road, then takes the first right off the carriage road onto a trail. At the next junction, the left fork switchbacks to an overlook at 1421 ft. The right fork eventually ends on the carriage road to the South Peak of Mount Tom or at the Pogue. The National Historic Park map, which is available at the trailhead, is useful for following this trail.

Mount Peg

This pleasant walk, especially good for children, has a nice view. For a longer return hike, take the alternate route described. In winter, this trail is a good snowshoe outing.

Distance: 0.5 mi.

To the Trail: Located in the southern part of the village, the blazed, graded path to the summit (1,080 ft.) begins at the intersection of Golf Avenue and Maple Street (USGS Woodstock South). From the village green, follow South Street (Vt. 106) south for about 0.1 mi., past the Woodstock Inn. Turn left on Cross Street, continue past Court Street on the left to cross Kedron Brook, then turn right on Golf Avenue at the next intersection. Continue a short distance to another intersection with Maple Street. Just before the Maple Street sign is a three-car parking lot on the left. The trail enters the woods from a driveway behind the parking lot on the left side of Golf Avenue. An informal sign marks the beginning of the trail.

Description: From the sign (0.0 mi.), the trail climbs on switchbacks through the woods, branching and rejoining itself several times. Bearing left at each fork makes for a longer hike and bearing right for a shorter one.

The trail continues to a junction with a small loop trail that leads around the summit. It turns left into the loop, then immediately right at a junction where a spur trail leads north to Slayton Terrace. The summit loop climbs southward to a small picnic area on the summit of Mount Peg (0.5 mi.)

before reaching a junction where a side trail departs left. The summit loop then swings north and descends to rejoin the start of the circuit.

Alternate Return Route: From the southeastern corner of the summit loop (0.0 mi.), a side trail departs south and is marked first by red arrows on trees, then diamond-shaped metal markers or red blazes. The trail passes through a wooded area, crosses a power line on private property and reaches the end of an old field. Turning left, the trail ascends steadily in the open past extensive views east, north and west. After reaching the woods on a ridge (0.4 mi.), cross-country ski trails and bridle paths lead south to the Woodstock Country Club/Ski Touring Area. While hiking is encouraged along the trails in warmer weather, during the winter these trails are maintained for skiing only and an access fee must be paid at the touring center. The red-blazed trail continues past the Woodstock Country Club's golf course and eventually leads to a field at the Health and Fitness Center. A bicycle path nearby along the shoulder of Vt. 106 leads north about 1.5 mi. back to Woodstock. A return to Mount Peg may also be made via other ski trails or paths, using the map issued by the touring center.

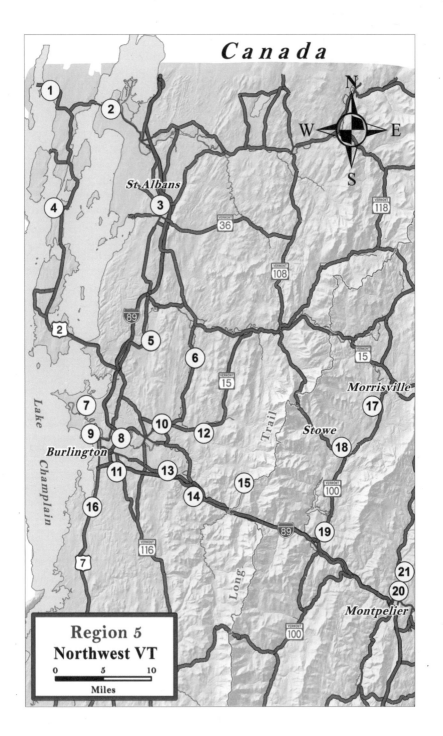

Canada

N
W ⊕ E
S

St Albans

Morrisville

Stowe

Burlington

Lake
Champlain

Long

Trail

Montpelier

VERMONT 118
VERMONT 36
VERMONT 108
VERMONT 15
VERMONT 15
VERMONT 100
VERMONT 116
VERMONT 100

89
89

2
7

Region 5
Northwest VT

0   5   10
Miles

Region 5
Northwest Vermont

① Alburgh

Alburgh Recreation Trail

This nearly 4.0-mi. multi-use trail follows the abandoned East Alburgh to Alburgh branch of the former Central Vermont Railway. Owned by the state of Vermont and maintained by the Department of Forests, Parks and Recreation in cooperation with a local snowmobile club, the trail is obvious but unsigned and unblazed.

To the Trail: The western terminus of the trail is at the easterly end of the Alburgh Industrial Park and is reached by the paved Industrial Park Road that leaves U.S. 2 opposite the Alburgh Volunteer Fire Department. Ample parking is available at this trailhead.

Description: The trail departs the parking lot (0.0 mi.) easterly along the flat roadbed before entering the Mud Creek Waterfowl Area (0.8 mi.). Managed by the Vermont Department of Fish and Wildlife, the waterfowl area attracts a variety of wildlife, especially in late summer and early fall. The trail continues through areas of marsh and open water before crossing a bridge over Mud Creek (1.6 mi.) and reaching the eastern boundary of the waterfowl area at Vt. 78 (1.7 mi.), about 1.0 mi. east of its junction with U.S. 2. Parking areas are located a short distance east and west.

Continuing across Vt. 78, the trail, now used less frequently, passes intermittently through areas of open farmland before crossing a farm road (2.3 mi.). It continues through a narrow band of trees to cross the paved Blue Rock Road (2.6 mi.), then the private gravel McGregor Point Road, both within sight of Vt. 78. The trail passes behind a series of private residences and through a wet area to reach an uncertain end in East Alburgh, terminating at an active railroad spur track a short distance west of the posted East Alburgh trestle (3.6 mi.). A road leads a short distance to Vt. 78 at the west end of the Missisquoi Bay Bridge.

Alburg Dunes State Park

The natural sand beach at Alburg Dunes State Park is one of the longest on Lake Champlain. Before the area became a state park in 1996, sand from the dunes was bulldozed to replenish the swimming beach. A fence built along the beach now protects the dunes and rare plant species from further degradation. The wetlands south of the beach provide habitat for black spruce, deer and wild turkeys. The park is open for day-use and there is an entrance fee from Memorial Day to Labor Day, when pets are prohibited. Maps are available from park staff. During the off-season, the gates are usually closed, requiring a longer walk to the trail. For more information, contact Alburg Dunes State Park, 151 Coon Point Rd., Alburgh VT 05440, 802-796-4170, www.vtstateparks.com.

Distance: 0.5 mi.

To the Trail: From U.S. 2 in South Alburgh, turn left (north) on Vt. 129 (0.0 mi.) and follow it 1.0 mi. Turn left on Vt. 129 Ext. for 0.1 mi. (1.1 mi.). Bear left on Coon Point Road and follow it 0.4 mi. to the park entrance (1.5 mi.). From U.S. 2 in Alburgh, bear right on W. Shore Road toward Isle Lamotte (0.0 mi.). In 4.4 mi., W. Shore Road becomes Vt. 129. Follow Vt. 129 1.6 mi. to Vt. 129 Ext. and turn right (6.0 mi.). Follow directions above from Vt. 129 Ext. to the park entrance (6.5 mi.).

Description: The trail begins at the west end of the parking area beyond an iron gate. In spring or after a heavy rain, the first segment of trail may be underwater. A detour along the beach to the first mowed path on the left avoids the wet area. From the gate, the trail follows Beach Road westerly through the marsh for 0.5 mi. before ending at a second iron gate and a four-way intersection. To the left, a farm road follows the route of the former Island Line Railroad. Although most of the railbed crosses state-owned land, parts of it are privately owned. The road to the right leads out to Point of the Tongue; the road straight ahead leads to South Alburgh. On the return, the first mowed path on the left leads to the beach and the shoreline may be followed back to the parking lot.

② Missisquoi National Wildlife Refuge

This 6,345-acre area, managed by the U.S. Fish and Wildlife Service, was established in 1943 to provide feeding and resting habitat for migratory waterfowl. Lying in the Atlantic Flyway, the refuge occupies much of the Missisquoi River delta on the eastern shore of Lake Champlain (USGS East Alburgh) and

Missisquoi National Wildlife Refuge.

consists of marsh, open water and wooded swamp. Most of the refuge is inaccessible to foot travel.

To the Trail: The refuge headquarters building is on the south side of Vt. 78, 2.4 mi. west of its junction with U.S. 7 in Swanton village. Parking is available behind the building. About 1.5 mi. of foot trails on a small tongue of land extending southwest between Maquam Creek and Black Creek are open during daylight hours throughout the year.

Description: The trail begins at an informational kiosk at the rear of the parking lot. An unblazed but obvious access trail follows a refuge road across the field behind the headquarters building, over the active New England Central Railroad tracks and past a woodcock management area.

At a signed junction, the Maquam Creek Trail departs right and closely follows the shore of the meandering waterway. The trail soon arrives at a signed junction where the Black Creek Trail leaves left. Straight ahead, the Maquam Creek Trail continues 0.5 mi to its end at Lookout Point, deep in the heart of the swamp.

Bearing left at the junction, the Black Creek Trail crosses an impressive series of bridges before meandering along the south shore of the peninsula. The trail leaves the water's edge to reach its end on the refuge road at the start of the Maquam Creek Trail, a short distance from the headquarters.

③ St. Albans

Missisquoi Valley Rail Trail

Following 26 mi. of the former Central Vermont Railway-Richford Subdivision, this smooth gravel trail generally follows Vt. 105 and the Missisquoi River northeast from the town of St. Albans through Swanton, Fairfield, Sheldon, Enosburg and Berkshire before ending in Richford. This multi-purpose trail, the longest continuous rail trail in Vermont, is owned by the Vermont Transportation Agency and maintained by the Department of Forests, Parks and Recreation with volunteer assistance. A flyer describing the access, history and permitted uses is available from the Northwest Vermont Rail Trail Council, www.stalbanschamber.com/railtrail, and sometimes from register boxes located at major road accesses. The trail is described eastbound from St. Albans.

To the Trail: Although access to the trail is possible at a number of road crossings, parking is not always available. There is ample parking at a designated lot at the junction of U.S. 7 and Vt. 105. in St. Albans.

Description: From the parking area (0.0 mi.), the trail bears northeasterly, passing under I-89 and traversing a series of farm fields before crossing Vt. 105 near an old cemetery at the hamlet of Greens Corners (3.0 mi.). It soon crosses an interesting marshy area before passing high above the forest floor on the built-up roadbed and eventually crossing Vt. 105 again near Sheldon Springs. After passing through the village, the trail reaches Vt. 105 a third time (8.6 mi.). It crosses a restored railroad bridge over the Mississquoi River, then departs the river to the left into the midst of an active grain mill (9.0 mi.). The trail follows the Missisquoi River upstream, eventually crossing a road in North Sheldon (11.4 mi.) before recrossing Vt. 105 (14.4 mi.) a short distance south of a parking area near a bend in the river.

The trail continues through a series of pastures, crossing Vt. 236 in South Franklin (13.5 mi.) and Vt. 105 twice more (13.9 mi., 15.8 mi.) before crossing a wooden railroad trestle (16.2 mi.) near Enosburg Falls. After passing through the center of town (16.6 mi.), the trail again departs through farm fields and follows the river before making the first of six crossings of Vt. 105 (18.9 mi.). At the last of these crossings, beyond East Berkshire, the trail reaches the east side of Vt. 105 (22.0 mi.) and passes a view up the Trout River to Hazen's Notch and Sugarloaf Mountain. A short distance beyond, the trail crosses the Missisquoi River on a large single-span truss trestle (23.2 mi.), then continues through rural landscape to reach its terminus on Troy Road/Vt. 105 (26.1 mi.) in the village of Richford.

Burton Island State Park

Burton Island is one of three island state parks in the northern part of Lake Champlain, accessible by boat or ferry from Kill Kare State Park in St. Albans. At 253 acres it is the largest of the three state-owned islands. Both Woods Island State Park and Knight Island State Park are nearby.

Burton Island has 3.0 mi. of shoreline, hiking trails, a nature center/museum, a park store and food service, rowboat and canoe rentals and places to swim and picnic. It is popular for family recreation with 17 tent sites, 26 leantos, 15 boat moorings and a 100-slip marina with dockside electricity, fuel service and a marine holding-tank pumpout facility. For more information, including a ferry schedule, rates and maps: 802-524-6353 in season, 802-241-3655 in the winter months, www.vtstateparks.com.

To the Trail: At the T-intersection of Vt. 36 (Lake Street) and Lake Shore Road in St. Albans Bay (0.0 mi.), travel north on Lake Shore Road and bear left on Hathaway Point Road (0.8 mi.). Continue to Kill Kare State Park at the end of the road where parking is available (3.7 mi.).

Description: Three trails connect and circle approximately 2.5 mi. of the island. The North Shore Trail starts at the westerly end of the campground and connects with the West Shore Trail at the northern shore. This trail leads to a clearing where it connects to the Southern Trip Trail, which circles back to the southerly side of the park facility. A descriptive brochure of the trails is available at the island's Nature Center.

Hard'ack and Aldis Hill

Generations of St. Albans residents have grown up playing at Aldis Hill and Hard'ack, a community park with enough woodland paths and rock crannies to spark any child's imagination. The paths are unnamed and unmarked as are all junctions, making it an easy place in which to get lost. From the loop described here, the left-hand trails generally lead uphill to the wooded summit plateau; the right-hand trails generally lead downhill to community access points where there is no public parking. The ski hill is run by Hard'ack, Inc., a non-profit volunteer organization: www.hardack.org.

Distance: 1.8 mi.

To the Trail: From I-89, exit 19, turn right (north) on Vt. 104 and follow it 1.2 mi. to Congress Street. Turn left on Congress Street, then immediately right into a small parking area before the gate. Please do not block the gate.

Description: The route to the trails skirts the left side of the gate and follows the gravel road 0.2 mi. to the base lodge at the sliding/skiing/boarding hill. From the lodge, the trail ascends steeply up the left side of the hill along the treeline to the top of the rope tow (0.4 mi.), where there is an open view east toward French Hill. This short, stiff climb is slippery when wet. At the T-junction at the top of the hill, the loop trail leaves either left or right. The right-hand path follows the edge of the hill north, passing several narrower side trails on both the right and left.

At 0.5 mi., the trail levels, then begins a steady descent to a wooden bridge and four-way junction (0.7 mi.).

SYLVIE VIDRINE

View from Burton Island State Park.

Junction: The trail left leads 0.2 mi. to a shallow ravine and left-hand spur trail to the summit (0.5 mi.). The right-hand trail crosses a wooden bridge, bears left at a fork (0.1 mi.) and leads to a communications installation accessed by a gravel road. This road leads to private property off Quarry Court.

The loop trail continues straight along the top of the plateau on a slight downhill grade, then climbs gently uphill before descending steeply to a trail junction (1.0 mi.).

Junction: This trail and the next two descend 0.3 mi. to an access point at the end of Isham Ave. where there is no public parking.

After passing the third junction, the loop trail begins a steady climb back to the beginning of the loop at the top of the ski hill (1.4 mi.). A final right-hand spur trail just below the hilltop drops 0.3 mi. to an access point on Congress St. at the site of the former Governor Smith mansion where there is no public parking. At the top of the hill, just before the loop trail emerges from the woods to close the loop, a left-hand spur leads 0.4 mi. to the wooded summit. The loop trail ends at the top of the ski hill and turns right to descend steeply back to the base lodge and parking area (1.8 mi.).

Rotary Health Path

Distance: 1.4 mi.

To the Trail: From I-89, exit 19, turn left on Vt. 104 and follow it 0.25 mi. to the entrance to the Collins-Perley Sports and Fitness Center. Turn right into the parking area and continue straight 0.1 mi. to a sign and map for the Rotary Health Path. Another trail access point is at the northeast corner of the sports center.

Description: The paved path, which is open for walking, running and cross-country skiing, follows the perimeter of the playing fields. The posted trail map also shows other, shorter loops.

Lake Champlain Islands

North Hero State Park Nature Trail

The floodplain forest and habitat of the 399-acre North Hero State Park is only found in Vermont around Lake Champlain. Please note that because sections of the park lie less than 100 ft. above sea level, they are sometimes under water. There is a park entrance fee from Memorial Day to Labor Day and maps are available at the entrance booth. The main park road is plowed in winter. For more information, contact North Hero State Park at 3803 Lakeview Drive, North Hero VT 05474, 802-372-8727, www.vtstateparks.com.

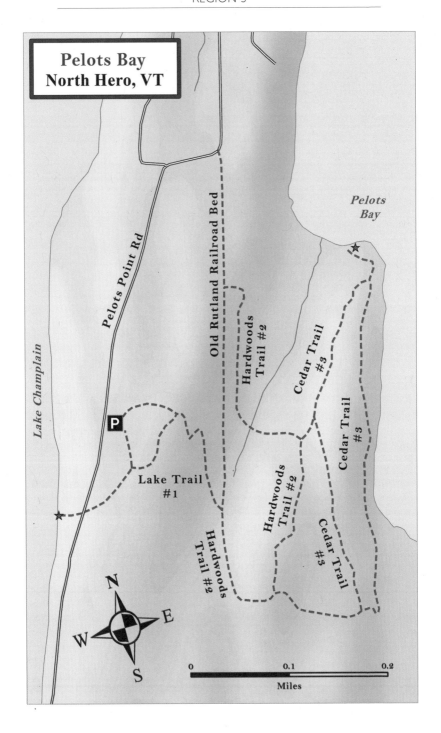

Pelots Bay
North Hero, VT

Pelots Point Rd

Old Rutland Railroad Bed

Pelots Bay

Lake Champlain

Hardwoods Trail #2

Cedar Trail #3

Cedar Trail #3

Lake Trail #1

Hardwoods Trail #2

Cedar Trail #3

Hardwoods Trail #2

P

N
W   E
S

0   0.1   0.2
Miles

Distance: 1.0 mi.

To the Trail: From U.S. 2, 3.0 mi. north of North Hero village, bear right on Lakeview Drive and follow it 3.7 mi. to the state park entrance on the left. From the north, take the first left after the North Hero Volunteer Fire Company Station on Jerusalem Place, then turn left on Lakeview Drive. Follow the state park road 0.7 mi. around Loop 3 to a split-rail fence and the nature trail entrance, where there is a wooden box containing trail brochures.

Description: From the entrance, the trail bears right at the first junction and follows the mowed path to a series of numbered interpretive sites. Especially noteworthy are the quaking aspens, shag bark hickory and a magnificent white oak. After the first junction, the path bears right at all other junctions to complete the loop. The three side trails, which leave right, lead to campground Loops 1 and 2 and to the main park road, respectively.

Pelots Natural Area

Pelots Point is named for Paschel Pelot who settled there in the 18th century. The natural area, which is owned by the Town of North Hero, is open for day-use to walkers year-round. The three main trails, Lake, Hardwood and Cedar, designate three communities that make up the natural area. The abandoned railbed of the Island Line Railroad (1901-1961) crosses the property and is lined with nature interpretive stations. Hunting is permitted from October through December. The loop described here incorporates both the Hardwoods and Cedar Trails.

To The Trail: From the drawbridge connecting the towns of Grand Isle and North Hero (0.0 mi.), follow U.S. 2 north 3.0 mi. to Station Road. Turn left (west) on Station Road for 1.1 mi., then bear right on Pelots Point Road (4.1 mi.). Follow Pelots Point Road 1.2 mi. (5.3 mi.) to a large parking lot and signboard on the right. The trails leave from the north end of the parking lot and are marked with numbered signposts. Station Road is 0.5 mi. south of the village of North Hero.

Description: At the north end of the parking area, a grassy path crosses the open field to the treeline. A wooden signpost indicates that the Lake Trail (# 1) leads right and the Hardwoods and Cedar Trails (# 2 and 3) continue straight ahead.

> **Junction:** The Lake Trail follows a grassy path that parallels the treeline briefly before turning toward Lake Champlain. At a junction in the middle of the field, the right fork loops back to the parking area. The left fork continues west, crosses Pelots Point Rd. and ends at a ledge overlook high above the water (0.2 mi.).

From the first junction, the Hardwoods and Cedar Trails enter the woods, curve downhill and lead to the former Island Line Railroad railbed. Please respect the sugaring operation by stepping over or around the saplines. Turning right on the railbed, the route passes two interpretive stations before bearing left onto a wide path. As the trails leave the woods to enter an open field, they split at a junction. The trail left takes a diagonal course and rejoins the Hardwoods Trail. Straight ahead, a connector trail leads downhill, past an unmarked junction, through a marshy area to a junction with the Cedar Trail loop. At this junction, the left-hand trail makes for a shorter loop back to the parking area.

Bearing right, the Cedar Trail drops to the marshy shore and continues mostly level. Pelots Bay is visible through the trees. As the trail curves away from the water, it reaches a marked junction where a right-hand trail leads 200 ft. down to the water. The narrower Cedar Trail bends sharply left, leaves the woods and enters a field to another junction. The trail to the left completes the Cedar Trail loop. Bearing right, the Hardwoods Trail comes immediately to another junction where it bears right again. The trail straight ahead diagonals back across the field to the junction where the connector trail led downhill to the Cedar Trail.

The Hardwoods Trail drops to a series of bog bridges and widens as it curves left back toward the railbed, which can be seen above. At the junction with the railbed, the right-hand path leads to private property. The left-hand path now follows the railbed and passes the nature interpretive stations. At station #4, the route turns right to rejoin the trail through the sugarbush back to the parking lot.

Camp Ingalls

This loop at North Hero's Ingalls 4-H Camp traces a nature interpretive trail with stations that identify trees and other plants. Hunting is not permitted.

Distance: 0.5 mi.

To the Trail: From the drawbridge connecting the towns of Grand Isle and North Hero (0.0 mi.), follow U.S. 2 north 1.1 mi. to South End Road. Turn left on South End Road and follow it 1.8 mi. to where the town road ends at Stevens Camp Road (2.9 mi.). The crushed stone parking area for Camp Ingalls is on the left behind a wire mesh fence. The green camp buildings are visible from the road.

Description: From the parking area, the route passes between the green camp buildings and the athletic field, up an incline toward the picnic tables. Beyond the picnic tables, a wide path enters the woods and leads to the first nature interpretive station. Bearing right on level ground, the wide trail reaches a second junction where a trail right leads back to the parking area. Bearing left and following the interpretive stations, the trail parallels an open field, dips and turns left to make the loop. It crosses a wet area and ends back at interpretive station #1 (0.5 mi.).

Knight Point State Park

In 1785, John Knight with his partner Alexander Gordon began ferry service between Grand Isle and North Hero. The service continued until 1892 when the first bridge was built. The Knight Point Tavern, built in 1790 to accommodate ferry travelers, is now home to park staff. During summer, the park becomes the Island Center for Arts and Recreation, hosting concerts on Tuesday evenings. Knight Point became a state park in 1978 and maps are available at the entrance booth. There is an entrance fee between Memorial Day and Labor Day. Pets are prohibited during the park operating season. For more information, contact Knight Point State Park, 44 Knight Point Rd., North Hero, VT 05474, 802-372-8389, www. vtstateparks.com.

Former Knight Point Tavern

Distance: 1.0 mi.

To the Trail: The park entrance is on the west side of U.S. 2, 2.6 mi. south of North Hero village and 0.4 mile north of the drawbridge connecting the towns of Grand Isle and North Hero. The mowed nature trail, on the right immediately after the entrance booth, is marked with a sign. Parking is on the left in the large lot.

Description: At the sign, the trail enters the woods for 200 ft. before crossing a grassy area with a bench, then re-entering the woods. It bears left to follow an ancient rail fence and crosses several bog bridges. At the first junction, the route bears right toward Lake Champlain. The path to the left, as well as the remaining left-leaving paths, leads to an open field and picnic shelter. At the second junction, the trail also bears right and eventually emerges onto a grassy knoll with benches and views over the water to the north and west. Bearing left around the point, the trail continues through the trees, finally exiting into an open field where there is another small trail sign. The picnic shelter is on the left. For the return to the parking lot, a gravel road leads from the picnic shelter or a grassy route follows the treeline to the public swimming beach and restrooms.

Grand Isle State Park

Grand Isle State Park takes its name from, and is located on, the east shore of Lake Champlain's largest island. A short trail opposite the park entrance leads to an observation deck and is the only park facility open for day-use.

To the Trail: From the intersection of Vt. 314 and U.S. 2 in South Hero (0.0 mi.) near Keeler Bay, proceed north on U.S. 2 to an intersection on the right with State Park Road (1.8 mi.) where there is a large sign for Grand Isle State Park. Turn east on State Park Road and proceed straight through an intersection with East Shore Road (2.7 mi.) before reaching the contact station (2.8 mi.) where parking is available. A day-use fee is charged in-season.

Description: Opposite the park entrance, on the southwest corner of the State Park Road and East Shore Road intersection, a nature trail, marked with a sign, leaves the road to begin a counterclockwise loop. The trail immediately reaches a junction where a spur left leads directly to the observation deck. Continuing straight ahead, the trail crosses several marshy areas on puncheon, then two watercourses. It passes from cedar woods into young hardwood forest as it crosses an open rock knob and the corner of a field. After ascending a flight of wooden steps, the trail reaches an unmarked four-way intersection. About 70 ft. to the right is a well-constructed, 10-ft.-tall wooden observation deck with good views over the lake to the east. Straight ahead, the trail emerges from the woods to its terminus, 60 ft. south of the trailhead.

South Hero Recreation Path

Distance: 1.5 mi.

To the Trail: For the northern end of the trail, from U.S. 2 just north of the village of South Hero and 0.4 mi. from its intersection with South Street, turn west on Tracy Road for 0.2 mi. When the road forks, a large parking lot is on the left. For the southern end of the trail, from U.S. 2 in the village of South Hero, turn west on South Street for 1.9 mi. to West Shore Road. Turn north (right) on West Shore Road and follow it 0.6 mi. to the trail and a small parking area on the right. The sign for the trail may be obscured by trees.

Description: The recreation path, shared with bicyclists, follows the route of the former Island Line Railroad through South Hero between Tracy Road and West Shore Road. The railroad, which operated from 1901 to 1961, brought visitors to the Champlain Islands and transported produce from island farms to the markets in Burlington and beyond. From the Tracy Road parking area, the trail heads southwest on the old railbed through marsh for most of its length. It is straight and virtually flat.

⑤ Milton Recreational Park Trails

The Milton Recreational Park Trails are marked with red squares, blue diamonds and yellow triangles. The red trail, which is the longest, forms a 3.5 mi. loop. The shorter blue trail leads to a smaller bog loop and the yellow trails are connectors between the two. The short loop described here follows the blue trail and a short section of the red trail. An excellent, color-coded map is posted at the trailhead.

Distance: 0.5 mi.

To the Trail: From the intersection of U.S. 7 and U.S. 2 at Chimney Corner in Colchester (0.0 mi.), follow U.S. 7 north to Milton and turn right on Hobbs Road (sign is missing) (3.8 mi.). Follow Hobbs Road 0.2 mi., turn right on Park Place (4.0 mi.) and enter the Milton Recreational Park. Park on the left near the baseball fields (4.2 mi.) where there is a large signboard and map.

Description: From the signboard, both the blue and red trails bear right around the baseball diamond to follow the treeline into the pine forest at a corner of the mowed field. While the red trail continues straight ahead, the blue trail bears left and passes a junction with a yellow trail on the right (0.1 mi.). At a second junction with yellow trail, the blue trail curves left, passes an unmarked trail on the right and descends to cross several bog bridges. It emerges from the trees under a power line and comes to an unmarked junction, which is the beginning and end of a short loop. Bearing left, the blue trail crosses the power line and enters the woods at a junction with the red trail. The right-hand blue trail circles and rejoins itself at the power line junction. The red trail to the left leads to an open field and bears left along the edge of the mowed grass to return to the parking area (0.5 mi.).

⑥ Schultz Trail

This obvious, well-marked trail, which follows an old roadbed, is not as easy or straightforward as it appears on the map posted at the trailhead. It begins with a steady uphill, passes through areas oozing with mud and crosses an unbridged stream that is just a bit too wide for the average person to step over. The trail is marked and maintained by the Westford Conservation Commission.

Distance: 1.0 mi.

To the Trail: From the intersection of Vt. 128 and Cambridge Road in Westford (0.0 mi.), follow Cambridge Road 0.3 mi. and turn right on Old #11 Road. Cross Covey Road (1.2 mi.), bear right at Kilburn Lane (2.3 mi.) and continue to the trailhead at the end of the road (2.8 mi.). Please do not block access to the road or driveways.

Description: From the parking area, the trail continues past the end of Old #11 Road, climbs steadily to its high point (0.4 mi.) and begins a long descent. At the bottom of the hill (0.6 mi.), it bears right through a wet area; a small pond is visible on the left through the trees. It passes a second pond, narrows and crosses a private drive (0.8 mi.). The trail drops to an unbridged stream, crosses it and climbs on a wider, rutted woods road to its end at Machia Hill Road, where there is enough space for one or two cars to pull off on the edge of the travel lane (1.0 mi.).

⑦ Colchester

Niquette Bay State Park

Niquette Bay State Park sits on the northwestern shore of Malletts Bay in Lake Champlain. The 553-acre property, which was farmed in the 1800s, includes 4,700 ft. of shoreline—with both a sand beach and sheer cliffs dropping to the water—and three viewpoints. The state initially purchased land for the park in 1975, with the Lake Champlain Land Trust adding an additional 290 acres in 2000. The park is open from Memorial Day to Labor Day for day use only from 10 a.m. to dusk. Trail maps are available at the park entrance and one is posted at the trailhead kiosk. The three high vistas are marked on the map. Pets are permitted off-leash on the Muhley, Island View and Burns Trails, although they must be under voice command. Pets must be leashed on all other trails and owners are expected to clean up after them. Hunting is permitted in season.

MARY LOU RECOR

The Beach Trail, Niquette Bay State Park.

To the Trail: From I-89 exit 17, turn west on U.S. 2 toward the Champlain Islands. In 1.0 mi., bear right for Raymond Road and turn left to cross U.S. 2. Follow Raymond Road 0.2 mi. to the park entrance on the left. Trailhead parking is 0.2 mi. from the entrance on the right near a signboard. The trail system allows for several loops; the one described here incorporates the blue-blazed Muhley, Beach and Ledges Trails, a total of 3.1 mi.

Description: From the signboard, the wide main trail enters the woods to the right and reaches a junction with the Ledges and Allen Trails (0.1 mi.).

Junction: The Ledges Trail leaves left just before the junction. The Allen Trail, which is the shortest and most direct route to the beach, continues straight and follows a wide old road 0.5 mi. to a junction with the other end of the Ledges Trail and the Beach/Beach Bypass Trails.

The Muhley Trail bears right to parallel a ravine, which has a small brook running through the bottom. At 0.25 mi., the trail bears right and switchbacks down into the ravine to cross the brook over a small bridge, then turns sharply left. A trail leading to private property leaves right. After crossing a second bridge, the Muhley Trail reaches a junction with the Burns Trail.

Junction: The heavily-rooted Burns Trail leads straight ahead 0.6 mi., with little elevation change, to intersect the southern end of the Muhley Trail near the lake.

The Muhley Trail turns right and climbs on wooden steps through a shallow ravine. It levels briefly, climbs gradually on puncheon, then more steeply and passes a view of the Green Mountain ridge line on the right (0.5 mi.). At a sharp left turn, and the trail's high point, it passes the junction with the Islands View spur (0.6 mi.).

Junction: The Islands View spur trail leads north to a loop junction. At the junction, either trail leads to a bench with a spectacular view across Malletts Bay to the Colchester Causeway, South Hero, Stave Island and beyond to New York state.

From its high point, the Muhley Trail descends gradually through mixed hardwood and softwood forest toward Lake Champlain. At 1.1 mi., it bears sharply left, crosses a small bridge at 1.3 mi. and reaches a junction with the southern end of the Burns Trail (1.4 mi.). Bearing right, the Muhley Trail ends at a junction with the Beach Trail (1.5 mi.). From here, an unblazed trail follows the shoreline above the lake with spur trails leading down to the shore. This heavily eroded trail, which hugs the hillside, is more rugged than the other trails in the park and is not recommended. Eventually, it rejoins the Beach Trail.

The shorter and gentler Beach Trail departs left, passes the remains of an old jalopy and switchbacks down to the trail along the lake and a sign for the Muhley Trail (1.7 mi.). Bearing left, the trail crosses a small bridge to a fork where two trails parallel the shoreline. The right-hand trail crosses the beach near the treeline. It tends to be marshy and is sometimes obstructed by fallen trees, which are left deliberately to slow beach erosion. When the beach is flooded, it is recommended to follow the Beach Bypass instead of scrambling along the bank, which impacts the bank's stability and hastens erosion. The left-hand, blue-blazed Beach Bypass Trail climbs sixty steps to a mostly flat, wooded ridge high above the lake. It then drops to the shore on a second stairway where a short trail leads right to the sand beach.

At the bottom of the stairs, the trail swings sharply left, crosses a bridge over an inlet and comes to a welcome sign reminding visitors that this is a "carry in, carry out" park (2.2 mi.). Beyond the sign, the Allen Trail leads left 0.6 mi. back to the trailhead. The blue-blazed Ledges Trail bears right and climbs briefly; a short side trail parallels the main trail on the right and leads to a picnic table. The main trail levels, then drops to a wooden walkway across a marsh before climbing steeply through its namesake ledges to the high point where there is a view toward the bay (2.7 mi.). From here, the Ledges Trail meanders with little elevation change, then bears left downhill. Although marked with a double blaze, this bend is easy to miss. The trail continues descending to its northern terminus at the junction with the Allen and Muhley Trails. The parking lot is a short distance to the right (3.1 mi.).

Colchester Pond Natural Area

This 694-acre park, opened by the Winooski Valley Park District in 1997, encircles the mile-long Colchester Pond. This natural area is contiguous with the Indian Brook Reservoir Park to the east owned by the town of Essex. No vehicles, motorized boats or electric motors are permitted in the natural area, which is open dawn to dusk. The one hiking trail in the park circumnavigates Colchester Pond and is marked with yellow blazes and wooden directional signs.

Distance: 2.5 mi.

To the Trail: From the junction of U.S. 2 and U.S. 7 with Vt. 2A in Colchester (0.0 mi.), proceed east on Vt. 2A to the center of Colchester village and turn north (left) on East Road (1.0 mi.). Turn right at the next intersection (1.2 mi.) on Depot Road and continue past the railroad tracks (1.9 mi.) to a fork (2.3 mi.). Bear left on Colchester Pond Road and proceed past Curve Hill Road on the right to the parking lot on the right (2.6 mi.). The gravel lot contains parking for 20 cars and provides access to both the pond and the hiking trail.

Description: From the parking lot (0.0 mi.), the trail descends along a tree line to the western shore of the pond, which it then follows northerly for some distance through three meadows before ascending the shoulder of a small hill. The trail reaches an unmarked junction (0.8 mi.), where it bears right, then meets another unmarked junction, where a spur trail right leads to the shore. Continuing left through mature pines, the trail follows the north end of the pond until it intersects the Peninsula Trail (1.2 mi.), which leads 0.1 mi. to the pond's edge.

Continuing straight, the trail crosses a stream on a wooden bridge (1.3 mi.) before meeting and following a logging road (1.6 mi.) along the east side of the pond. The trail follows this road through three hay fields, bisecting each on an indistinct path. Near an electrical transmission line at a gate and fence, the trail turns right to follow the southern shore of the pond back to the dammed outlet and bridge (2.4 mi.). The parking lot is a short walk to the right on the road. This last stretch along the southern edge of the pond is often muddy. Special care should be taken to respect the private property of the residents.

Rossetti Natural Area

Distance: 0.3 mi.

To the Trail: From I-89, exit 16 (Colchester/Winooski), turn right at the end of the ramp on U.S. 7 (0.0 mi.) and follow it 1.7 mi. to Vt. 127. Turn left at the traffic light on Vt. 127 and follow it 4.6 mi. (6.3 mi.) to the parking area on the right, just beyond the Church Road intersection. Please don't park in front of any of the emergency access signs along the edge of the lot.

Description: The route enters the woods at a metal gate, near a sign listing rules and regulations. It follows a wide dirt road down a slight grade as it bends right and levels out. It continues through a grove of tall white pine and across a stone culvert before ending at 0.25 mile. The route crosses a bridge onto Thayers Beach, an expanse of undeveloped shoreline and wetland habitat on Lake Champlain. Dogs are not permitted on the beach.

Airport Park and Colchester Bog

The 64-acre Airport Park, managed by Colchester Parks and Recreation, has playing fields, tennis courts, a playground, restrooms and a 1.3-mi. gravel path that circumnavigates the open fields. The park also offers access to Colchester Bog. Note: the boardwalk into Colchester Bog is closed to foot traffic.

Distance: 1.3 mi. loop

To the Trail: From Vt. 127, 1.2 mi. north of the Heineberg Bridge over the Winooski River, turn left on Porter's Point Road (0.0 mi.) and follow it to a four-way intersection (1.9 mi.). Turn left on Airport Road and continue to Airport Park on the right (2.4 mi.) where ample parking is available.

Description: From the parking area, the gravel-surfaced path parallels Airport Road a short distance to a signed junction with the Colchester Causeway.

> **Junction:** The mostly flat Colchester Causeway follows an old railbed, abandoned in 1961, along the edge of the bog and out into Malletts Bay. The Rutland Railroad opened the line across the marble riprap causeway, known as the Big Fill, to the Lake Champlain Islands in 1901. The causeway ends after 4.0 mi. at a once-bridged opening between Malletts Bay and the broad lake.

From the junction, the gravel path toward Colchester Bog bears right to follow the treeline, passing several woodland paths on the left. Each of these paths leads downhill to another path that runs along the edge of Colchester Bog. The boardwalk into the bog is closed indefinitely due to needed maintenance. It is not safe for walking.

The obvious gravel path continues to the far end of the playing fields, turns right to loop the periphery and follows the opposite side of the fields back to the parking area.

Mallets Bay Causeway

At the turn of the 20th century, the Rutland Railroad constructed a causeway between Mills Point in Colchester and Allen Point in South Hero, commencing rail service through the Champlain Islands in January 1901. Although rail service was discontinued in 1961 and the tracks were removed in 1964, the massive marble blocks of the causeway remain intact, stretching more than 3 mi. into the broad lake.

To the Trail: There are two ways to access the causeway: by the Burlington Recreation Path or by car. After crossing the Winooski River on the pedestrian/bike bridge, travel 0.5 mi. on boardwalks through Delta Park (a beautiful lakeshore natural area). Continue 0.5 mi. on bike lanes through a quiet residential neighborhood. The bike lanes connect to Airport Park where the causeway path picks up. For driving directions, see "To the Trail" for Airport Park and Colchester Bog.

Description: From the park (0.0 mi.), the route follows a gravel path leading west, paralleling Airport Road at the edge of Colchester Bog. The path joins the old railroad bed, which turns northwesterly to cross the bog, and reaches Mills Point Road (1.1 mi.). The trail continues to the edge of the lake (1.5 mi.) and out onto the marble-block causeway. Beyond the first bridge (2.7 mi.), the causeway narrows a bit, eventually reaching its end at a gap where the railroad's drawbridge once spanned the gap (4.0 mi.). From this point there are fine views in all directions. The shore of South Hero lies 0.5 mi. north, and to the east, the main range of the Green Mountains is clearly visible over the scattered foothills of the Champlain Valley.

Local Motion, a non-profit organization promoting walking and cycling, is developing a bike ferry, replacing the missing turnstile bridge, to link the Colchester side of the causeway with the South Hero side. Currently, the ferry runs on weekends in August. For information: Local Motion, 1 Steele Street, Burlington VT 05401, 802-652-BIKE, www.localmotionvt.org.

Macrae Farm Park

The trails at Macrae Farm Park are mostly flat and follow the edges of mowed fields. Because the low-lying property borders the Winooski River, the paths may be wet at any time of year. The Winooski Valley Park District maintains the park. Hunting is prohibited and pets must be leashed.

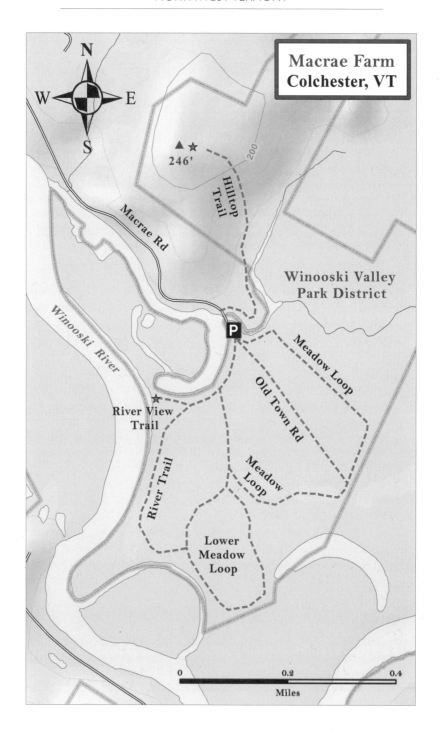

Macrae Farm
Colchester, VT

N
W E
S

▲ ★
246'

200

Hilltop Trail

Macrae Rd

Winooski Valley
Park District

Winooski River

P

Meadow Loop

Old Town Rd

★
River View
Trail

River Trail

Meadow Loop

Lower
Meadow
Loop

0   0.2   0.4

Miles

To the Trail: From the intersection of Vt. 127 and Macrae Road in Colchester, turn on Macrae Road and follow it 1.2 mi.—it turns to gravel in 0.8 mi.—over a one-lane bridge to the parking area. The trailhead is at far end of the parking lot marked by a sign: To Trails.

Description: From the parking area, an old farm road leads to the start of the River View, River and Meadow Loop Trails. From the junction, the River View Trail leads right 0.1 mi. to a bench on the bank of the Winooski River. The Meadow Loop leaves left and circles the perimeters of two mowed meadows. The River Trail, which is sparsely marked "WV," leads straight ahead and follows the Winooski River upstream, passing an osprey nesting site and reaching a bench on the river bank (0.3 mi.). The trail curves away from the river and ends in a meadow at a junction with the Lower Meadow Trail. The left-hand Lower Meadow Trail is the shortest route back to the parking area. The right-hand trail follows the perimeter of the meadow, bearing left at a small arrow, and exiting the field near a signed junction with the Meadow Loop (0.9 mi.). The trail to the left leads directly back to the parking lot. The Meadow Loop turns right to follow the perimeter of another meadow. The buildings atop Water Tower Hill can be seen in the distance. At a junction between two meadows, the Old Town Road leaves left and returns to the parking lot. The Meadow Loop continues straight into another meadow (1.1 mi.) and follows its perimeter back to the parking area (1.3 mi.).

Hilltop Trail: The Hilltop Trail leaves Macrae Road just before the one-lane bridge and is marked by a sign. It follows a tributary 0.3 mi., then turns away from the water and begins a steady climb. At a T-junction, the trail turns left and climbs more steeply to an open hilltop bordering a gravel farm road where there is a view of the farm and parking area below (0.5 mi.). From here, the hillside is crisscrossed by farm roads and ATV trails.

8 Winooski

Gilbrook Nature Area

Winooski's Gilbrook Nature Area is a small piece of forest between I-89, St. Michael's College, Camp Johnson and the Winooski Department of Public Works. The mostly flat trails crisscross the forest and, although none of the junctions are marked, they all lead back to the main loop trail. A shorter trail circumnavigates the pond.

Distance: 1.0 mi. loop

To the Trail: From I-89, exit 15 (0.0 mi.), turn west on Vt. 15 toward Winooski, then right on Dion Street (0.1 mi.). Turn right on Lafountain Street (0.2 mi.) at the four-way stop, then left on Gilbrook Road (0.3 mi.). A parking lot for the nature area is on the right at a dam (0.4 mi.). A second, larger parking area is at the far end on the right.

Description: The trail passes along the right side of the pond to a junction where the loop begins (0.1 mi.). A trail straight ahead leads a short distance uphill to a beaver pond then curves right to intersect the main trail. Turning right, the main trail follows a wide woods road past a stonework dam on the right and reaches a four-way junction with the trail from the beaver pond on the left. Another, narrower trail straight ahead loops through the woods to rejoin the main trail. The main trail bears slightly right, then right again at a Y-junction. The left-hand fork will intersect the main trail at a farther point.

At 0.25 mi., the main trail emerges from the woods at a third trailhead on the campus of St. Michael's College. It bears left along the fence and re-enters the woods. It passes a spur loop on the right (0.3 mi.) that curves along the back fence at the Camp Johnson National Guard base. At 0.4 mi., another trail on the right intersects the Camp Johnson loop. The main trail continues straight, reaching a T-junction with the Camp Johnson loop at the fence. Turning left, the trail follows the fenceline behind the Winooski Department of Public Works garage and passes the beaver pond and a spur to the pond on the left (0.8 mi.). A second, wider path on the left leads back to the beginning of the loop. Straight ahead, the trail ends at the second (northern) parking area on Gilbrook Road. The loop ends where it began between the two ponds. The route turns right back to the parking area. (1.0 mi.).

Winooski Nature Trail and River Walk

Distance: 1.1 mi.

To the Trail: From the rotary at the intersection of U.S. 7 and Vt. 15 in Winooski, follow Vt. 15 east 0.3 mi. to a small parking area on the right before the railroad tracks. Or from I-89, exit 15, turn left toward Winooski on Vt. 15 and follow it 0.6 mi. to the parking area on the left just past the railroad tracks. This parking area is easy to miss. The trail may also be accessed from the boardwalk at the Champlain Mill near the rotary in downtown Winooski.

Description: The nature trail leaves the east end of the parking area and is marked by a sign for pedestrians only. It passes through a wood-fence turnstile and drops steeply to the edge of the marsh. At 0.1 mi., the trail crosses a wooden bridge, levels, then climbs a few steps. It crosses an inlet (0.4 mi.), climbs again and descends to the shore of the Winooski River (0.6 mi.) at the base of the I-89 bridge over the river.

> **Junction:** A sign nailed to a tree indicates that the nature trail leaves left and passes under the bridge. This trail continues upstream, climbing away from the river. It eventually deteriorates into a narrow path on a steep hillside above the river and is not recommended.

Bearing right, the trail follows the Winooski River downstream. At 0.8 mi., a spur trail leaves right to a gravel construction road, which bears right toward the Winooski River Falls development, reaching it at the corner of Abenaki Way and Winooski Falls Way. The trail along the river continues to a board-walk that ends at the the Champlain Mill (1.1 mi.). A sidewalk skirts the mill, passes under the U.S. 7 bridge linking Burlington and Winooski and ends at a viewpoint overlooking Winooski Falls.

⑨ Burlington

Ethan Allen Park

The two salient features of Ethan Allen Park are the Pinnacle and the tower, both of which offer spectacular views over Burlington's north end and the Champlain Valley. The original park was laid out by William Van Patten and commemorates patriot and scalawag Ethan Allen. The medieval-appearing tower was built in 1905 by a group of citizens.

To the Trail: The signed entrance to Ethan Allen Park is on the east side of North Avenue in Burlington, at the intersection of North Avenue and Ethan Allen Parkway, 0.3 mi. north of the North Avenue/Beaches exit off Vt. 127.

Pinnacle Trail

Distance: 0.8 mi.

Description: From the parking lot, the paved Pinnacle Trail leaves left just past the gravel path to the playground. It enters the trees on a gravel path and climbs briefly before leveling off, then dropping to Ethan Allen Pkwy. at a gate and sign indicating the Pinnacle Trail and the route back to the parking lot (0.3). The Pinnacle Trail now follows a wide paved roadway past the gate and begins to climb, gently at first, then more steeply. At 0.5 mi., it passes a path on the left that leads 0.4 mi. to Ethan Allen Pkwy. near its intersec-tion with Farrington Pkwy. The Pinnacle Trail then tops a rise and reaches a junction with another paved path on the right. This path divides and leads either to the Ethan Allen Homestead on the east side of Vt. 127 or back to the parking area.

The Pinnacle Trail continues straight uphill another 0.3 mi. to the Pin-nacle, where there is a stone gazebo, picnic table and ledge-top view over the valley (0.8 mi.).

Observation Tower and Perimeter Trail

Description: The short walk to the observation tower begins in the parking area and follows the paved walkway straight ahead. At 0.1 mi. it reaches a sign for the tower on the left.

Junction: The trail to the tower is a short, but steep 0.1 mi.

From the tower trail, the paved perimeter route continues straight past a dilapidated shelter (0.3 mi.) to a junction marked with a "Cycle the City Marker." The path straight ahead ends at the Pinnacle Trail. The path to the right circles the Pinnacle, passes a steep woodland path to the Pinnacle at a signed junction (0.6 mi.) and reaches the junction with the trail to the Ethan Allen Homestead at another "Cycle the City" marker (0.8 mi.).

MARY LOU RECOR

Junction: The paved path to the Ethan Allen Homestead drops to a pedestrian bridge crossing over Vt. 127. At the end of the bridge, it turns right and leads to the homestead and network of Winooski Valley Park District trails.

The Pinnacle Trail ends at the gazebo.

The trail around the park's perimeter, now dirt, continues straight and descends to Ethan Allen Pkwy. near its intersection with Farrington Pkwy., 0.7 mi. from the parking lot.

Ethan Allen Homestead

The Winooski Valley Park District was formed to preserve or acquire natural areas of regional significance and special interest. The park district includes Burlington, Colchester, Essex, Jericho, South Burlington, Williston and Winooski. The district maintains more than seventeen properties totaling 1,736 acres for muscle-powered recreation and environmental protection. Several locations in Chittenden County provide boat access, picnic areas or wildlife sanctuaries and are described in "Six Easy Walks," a flier available from the district. For more information, contact the Winooski Valley Park District, Ethan Allen Homestead, Burlington, VT 05401, 802-863-5744, wvpd@together.net.

The Ethan Allen Homestead was once the home of Ethan and Fanny Allen. The property offers walking trails, guided tours of the restored farmstead, a multi-media show and museum exhibits as well as picnicking. The trails are open year-round from dawn to dusk. The homestead is open Monday through Saturday, 10:00 a.m. to 5:00 p.m., and Sunday from 1:00 p.m. to 5:00 p.m. during spring, summer and fall. The homestead is closed during the winter. For more information and a trail map: www.ethanallenhomestead.org.

To the Trail: From Burlington, follow Vt. 127, also known as the Northern Connector or the Beltline, north and take the North Avenue/Beaches exit. The access road to the homestead begins off this exit ramp, immediately after a big curve, but before crossing over Vt. 127. Continue 0.4 mi. to the Ethan Allen Museum parking lot. From Colchester, take the North Avenue/Beaches exit off Vt. 127 and turn left to pass over Vt. 127. Turn left again at the Ethan Allen Homestead sign.

Description: There are five trails on the property. Two are short wetland trails named Wetlands Walk South and Wetlands Walk North. The three others, each less than a mile long and within easy walking distance of the education center, are the Peninsula Loop (0.9 mi.), Homestead Loop (0.9 mi.) and River Loop (0.7 mi.). A well-worn footpath off the River Loop parallels the Winooski River, then follows farm roads to Intervale Road off Riverside Avenue. Natural features of the Intervale, such as the mature floodplain forests, may be seen from all these trails.

Rock Point

The Episcopal Diocese of Vermont has owned and maintained 130-acre Rock Point since 1854, when the Rev. John Henry Hopkins deeded it to the church. The property is known for the diversity of its natural features, including the exposed face of a thrust fault, and a spectacular view west over Lake Champlain. While Rock Point is open to the public, the diocese requests that all

MARY LOU RECOR

The Ethan Allen Homestead

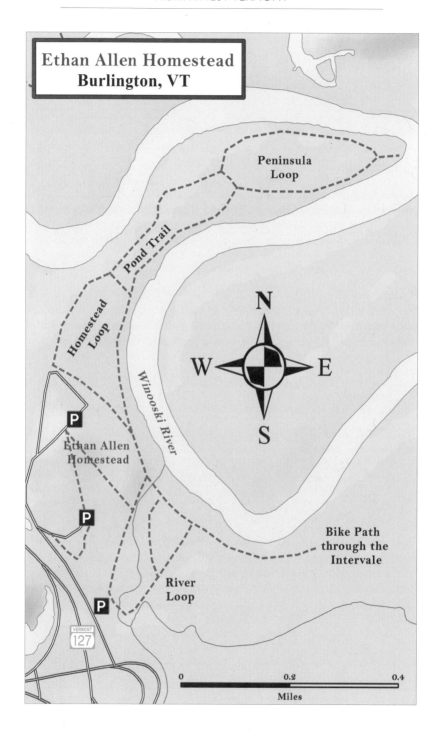

Ethan Allen Homestead
Burlington, VT

Peninsula Loop

Pond Trail

Homestead Loop

Winooski River

N
W   E
S

P

Ethan Allen Homestead

P

Bike Path
through the
Intervale

P

River
Loop

VERMONT
127

0   0.2   0.4

Miles

visitors obtain a pass and map before visiting the property. Passes are available Monday to Friday, 9 a.m. to 4 p.m. at the diocesan office. Weekend visitors should phone during office hours for permission to visit: 800-286-3437 or 802-863-3431. The trails are open during daylight hours only for walking, snowshoeing or skiing. Bicycle riding is not permitted. Dogs must be leashed and owners are requested to clean up after them. Use caution along the cliff top trail as there are no guardrails. For more information, contact property manager Chuck Courcy at 802-355-8737 or ccourcy@dioceseofvermont.org

Distance: 1.5 mi.

To the Trail: From the intersection of North Avenue and Institute Road in Burlington (Burlington High School and North Beach entrance), follow Institute Road 0.2 mi. to the entrance to the Episcopal Diocese of Vermont, marked private. Turn right between the stone pillars and follow the driveway 0.3 mi. to a parking area on the right (0.5 mi.), opposite the diocesan office where you can register and obtain a trail pass.

Description: From the parking area (0.0 mi.), the route follows the gravel access road 0.1 mi. over a bridge, then bears left at a fork (signed). It passes the bishop's house and continues on the road to the trailhead, which is marked by a trailhead sign (0.5 mi.). The route continues straight past the trailhead sign on a wide path. It bears left at a series of trail signs before arriving at a signed junction.

    Junction: The path straight ahead leads to the outdoor chapel and is the return route for this loop.

Bearing left, the trail emerges from the woods onto the open Parade Ground at a four-way junction (0.6 mi.).

    Junction: The trail left leads 0.3 mi. to Lone Rock Point, a rocky promontory overlooking Lake Champlain. It then circles north around the point on a less-worn path and intersects the trail across the Parade Ground at the canoe landing (0.6 mi.).

The trail right intersects the direct trail to the outdoor chapel.

    The trail straight ahead continues through the Parade Ground and ends at the canoe landing and thrust fault (0.7 mi.). A short spur trail straight ahead leads down to the water. From the landing, the trail along the cliff top turns right and climbs steeply, but briefly, to a high point, levels, then drops to an iron fence along the cliff where there is a view west across the lake (0.9). The outdoor chapel is on the right. Turning away from the lake and crossing the chapel grounds, a wide path leads back to the signed junction where the loop began (1.0 mi.). The trail straight ahead returns to the trailhead and gravel road to the parking area (1.5 mi.).

Donahue Sea Caves

The short trail to the sea caves is best done in winter when the marsh is frozen or in summer with a small boat in tow.

Distance: 0.25 mi.

To the Trail: From the intersection of North Avenue and the Vt. 127 access road in Burlington, follow North Avenue south 0.3 mi. to Institute Road (Burlington High School) and turn right. There is a small parking area on the left. The trail to the caves is across North Avenue, behind the bus shelter, and marked with a sign.

Description: From the bus shelter, the wide trail drops gradually down to the marsh and ends at the pond. In mid-winter, it is possible to continue across the pond ice to the sea caves carved into the embankment. In summer, they may be reached by canoe or kayak.

Rena Calkins Trail

This trail, which follows the bank of the Winooski River in Burlington's Intervale, is named for the last dairy farmer in Burlington. It is mostly flat and sparsely marked with small "RC" markers. From the trailhead, two loops are possible: a short one that circles to the Intervale Center and a longer one that follows a woodland path, farm road and the lightly traveled Intervale Road back to the parking area.

SYLVIE VIDRINE

Rena Calkins trailhead.

Distance: 1.0 mi.

To the Trail: From the intersection of Riverside Avenue and Intervale Road in Burlington, turn north on Intervale Road and follow it 0.5 mi. to a parking area and signboard on the right.

Description: From the parking area, the trail heads toward the Winooski River and reaches a T-junction at its bank (0.15 mi.). The right-hand trail follows the river upstream to a pond behind Gardener's Supply and the Intervale Center (0.3 mi.). The left-hand trail meanders downstream 0.4 mi., then turns left away from the river, climbs a small embankment and enters a field. A farm road straight ahead leads back to Intervale Road, 0.4 mi. from the parking area

(1.0 mi.). The limited-access, right-hand branch of Intervale Road leads to the Winooski Valley Park District trails at the Ethan Allen Homestead.

Salmon Hole Park

Distance: 0 .7 mi.

To the Trail: The trailhead parking lot is on the west side of Riverside Avenue (U.S. 2 and U.S. 7) in Burlington, 600 ft. south of the Winooski River Bridge. Dogs must be leashed.

For a longer walk: Follow the sidewalk north across the bridge, turn left onto a path and climb down the stairs where there are two plaques on a brick wall. Turn right and follow the path to the hydroelectric dam where there are informational signs. At high water, the view of the falls is breathtaking. Use caution when exploring the rock ledges and relics of mills from another era.

Description: From the parking area, the trail begins about 500 ft. south on the sidewalk (away from the bridge). Multiple pathways lead down to the river, making a short loop possible by following the trails to the right downhill and returning via one of the trails farther downstream. For a longer excursion, the path continues downstream a short distance. There are stairs and benches in various places. When the water is low, exposing the rock ledges, there is a great view of Winooski Falls and the old mill buildings.

Centennial Woods Natural Area

Centennial Woods is a designated natural area of the University of Vermont (UVM). It encompasses 70 acres of mature conifer and mixed hardwood forests, streams and wetlands used as an ecology laboratory for students. The Area is notable for its relatively pristine state despite its location along the eastern edge of Burlington, Vermont's largest city. It is open to the public for foot travel and UVM's Environmental Program maintains a trail loop. Just over 1.0 mi. long, the trail is blazed sparingly with white paint and some arrows at important turns. For more information, contact University of Vermont Environmental Program, 153 South Prospect Street, Burlington VT 05405, 802-656-4055.

To the Trail: From the jug-handle intersection of Williston Road (U.S. 2), Spear Street and East Avenue, turn north on East Avenue and proceed a short distance to the first traffic light. Turn right and continue to the second driveway in front of the Instrumentation and Model Facility at 280 East Avenue where there are four metered spaces reserved for natural area visitor parking. The trailhead is across the road near a wooden sign.

Description: At the entrance to the trail there is a ledger box, which may contain copies of a UVM field guide with descriptions corresponding to numbered stations along the trail. The trail heads northeast to cross a wet area on puncheon before reaching a bridge across a stream at the bottom of a ravine. It then ascends a short distance to a junction, marking the beginning of the trail loop. Following an arrow to the right for a counterclockwise circuit, the trail ascends steeply to a plateau, then meanders along a ridge covered with towering white pines, many of which are more than 100 years old. The trail passes municipal boundary markers, crossing into South Burlington, then back into Burlington, before descending steeply into a ravine and its northernmost point at an electric transmission line. The trail climbs over a small shoulder to follow a southerly course along the east side of a stream back to the junction with the access trail.

Burlington Recreation Path

This 7.6-mi. multi-purpose path has many access points along Burlington's scenic waterfront and provides links to other recreation trails in the area. Generally following the former Rutland Railway rail bed, the path offers striking views across Lake Champlain toward the Adirondack Mountains.

Local Motion, a nonprofit organization promoting walking and cycling, is working to extend this trail northward from Burlington to Canada on the historic Rutland Railroad Island Line and existing roads. The Island Flyer ran on these tracks through the Lake Champlain islands from 1901 to 1961.

The Burlington Recreation Path connects to the South Burlington Recreation Path to the south and recreation paths in Colchester to the north. The South Burlington path is more a spider web of trails than a path. From Oakledge Park, it is roughly 0.5 mi. on Austin Drive to link up with the network.

In 1999, a group of trail advocates established a bike ferry across the Winooski River (the northern terminus of the Burlington Recreation Path) to connect with the recreation path in Colchester. That ferry has now been replaced by a pedestrian/bike bridge. On the Colchester side, the recreation path continues 1.0 mi. before connecting with the Mallets Bay Causeway (p. 158).

To learn more about Local Motion's work to unite existing trails into a regional Island Line Trail, contact Local Motion, 1 Steele Street, Suite 103, Burlington VT 05401, 802-652-BIKE, www.localmotionvt.org.

To the Trail: To reach the path's southern terminus, from the rotary on U.S. 7 at the head of Shelburne Road, proceed south about 0.7 mi. Turn west on Flynn Avenue and continue about 0.5 mi. to Oakledge Park where ample parking is available (a fee may be charged). Parking is also available at the Burlington Boat House.

Description: The southern terminus of the paved recreation path is at Austin Drive (0.0 mi.) 0.3 mi. south of Oakledge Park. The trail continues north, reaching the waterfront at Roundhouse Point and Perkins Pier (2.2 mi.), where there is a ferry dock and parking, and continuing north past the foot of College Street, the Lake Champlain Science Center and Burlington Boat House. The path ascends a tiny hill (3.6 mi.) before reaching North Beach (4.1 mi., parking) and continuing through a wooded area to Leddy Park (5.2 mi., parking). After crossing Starr Farm Road (6.2 mi.), the path crosses another side road (7.3 mi.) before crossing the Winooski River (7.6 mi.) on the pedestrian/bike bridge. The route continues on paved streets to Airport Park in Colchester.

Essex

Indian Brook Reservoir Park

This 575-acre preserve was formerly used as a municipal water supply and is now managed by the Essex Town Parks and Recreation Department. The 66-acre reservoir was created by damming Indian Brook and is attractive for non-motorized watercraft. The principal hiking trail in the park circumnavigates the reservoir but is only intermittently signed or blazed. A second trail ascends a ridge east of the reservoir, where there is a view west.

Circumferential Trail

Distance: 1.8 mi.

To the Trail: From the junction of Vt. 289 and Vt. 15 in the town of Essex (0.0 mi.), travel east on Vt. 15 and turn left on Old Stage Road (0.2 mi.). Passing Lost Nation Road on the left, take the next left (0.6 mi.) on Indian Brook Road and continue into the park at a boundary sign (1.8 mi.). Bear right past two parking lots to reach a third lot located near the boat launch.

Description: From the north end of the parking lot (0.0 mi.), the Circumferential Trail begins its loop around the reservoir by paralleling the east shore. Bearing right at an intersection (0.4 mi.) where a spur leads left to the shore, the trail follows an old road northward to a corner, where a blue arrow on a tree points left. Bearing left, the trail swings south to an unmarked intersection (0.8 mi.) where it turns right and crosses Indian Brook on a plank bridge. Bypassing an unmarked trail to the right (1.0 mi.), the trail reaches another intersection (1.2 mi.) marked by a second blue arrow. Bearing left as the arrow indicates, the trail flanks the western edge of the pond, bypassing a spur on the right (1.6 mi.) before reaching a signpost (1.8 mi.) marking the western end of the trail. A short gravel path leads below the reservoir's dam back to the access road and lower parking lots.

Overlook Trail

Distance: 1.0 mi.

Description: The Overlook Trail leaves the east side of the parking lot (0.0

mi.) and proceeds southeast as a mowed path before swinging north after being joined by another path from the right. Marked by blue blazes, the trail soon merges into an old road and crosses a stone fence (0.3 mi.). It makes a sharp left turn (unmarked) off the road and follows a narrow path past a sharp right turn (0.4 mi.) to two lookouts (0.7 mi.). From the second of these lookouts, the trail makes a sharp turn right and continues its northward ascent of the ridge. The trail ends at a ledge from which Lake Champlain is seen in the distance (1.0 mi.).

Woodside Natural Area

This Winooski Valley Park District loop trail passes through floodplain along the Winooski River. It is well marked and easy to follow. Hunting is prohibited and pets must be leashed.

Distance: 1.1 mi. loop

To the Trail: From I-89, exit 15 (0.0 mi.), follow Vt. 15 east 1.3 mi. to the traffic light at the western entrance to Fort Ethan Allen and turn right on Woodside Drive (unsigned). Follow Woodside Drive 0.25 mi. to a small parking area on the right at a gate (1.6 mi.).

Description: From the gate and signboard, the trail follows a wide, flat woods road toward the Winooski River, passing a sign on the left for the beginning of the loop trail (0.1 mi.). At the river, it emerges onto a grassy area and turns upstream (0.2 mi.) to re-enter the woods at a sign for the "Woodside Trail." It then curves away from the water, crosses a wet area on puncheon (0.4 mi.) and begins a gradual climb to an old woods road where it turns left. Following a narrow ridge, the trail passes a bench on the left, then another—both with views over the marsh—before closing the loop (1.0 mi.). Turning right, it returns to the trailhead (1.1 mi.).

Pearl Street Park

The well-maintained trails of Pearl Street Park are open 7 a.m.-9 p.m. The paved portion is wheelchair accessible.

Distance: 0.75 mi.

To the Trail: Located in Essex Junction, Pearl Street Park is just west of the Champlain Valley Exposition on Vt. 15 (Pearl Street) at the intersection of Pearl Street and West Street Extension. The best landmark is the jug handle at this crossroads. If coming west from the Colchester/Winooski area, look for the intersection just past Susie Wilson Road. Note: the park sign cannot be seen from Vt. 15. Drop down a slight knoll from the jug handle to the parking area and sign.

Description: From the parking area, the trail follows a paved path with a swamp on the left and woods on the right. It climbs a slight knoll where tennis and basketball courts are on the left, a playground on the right. There are picnic tables and benches scattered throughout this area, with evidence that a dog-friendly trail awaits as pooper-scooper bags are hung on posts here and there. The trail winds to the left down a slight knoll with a baseball field ahead. This is where the paved path ends, with a slight jog into the woods (marked with a large vertical "Public Access" black and white sign). The trail takes a short diversion onto the parking area of a condo/apartment complex, then heads into the woods, where it changes to a dirt surface. Crossing a small brook accessed by a short sturdy wooden bridge, the trail proceeds slightly uphill to the right and arrives behind the tennis and basketball courts.

Sand Hill Park/Mathieu Town Forest

Although this trail is only a mile long, it seems longer as it drops into and climbs out of several small ravines. It is well blazed with orange paint and easy to follow, despite a number of twists and junctions.

Distance: 1.0 mi.

To the Trail: From I-89, exit 15, turn east on Vt. 15 toward Essex Junction (0.0 mi.). Follow Vt. 15 through the Five Corners intersection (3.6 mi.) to Sand Hill Road in Essex (7.1 mi.). Bear right on Sand Hill Road, then turn right into the driveway for the Sand Hill Park parking lot (7.3 mi.). Park in the lot at the far end of the driveway.

Description: The orange-blazed trail begins at an opening in the trees between the two basketball hoops. At 0.1 mi., it reaches a junction and a sign that reads "Essex Public Trail."

> **Junction:** The trail to the right follows the fence around the tennis court toward the playground. The trail straight ahead descends gently, then loops back to rejoin the orange trail.

The orange trail turns left and descends slightly before intersecting with the other end of the short loop trail. It bears right behind some houses and reaches a junction with the blue trail (0.2 mi.). Bearing right, the blue and orange trails coincide and pass an overlook above Alder Brook on the right. At a sign for the Essex Town Public Trail, (0.4 mi.), the blue trail continues straight ahead to close the loop. The orange trail leaves right and follows a fence briefly before bearing right and dropping into a ravine. At a double blaze, it turns left, follows a small brooklet, then crosses it. The trail continues to meander through pine forest, dropping into and climbing out of several small ravines. At 0.7 mi., it intersects with a wider woods road and turns left to follow the road past a Birchwood Land Company sign (0.8 mi.). The trail climbs a stiff uphill, turns left at a junction, levels and reaches a "No Trespassing" sign on the left.

It turns right, away from the sign, and continues straight with little elevation change. At 1.0 mi., it emerges from the woods on an embankment above Vt. 289, where a path follows the treeline and drops down to the highway at a small parking area, 0.6 mi. from the intersection of Vt. 289 and Vt. 117.

Forestdale Natural Area

Distance: 1.1 mile loop

To the Trail: From I-89, exit 11 (Richmond), turn right on U.S. 2, then right on Vt. 117. Continue 4.7 mi. to Sand Hill Road. Turn right on Sand Hill Road for 1.0 mi., then left on Allen Martin Parkway. Follow Allen Martin Parkway 0.3 mi. and park in a small pullout on the right near some mailboxes, just before the street ends at Partridge and Laurel Drives. From Essex Junction, follow Vt. 117 east 1.5 mi., then turn left on Sand Hill Road and follow the directions above.

Description: From the parking area, the route crosses Partridge Drive at the crosswalk and continues straight ahead along a wide clearing. It enters the woods at an Essex Public Trail sign and descends on an old road. Almost immediately, it turns left on a narrow path. This turn is easy to miss. At the turn, houses are still visible uphill to the left. The path continues slightly uphill, then traverses the slope before reaching a more level area at a T-junction with a wider trail (0.25 mi.). Turning left, the trail eventually emerges from the woods at a cul-de-sac (0.35 mi.). It follows a drive to the right for a couple hundred feet and turns downhill on the next path back into the woods. At the beginning of a small rise, the trail bears left at a fork. It curves downhill with a steep gully on the right before leveling in a valley. The trail bears left at a junction where a bridge is visible on the right (0.7 mi.). At the next fork, it climbs slightly uphill (0.9 mi.), then exits the woods on a paved drive. Laurel Lane to the right leads back to the parking area (1.1 mi.).

Saxon Hill School District Park

The trails for the Saxon Hill School District park were laid out in 2004 and 2005 by volunteers from The Fellowship of the Wheel, an organization dedicated to the promotion of mountain biking. Consequently, they are nicely graded, but meandering. At times, it seems they will loop back on themselves. The Mo Flo, which is described, leads to the two other trails: Flo and Paper Route. These trails are part of a larger trail network: The Saxon Hill Forest Trail Network. For maps and information: www.fotwheel.org or www.essex. org. The trails are open to mountain bikers, skiers, snowshoers and walkers. Please share the trails and yield to mountain bikers.

Mo Flo Trail
Distance: 1.2 mi.

To the Trail: From I-89, exit 15, turn east on Vt. 15 toward Essex Junction (0.0 mi.). Follow Vt. 15 through the Five Corners intersection (3.6 mi.) to Allen Martin Drive in Essex and turn right (8.0 mi.). Follow Allen Martin Drive 0.3 mi. and turn left on Thompson Drive. Park in the small parking area on the left before the gate (8.6 mi.). Do not block the gate. Other trails in the Saxon Hill School District may be accessed at the intersection of Allen Martin and Thompson Drive, however, there is no parking.

Description: The route passes around the gate and follows a gravel extension of Thompson Drive straight ahead, then turns right onto a narrow path, marked with a blue Fellowship of the Wheel marker. The trail meanders through the woods with no elevation change, passes two ponds—one of them twice—and eventually reaches a junction where there is a kiosk and map of the three trail loops. Mo Flo now loops back to the closed gravel section of Thompson Drive. The Flo loop begins across the gravel road. The road left leads back to the parking area.

George R. Clapp Nature Trail
Distance: 0.5 mi. loop

To the Trail: From the center of Essex Junction, follow Vt. 15 northeast 3.1 mile to Vt. 128. Continue straight on Vt. 128, then turn right into the school bus turnaround. There is room for a couple of cars to pull off the paved area and park. Please don't block the school buses.

Description: The trail enters the woods at a sign for the George R. Clapp Nature Trail near two boulders. After 250 ft., the route leads straight ahead at a sign pointing right to The Commons. At a T-junction, it turns left through a small pine grove and descends to an observation platform looking over the wetlands at 0.1 mile. Returning to the T-junction, the nature trail continues straight. At a clearing with a totem pole ahead, it turns left, descending toward a footbridge at 0.2 mile. Crossing the bridge (slippery if wet), it continues through pines and mixed woods on the other side, along the edge of the wetland. The good trail ends at 0.3 mi. where the path takes a sharp left toward the wetland and deteriorates to a muddy path. Returning to the bridge and turning left just after the bridge, the trail continues the loop. It ascends a short hill, continues straight, passing a side trail on the right, then returns to the parking area at 0.5 mi.

⓫ South Burlington

Winooski Gorge

Distance: 0.25 mi.

To the Trail: From I-89, exit 15 (0.0 mi.), follow Vt. 15 east 0.5 mi. and turn right on Lime Kiln Road. The trailhead for the gorge is 0.2 mi. on the right just beyond the bridge (0.7 mi.) at a paved parking area. The best view of the gorge is from the concrete platform next to the bridge.

Description: The trail enters the woods between the parking area and the river at a Winooski Valley Park District sign for Winooski Gorge. It climbs gently to a T-junction. The right-hand trail circles back toward Lime Kiln Road and ends at the viewing platform near the bridge. Straight ahead, a short spur leads to a view looking downstream. The left-hand trail follows a metal fence and ends at another viewpoint (0.25 mi.). It does not extend beyond the fence and any informal paths peter out after a short distance.

Muddy Brook Park

The walk described here goes the full length of the park, using the River Loop and River View Trails, and offers great views of the Winooski River. This is part of the Champlain Birding Trail and is popular with bird watchers. During early spring, low lying areas of the trail may be flooded.

Distance: 1.0 mi. loop

To the Trail: From I-89, exit 15, follow Vt. 15 east 1.0 mi. to Lime Kiln Road. Turn right on Lime Kiln Road and take the second left after the bridge on National Guard Avenue. Follow it to Poor Farm Road and continue 1.5 mi. to a parking lot on the left. **Alternate route:** From I-89, exit 12, in Williston, follow Vt. 2A north 2.2 mi. Turn left on River Cove Road for 1.3 mi. to the parking lot on the right.

Description: The trail passes through a wooden gate and continues straight to the edge of a grassy field. Turning left, it crosses a wooden bridge at a sign for the River Loop and Heron Loop. At a three-way junction, the trail continues straight or follows the right branch to stay on higher ground. The two branches rejoin shortly. At 0.1 mi., the Heron Loop joins from the left, returning to the parking area in 0.1 mi. Continuing straight on the River Loop, the trail reaches a junction where the River Loop turns left and returns to the parking area (0.2). Continuing straight on the River View Trail, the route follows the top of a small embankment, passes a fence at a field corner at 0.3 mi. and continues between the river and the fence. At 0.4 mi., the park ends at a sign posted on a tree. Retracing to the field corner, the trail follows the right-hand,

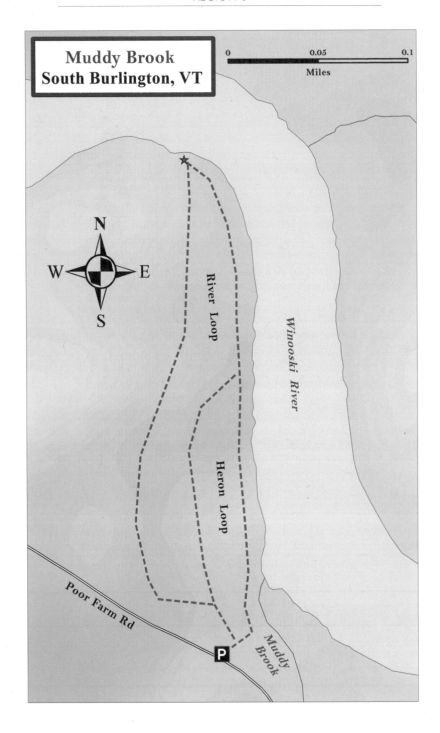

inland branch of the River Loop through the woods and finally emerges in an overgrown field before returning to the parking area at 1.0 mi.

Red Rocks Park

Red Rocks Park is the former site of a private estate, with interconnected carriage paths that lead through pleasant pine woods to vantage points on the shore of Lake Champlain. The park is maintained by the South Burlington Recreation Department.

To the Trail: From U.S. 7 (Shelburne Road), immediately south of the I-189 interchange, turn west on Queen City Park Road. After crossing a one-lane bridge, turn left on Central Avenue and continue a short distance to the park entrance on the right. A parking fee is charged from late June to Labor Day, but pedestrians may enter the park without charge at any time.

Description: From the parking lot designated Parking 1 (0.0 mi.), a trail leads west along the top of a bluff on the north shore of Shelburne Bay, eventually reaching an overlook with a fine view south (0.4 mi.). The trail continues to a turnaround loop at the west end of Red Rocks Point, about 50 ft. beyond a right turn, where another trail descends to a loop on the east shore of the lake (0.6 mi.). From this latter lookout, there is a magnificent vista across the broad lake to the Adirondacks.

North of this main trail are three loops, each 0.6 mi. long, which may be used to return to the park's entrance. The westernmost loop departs the main path before the turnarounds on Red Rocks Point and circles a 240-ft. knob before returning to the main trail. At this junction, the middle loop leaves north to cross the park's 280-ft. wooded summit, passing red rock ledges. This path continues east, ending at a junction. To the right, a short path returns to the main trail; while to the left, the easternmost loop heads north to the park boundary before bearing east and ending at the park entrance.

East Woods Natural Area

Owned by the University of Vermont, East Woods is a 40-acre woodland in South Burlington, exemplary of a mature northern forest. UVM students use the area as an ecology laboratory; it is open to the public for foot travel. An interpretive loop trail, under 1.0 mi. long, winds through the site's towering pines, hemlocks and oaks and is sparsely marked with wooden rectangles inscribed with arrows.

To the Trail: From the jug-handle intersection of Williston Road (U.S. 2), Spear Street, and East Avenue (0.0 mi.), turn south on Spear Street and continue to a traffic light (2.1 mi.). Turn right on Swift Street and proceed west a short distance to the entrance to East Woods Natural Area, which is on the right and marked by a large wooden sign (2.5 mi.).

Alternatively: from the intersection of Shelburne Road and Swift Street (0.0 mi.), just south of the I-189 interchange, turn left on Swift Street to the entrance, which appears shortly on the left (0.6 mi.). Ample parking is available along the side of the street at the entrance.

Description: From the entrance, the trail leads a few hundred feet to an informative bulletin board and ledger box, which is usually empty. The trail continues westerly and passes a junction on the left (0.1 mi.) with the return trail. Bearing right at this junction to make a counterclockwise circuit, the trail descends steeply to approach Potash Brook, which meanders through the woods on its way to Lake Champlain. It crosses a slight depression (0.2 mi.), a remnant of the railbed of the Burlington and Hinesburg Railroad, which was graded in 1898 but abandoned before any track was laid.

Adjacent to this railbed, the trail crosses the more conspicuous and parallel railbed of the Burlington and Lamoille Railroad (B&L), which was completed in 1877. The tracks were used for only a few years before being removed. Directly across the B&L railbed, the trail descends to an elbow of Potash Brook, then swings back to recross the two railbeds (0.4 mi.). (Turning left on the B&L railbed is a shortcut.) After ascending a small shoulder, the trail descends to follow the south shore of Potash Brook downstream to the west. It then arcs 180 degrees, rising easterly on undulating terrain to reach the return end of the loop (0.9 mi.). From here, the trail may be retraced to the entrance (1.0 mi.).

Stonehedge Woods

The woodland paths that crisscross Stonehedge Woods between Swift Street, Brewer Parkway and the Stonehedge development are unmarked. The terrain is challenging, with many short, steep ascents and descents.

To the Trails: From the intersection of U.S. 7 and Swift Street (0.0 mi.) in South Burlington, turn east on Swift Street and follow it 0.2 mi. to the signed entrance to Farrell Park. Turn into Farrell Park and follow the access road 0.1 mi. to the farthest parking lot. The entrance to Farrell Park is 0.7 mi. west of Spear Street.

Description: From the parking area, the route to Stonehedge Woods passes through an opening in the fence and turns left onto the paved South Burlington Recreation Path, which it follows uphill 0.2 mi. to an opening in the woods on the right. A trail on the left of the paved path circles back to the parking area. The trail on the right enters the woods, drops into a shallow gully and continues to parallel the paved recreation path to an intersection. The trail left leads out of the woods to the paved path and the trail right leads deeper into the woods on the trail network.

Dorset Park Trails

Dorset Park, off Dorset Street in South Burlington, is a community park with playing fields and an ice arena on the north side of Swift Street Extension. On the south side, the 103-acre natural area, also known as the "Calkins Parcel," was set aside in 1992. It has over 2 mi. of trails through overgrown fields, woods and wetlands, with many opportunities for enjoying nature. Parts of the trail can be wet, but there are boardwalks on the wettest. Many of the trails and junctions are not well marked. In some places, there are dark red wooden sign boards on green metal posts, apparently put up in 2001 or 2002, but most of the signs have been torn off. Even without signs, the natural area is an interesting place to explore.

To the Trails: There are three main access points to the park: (1) from a parking lot near the corner of Dorset Street and Swift Street Extension; (2) from the end of Swift Street Extension; and (3) from the view point on Park Street. From the intersection of Dorset and Swift Streets in South Burlington, Swift Street Extension continues from the end of Swift Street east of Dorset Street. The gravel parking area is on the right. The Park Street access is a little further down Swift Street Extension, also on the right. A bench with a view of the Adirondacks is on the left side of the street near the top of the hill. There is parking for one car on Park Street. There is no parking at the end of Swift Street Extension, but this is a very short walk from the parking lot near the corner. The trails can also be accessed from Butler Farms (but only through private land), the National Gardening Association and from the bike path just east of the Park Street lookout.

The Main Loop

Description: The Main Loop is a 0.8 mi. loop trail, most easily accessed from the lookout on Park Street. The trail begins just below the bench and is marked with signs and blue blazes. There is a trail map on the sign at the beginning. The trail heads to the right and slightly downhill and is mostly in the woods. It follows a brook for a short distance.

> **Junction:** At a signed crossing, a rock hop over the brook leads to the Butler Farms/Oak Creek Connector Trail. The right branch heads to Butler Farms and Oak Creek Village and the left to the end of Swift Street Extension.

The Main Loop circles left and continues over much boardwalk to another junction at a sharp left turn in the trail.

> **Junction:** At an unmarked junction Connector (Spur) Trail #2 leads right to the end of Swift Street Extension. A red sign board (no signs) indicates the continuation of the Main Loop. Just beyond is another branch of the trail to Swift Street Extension.

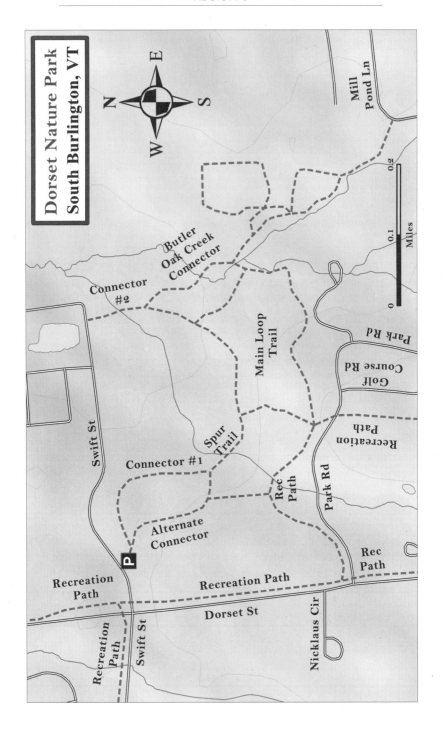

Dorset Nature Park
South Burlington, VT

The Main Loop continues a little farther to another junction.

Junction: A spur trail leads 0.1 mi. to the alternate Connector Trail #1 from the Swift Street Parking Lot and the National Gardening Association. There is a sign at this junction.

The Main Loop continues uphill through woods and reaches another junction just before the road.

Junction: The trail right leads to the bike path just east of the lookout; the trail left leads back to the beginning of the trail just before the lookout. Each of these trails is less than 200 yds. long.

Spur Trail

Description: The Spur Trail starts on the Main Loop at a signed junction about 2/3 of the way around the loop. It leads 0.1 mi. to Alternate Connector Trail #1 and the National Gardening Association. After 0.9 mi., it reaches a junction.

Junction: Connector Trail #1 is to the right and leads to the Swift Street Extension parking lot. It is marked with a red sign board (no sign).

The Spur Trail continues a little farther to an unmarked junction on the left.

Junction: This junction and the trail, next to a small clump of red cedars, are faint and easy to miss. The trail to the left leads to the bike path near Park Street, east of the lookout.

The Spur Trail continues 45 yds. to its end at alternate Connector Trail #1 (no sign).

Trails from Swift Street Extension Parking Lot

Connector Trail #1

Description: From the northwest corner of the parking lot, the route follows a water pipeline up a very small hill. To the left is a shagbark hickory tree, perhaps the first hint of the variety of nature in this area. To the right is a very short trail leading back to the alternate Connector trail.

Junction: At the bottom of the hill, a short trail to the right leads back to the Connector trail.

From the top of the hill there is an excellent view of Camel's Hump to the right and Bolton Mountain straight ahead. The alternate trail turns right near an unsigned red sign board. This is the actual original beginning of Connector Trail #1 and leads to the Spur Trail in 0.4 mi. A short distance down this trail is a view of Mount Mansfield. The trail crosses a field and enters the woods. It then reaches a T-junction with the Spur Trail.

Alternate to Connector Trail #1

Description: This trail begins at the southeast corner of the parking lot and leads across a large field directly to the National Gardening Association.

> **Junction:** A wide mowed path to the right leads to the National Gardens and a large red building.

The trail continues 60 yds. to another junction.

> **Junction:** The Spur Trail, which leads 0.1 mi. to the Main Loop, is on the left.

The trail circles right around the edge of the gardens to Dorset Street.

Trails from end of Swift Street Extension

Connector (Spur) Trail #2:

Description: This trail starts at the end of Swift Street Extension at the entrance to a housing development where there is a "hiking trail" sign beside the street. The trail is 0.2 mi. long and crosses a water line, then a bridge before reaching a Y-junction.

> **Junction:** The trail to the left is the Butler Farms Connector Trail and leads to Butler Farms and Oak Creek Village.

Continuing right, Connector Trail #2 soon reaches what appears to be a five-way junction.

> **Junction:** The trail farthest left leads back to the Butler Farms Connector. The second trail to the left splits again in a few feet at another Y, which looks like two trails but is actually a sharp bend in the Main Loop. The right hand side of the split has a red sign board; this is the continuation of the Main Loop. The trail farther to the right also leads to the Main Loop in a very short distance.

Butler/Oak Creek Connector Trail

Description: This 0.7-mi. trail leads from Connector Trail #2 to Butler Farms and Oak Creek Village. Part of the trail is outside park boundaries. In a short distance the trail comes to a junction.

> **Junction:** The trail to the right leads back to Connector Trail #2.

The Butler Farm/Oak Creek Trail crosses a bridge immediately after this junction. It enters the woods and climbs a slight hill. There are signs at a brook crossing to the Main Loop.

Junction: A rough trail to the right crosses the brook on rocks. The Main Loop is just across the brook.

The Butler Farms/Oak Creek Trail continues straight ahead. Just before a boardwalk and bridge another junction is reached.

Junction: A trail to the left crosses a wet area, then leads up a slight hill to an open field with good views. The houses of Butler Farms and Oak Creek Village are across the field.

The trail to the right crosses a boardwalk and bridge and continues to a field behind the houses of Butler Farms.

Whales' Tails Trail

Anyone driving north on I-89 toward Burlington can't help but notice the pair of black African granite whales' tails near the interstate. The sculpture is titled "Reverence" and was created in 1989 by Jim Sardonis of Randolph, Vermont. The best view of the sculpture is from the walking path, which begins on Community Drive and loops around the open pasture.

Distance: 1.7 mi.

To the Trail: From the south, from I-89, exit 12 (Taft Corners) (0.0 mi.), turn right on Vt. 2A and follow it 0.3 mi. to Marshall Avenue. Turn left on Marshall Avenue and follow it 2.1 mi.—Marshall Avenue merges onto Kimble Avenue— to Commercial Drive (2.4 mi.). Turn left on Commercial Drive and follow it 0.7 mi. (3.1 mi.) to a parking area on the left near the pond. The entrance is marked with a white sign for the walking paths and playing fields. **Alternate route:** From the intersection of Kennedy Drive and Kimble Avenue, turn south on Kimble Avenue and follow it 0.7 mi. to Community Drive. Turn right on Community Drive and follow as above.

JAMES SARDONIS

Description: The trail begins at the far end of the parking lot where a white sign marks the beginning. It follows the edge of the pond a short distance before reaching a fork. Either path leads to the beginning of the loop at the athletic field. Turning left, the trail follows

The Whales' Tails

the edge of the field south, then bears right toward I-89. A short right-hand spur at the corner of the field leads a short distance to Muddy Brook. The main trail parallels the interstate, passes a bench on the left and reaches the sculpture, where it turns left. A short spur path on the left leads uphill to the sculpture. The main trail continues near the interstate and passes two unmarked side trails on the right before bearing away from the highway at the north end of the field. When it reaches Community Drive, the trail turns sharply right to parallel the road back to the beginning of the loop near the pond.

A second, less-worn path leaves the parking area and circles the perimeter of the pond.

 Jericho

Old Mill Park

Old Mill Park in Jericho is a 12-acre property behind the Old Mill Craft Shop. The River and Pine Trails follow the rock-strewn Browns River and the Hilltop Loop traces a plateau above and away from the water. Pets must be leashed. The park, which is open during daylight hours, is maintained by the Winooski Valley Park District and the trails are marked with the stylized "WV" symbol. For information, contact the park district at 802-863-5744 or at wvpd.org

Distance: 0.7 mi.

To the Trail: From I-89 exit 15, follow Vt. 15 east 9.7 mi. to Jericho. The Old Mill is on the left, just before the bridge that crosses the Browns River. Parking is on the left side of the mill and all the trails begin behind the mill near a signboard for the Winooski Valley Park District.

Description: The trail bears right at the signboard toward the river, crosses a small wooden bridge and passes through a turnstile gate. At the first junction, the River Loop and Hilltop Trails bear right; the left-hand fork is the return trail. At 0.1 mi., the trail passes a bench near the river and comes to a junction.

> **Junction:** The Pine Trail leaves right to follow the river bank and several spur trails lead down to the water. One of them, at a bench, provides a clear view of kettle holes and worn rocks, evidence of the erosive power of moving water. The Pine Trail continues along the bank a short distance before turning away from the water and climbing to rejoin the River Trail.

The River Trail continues straight and meets the other end of the Pine Trail (0.2 mi.). It then crosses several bog bridges and descends on steps to the river where it follows the bank. Turning away from the water, the trail begins a steady climb to a signed junction with the Hilltop Loop and Beaver Pond Spur Trails (0.3).

Junction: The Beaver Pond Spur Trail bears right downhill to a bench and quiet spot overlooking a small stream. Past the bench, the trail leads a short distance to private property and the park border.

Junction: The Hilltop Loop Trail turns sharply left and rejoins the River Loop Trail nearer the parking lot.

The River Loop bears slightly left, continuing with little elevation change. It soon reaches a junction with the other end of the Hilltop Loop where it bears right at a sign for the parking lot (0.4 mi.). At a bench built as an Eagle Scout project, the River Loop Trail begins a steady descent back to its beginning. Bearing right at the last two junctions, the route leads back to the parking lot.

Mills Riverside Park

Mills Riverside Park in Jericho is a community resource providing athletic fields, a picnic pavilion, group camping site, skating pond, sledding hill, off-leash area and six miles of developed trails. The Meadow Loop, while the longest trail, is also mostly flat. The Fieldstone and South Hill Loops and Meadow Connector are shorter, but have greater elevation gain. All the trails are wide and well graded, making them ideal for cross-country skiing. Information is available from the Jericho Underhill

The covered bridge at Mills Riverside Park.

Park District, P.O. Box 164, Underhill VT 05489, 802-899-2693. A map is available at www.jerichovt.gov; click on Parks and Rec. Hunting is not allowed in the park.

To the Trails: From I-89, exit 15, follow Vt. 15 east 12.5 mi. to the hamlet of Riverside. At a sign for the park, turn right between stone pillars to a large parking area. All trails pass through the covered bridge, where a trail map is posted.

Meadow Loop

Distance: 1.7 mi.

Description: Just over the bridge, the Meadow Loop leaves right, passing a memorial to Lauryn Ashley Stockdale. It follows the river and loops along the edge of the athletic fields. Passing in front of the pavilion, it crosses the old gravel farm road, skirts the edge of the pond and joins a grassy path to a marked trail junction with a sign indicating trails to the left and right. The right-hand trail leads uphill to the Fieldstone Trail. The Meadow Loop Trail continues straight ahead into the meadow and soon passes a monarch butterfly waystation, an established stopping place on the annual migration. At a four-way junction, the trail on the left loops back to the waystation, the trail straight ahead is the return trail and the Meadow Loop Trail turns right to a second junction where the Meadow Connector leads straight ahead and uphill to the Fieldstone Loop.

The Meadow Loop Trail turns left through a line of trees and into a meadow. It skirts the perimeter, passing an unmarked trail on the left, which rejoins the Meadow Loop Trail, making for a shorter walk. At a barbed wire fence, it turns left to follow the fenceline with panoramic views east toward the Mount Mansfield profile. Continuing around the meadow, the trail returns to the four-way junction. The route straight ahead follows a grassy path back to the covered bridge.

Fieldstone Loop

Distance: 1.4 mi.

Description: From the covered bridge, the route to the Fieldstone Loop Trail follows an old gravel farm road, bearing right at the first fork and passing in front of the Wilson A. "Snowflake" Bentley pavilion. It climbs slightly, passes a storage building and group camping area on the right and comes to a trail junction. The trail on the left leads to the Meadow Loop Trail and off-leash area. To reach the Fieldstone Loop Trail, a wide old woods road bears right and begins climbing, gently at first, then more steeply. At an open meadow, it bears right and begins the Fieldstone Loop Trail. The trail to the left is the return trail and also a shortcut to the Meadow Connector. The Fieldstone Loop Trail continues to climb, at times on a wide woods road and at times on a narrower woodland path.

At a four-way junction, a sign (arrow) points right for the Fieldstone Loop west, which now follows yellow diamond-shaped markers on a moderate climb to a high point. It descends briefly, then climbs again to a marked junction with the South Hill Loop Trail.

Junction: The narrower South Hill Loop Trail leaves right and follows red diamond-shaped markers on a 1.25 mi. loop before returning to this junction.

The Fieldstone Loop Trail bears left downhill, immediately passing a bench on the left and an unmarked spur trail leading uphill to the South Hill Loop. A second unmarked trail follows an old farm road directly downhill to the beginning of the loop. The Fieldstone Loop Trail bears slightly right and descends to an old stone wall and an opening into a neighboring field where there is a clear view of Mount Mansfield. It now turns left to follow the fence line and levels. A spur trail right leads a short distance to a bench, a great spot from which to admire the magnificent ridge profile. The main trail drops briefly to cross a wooden bridge, then reaches a junction with the Meadow Connector, a shortcut to the Meadow Trail and signed "To Lower Meadow." The Fieldstone Loop trail then crosses a meadow to close the loop.

Mobbs Hill and Mobbs Valley Trails

The Mobbs property in Jericho is, like most old Vermont farms, a combination of open fields and forested hillsides, boggy low spots and rocky soil, a meandering brook and milkweed pods. The trails on both Mobbs Hill and Mobbs Valley are unsigned and the junctions mostly unmarked, making it nearly impossible to write accurate descriptions. Designed for multi-use, the trails meander through the forest and any number of loops, short or long, are possible. Expect to share the trails with mountain bikers and horseback riders. Maps and information are available from The Fellowship of the Wheel at www.fotwheel.org. Caution: the maps show fewer trails than actually crisscross the property. The Mobbs Committee is working to update the maps.

To the Trails: From the intersection of Vt. 15 and Browns Trace Road in Jericho, follow Browns Trace Road through Jericho Center (3.1 mi.) to Barber Farm Road (3.4 mi.). Bear right on Barber Farm Road, then left on Fitzsimonds Road (3.8 mi.). Access to the trails is at a small parking area on the right (4.5 mi.). Alternatively: From I-89, exit 11, follow U.S. 2 east 1.5 mi. to the traffic light in Richmond. Turn left on Jericho Road, which becomes Browns Trace Road, and follow it 3.2 mi. to Fitzsimonds Road (4.7 mi.). Turn left on Fitzsimonds Road to the small parking area on the left (5.6 mi.).

Description: The Mobbs Hill trails leave from a trailhead, marked with a small yellow disk surrounding the number 21, across the road from the parking area. They are intermittently marked with red plastic markers and the junctions with small yellow arrows. The loops on Mobbs Hill generally return to the road at a point 0.2 mi. north of the parking area.

The Mobbs Valley trails leave from the left side of the parking lot beyond the kiosk. The most direct trail into the woods follows an obvious route down and across the open meadow. After reaching its low point, it begins a gentle ascent to the treeline and a T-junction. The left-hand path follows the treeline and the right enters the woods and leads to a network of interconnecting trails.

⓭ Williston

Allen Brook Nature Trail

Distance: 0.9 mi.

To the Trail: From the intersection of U.S. 2 and Oak Hill Road in the village of Williston (about 2.3 mi. east of Taft's Corner), follow U.S. 2 west 0.3 mi. to the library entrance and turn right. At the T-intersection—the school is straight ahead—turn right and follow the pavement around the right side of the school to the large parking lot near the playground (0.6 mi.).

Description: From the parking lot, the route to the Allen Brook Nature Trail follows the paved recreation path through an arched gateway, turns right at the first T-intersection (near the Community Park Fieldhouse) and left at the second one (near the volleyball court). Skirting the edge of the playing fields, the paved path reaches a bench and gravel path on the right and the start of the Nature Trail, marked by a sign (0.2 mi.). The Nature Trail drops to a board-walk and bridge across the marshy floodplain of Allen Brook and turns immediately left to a fork. This fork is the beginning and end of the loop. Bearing right, the trail parallels an open field, curving away from the field to form the loop. It parallels a beaver pond on the right (0.5mi.), which has a large beaver lodge in the middle. The trail then bears away from the pond to rejoin itself and close the loop (0.7 mi.). The return route to the parking lot recrosses the boardwalk and follows the paved recreation path.

Five Tree Natural Area

Distance: 1.3 mi.

To the Trail: From the intersection of U.S. 2 and Oak Hill Road in Williston village, follow Oak Hill Road south 2.0 mi. to Sunset Hill Road. Turn right on Sunset Hill Road and follow it 0.6 mi. to a small parking area on the right. Because this trail crosses private property, please stay on the trail.

Description: The trail to the overlook, marked by black arrows on a yellow background, begins across the road from the parking area and is marked with a sign. It leads through a turnstile gate, passes a pond on the left and begins a gentle ascent through the woods. At 0.3 mi., it reaches a junction, marked by a sign, indicating that the next section is shared by skiers and snowmobilers. The now wider woods road continues straight, then turns sharply left at a bog bridge (0.4 mi.). It climbs briefly and descends to another bridge. At 0.6 mi., just past a small "3" nailed to a tree, it reaches a junction where the trail to the overlook, marked by a sign, leaves the woods road on the right and follows a narrower woodland path. It crosses the wider winter-use trail (0.8 mi.) and comes to a stone wall, where it turns left (0.9 mi.). At 1.2 mi., the trail reaches a junction where a sign indicates that the overlook is 480 ft. straight ahead. A spur trail to the right leads a short distance to Five Tree Road. The trail emerges on an open ledge where a bench has been placed for walkers to enjoy a panoramic view of the Champlain Valley. The return is via the same route.

Oak View Hill Trail

Distance: 1.2 mi. loop

To the Trail: From the intersection of U.S. 2 and Oak Hill Road in the village of Williston, follow Oak Hill Road south 3.3 mi. to a small parking lot on the right, opposite Fieldstone Drive, at the Isham Family Farm. Because this trail crosses private property, with public access permitted by easement, please stay on the trail.

Description: From the parking area, the trail follows the fenceline on a grassy path. At 0.2 mi. a path, marked with a sign in a tree, leaves left to the top of the knoll and a view of the hills that surround Williston. The main trail continues straight across a second pasture and enters the woods (0.3 mi.), now following an obvious woods road uphill, with an old stone wall on the right. At the next junction (0.5 mi.), the trail, marked by a black arrow on a white background, bears right and narrows to a path. It soon loops left, widens to a woods road and follows another stone wall. At the next junction, it continues straight and descends toward a pond, which is visible through the trees. A trail bears right down to the pond. The main trail, still marked with arrows, bears left to follow the edge of the pond, passes a sap holding tank and emerges from the woods at a T-junction. The farm road to the right leads to the sugarhouse and Oak Hill Road. The loop trail turns left and follows the treeline to intersect the incoming trail (1.0 mi.). The route turns right to return to the parking lot.

Mud Pond Conservation Land

From the parking area at Mud Pond, one trail leads a short distance down to Mud Pond and a second trail diverges from the first to cross South Road to the Mud Pond Country Park trails, which were laid out in 2002 and 2003 by The Fellowship of the Wheel. The Mud Pond Country Park trails are open to walkers, skiers and bikers. The trail to Mud Pond is open for foot traffic only. The Town of Williston manages the trails, which are open during daylight hours. Dogs under voice command are permitted. Hunting is prohibited.

To the Trail: From the intersection of U.S. 2 and Oak Hill Road, follow Oak Hill Road south 0.3 mi. to South Road. Turn left on South Road and follow it 1.9 mi. (2.2 mi.) to Mud Pond Road. Turn right on Mud Pond Road. The small parking area is immediately on the right. A signboard indicates the Mud Pond Conservation Land.

Mud Pond

Distance: 0.5 mi.

Description: The trail, marked by black arrows on a yellow background, climbs a short distance, bears sharply left and descends to a junction marked with a sign for Mud Pond (0.1 mi.). A trail straight ahead leads to South Road and the trailhead for Mud Pond Country Park. From the junction, the Mud Pond Trail turns left, descends slightly to reach a second junction, marked with a sign, where it bears right onto a wider woods road. The left-hand trail leads to a sign marking the end of the park and a swampy side trail, also marked but nearly impassable, that ends at Oak Hill Road, near Old Creamery Road. The Mud Pond Trail descends gradually—the pond can be seen through the trees on the left—crosses a series of bog bridges and ends at a set of raised bleachers for wildlife watching. A narrower trail continues past the bleachers and, while it looks promising, soon deteriorates into a bog.

SYLVIE VIDRINE

Walking back from Mud Pond

Mud Pond Country Park

Distance: 3.0 mi. loop

Description: From the parking area, the route follows the trail to Mud Pond 0.1 mi. to a junction marked with signs for Mud Pond and the parking area. For the Mud Pond Country Park trails, the route continues straight, crosses a brook, then bears right to cross South Road. The trailhead is on the east side of South Road. The trail, which is well marked with yellow diamonds surrounding black arrows, leads into the woods on a gentle climb to a junction (0.2 mi.) where the loop begins. The right fork follows a meandering path to a junction with the Herschkowitz Extension Loop (1.4 mi.).

> **Junction:** The Herschkowitz Extension Loop is a 1.5-mi. loop that begins and ends at this point and is marked with red markers.

The main trail turns sharply left and climbs to a ridge before joining a V.A.S.T. trail. It turns left to follow the wider V.A.S.T. trail 0.1 mi., then bears right back on a narrower path (1.9 mi.). The trail reaches another V.A.S.T. trail near an open field on the right and turns left to follow the wider trail (2.2 mi.). At 2.5 mi., the trail, still marked with yellow diamonds, turns right onto a narrower path. It then reaches the junction where the loop began (2.8 mi.). The right fork leads back to the South Road trailhead (3.0 mi.).

⑭ Richmond

Johnnie Brook Road

Distance: 1.0 mi.

To the Trail: From I-89, exit 11 (0.0 mi.), take U.S. 2 west 0.4 mi. to Johnnie Brook Road and follow it 1.3 mi. to the end of the public road (1.7 mi.), indicated by signs, where there is parking for two to three cars on the edge of the road. Please do not block the driveways.

Description: The route begins by following the dirt road (private drive) 0.1 mi. to a narrower path on the left marked with a signpost. As the path leaves the road, it descends gently to cross a wide wooden bridge (0.4 mi.), then narrows and parallels a farm road along the edge of a field. At 0.7 mi., it coincides with the farm road to cross a brook over a culvert, then diverges onto a path. It traverses a boardwalk, then rejoins the farm road just before reaching Huntington Road, 0.6 mi. from the Round Church in Richmond (1.0 mi.). There is room for one to two cars at this end of the path, but they must not block the farm road.

Old Jericho Road Path

Distance: 0.7 mi.

To the Trail: From I-89, exit 11 (0.0 mi.), follow U.S. 2 east 1.5 mi. to the traffic light in Richmond. Turn left on Jericho Road, which becomes Browns Trace Road, and follow it 0.5 mi. (2.0 mi.) to Southview Drive. Turn left on Southview Drive and park in the small parking area on the left just after the bridge (2.4 mi.).

Description: The trailhead is on the opposite side of Southview Drive from the parking area, a short distance uphill at a break in the guardrail. A small sign for the "Old Jericho Road Path" marks the start. The path follows the brook upstream, crossing over to the other side on a wooden bridge at about the halfway point. It ends at an unmarked junction with Jericho Road/Browns Trace Road, where there is no parking.

The wide woods road that leaves from the west end of the parking area leads 0.1 mi. to a V.A.S.T. trail.

Volunteer Green Trail

Distance: 0.4 mi.

To the Trail: From I-89, exit 11 (0.0 mi.), follow U.S. 2 east 1.5 mi. to the traffic light in Richmond. Turn right on Bridge Street and follow it 0.3 mi. to Volunteer Green and a parking area on the right before the bridge (1.8 mi.).

Description: The route to the trail skirts the left side of the playground and heads kitty-corner toward the Winooski River. It enters the woods at an opening, marked with a small trail sign, near the picnic table farthest from the parking area. It follows the river downstream 0.4 mi., then turns away from the river and intersects with a gravel road. To the left, the road leads to an open field; to the right, it leads along the edge of the athletic fields back to the parking area.

Warren and Ruth Beeken Rivershore Trail

The Warren and Ruth Beeken Rivershore Trail combines wooded trail and open field with short stretches on Cochran Road. It is an excellent trail from which to watch ducks float past on the Winooski River and great blue herons stalk their waterborne prey. There are three places to park for access to the trail: St. Mary's Cemetery (Cochran Road), the Winooski River canoe access (Cochran Road) and across from the Jonesville Post Office (U.S. 2). Expect to share the trail with mountain bikers and horseback riders.

Distance: 3.0 mi.

To the Trail: From I-89, exit 11 (0.0 mi.), follow U.S. 2 east 1.5 mi. to the traffic light in Richmond. Turn right on Bridge Street, cross the bridge and turn left on Cochran Road (2.0 mi.). Follow Cochran Road 0.5 mi. to St. Mary's cemetery on the right (2.5 mi.). Park along the road near the cemetery. The trail begins about 100 ft. back toward Richmond between the guardrail and the speed limit sign.

Description: From the road, the trail descends and passes a sign for private property. It draws near the Winooski River, which it follows upstream. At 0.4 mi., it turns away from the water, crosses a small wooden bridge and climbs the bank back to Cochran Road where a small sign marks this end of the trail.

The next segment begins 0.1 mi. farther east on Cochran Road across from Cochran's Ski Area and is marked by a small trail sign. There is no parking here. The trail drops toward the river through a wet area and follows the river upstream 1.0 mi. to an open field and a boulder commemorating the Warren and Ruth Beeken Rivershore Preserve. This segment ends at a Winooski River canoe access.

The third segment begins at the canoe access, 2.0 mi. from the junction of Bridge Street and Cochran Road. The trailhead is at the entrance to the access parking lot, near a sign: Canoe Access. This segment parallels the river's course upstream, following the edge of open fields and through the woods on the shoreline. After 0.7 mi., it curves away from the river to rejoin Cochran Road. There is no parking at this trailhead.

To the Trail: The easternmost trail segment is closer to Jonesville than Richmond and parking is across from the Jonesville Post Office. There is no public parking closer to the trail. From the post office, turn right on Cochran Road and follow it 0.4 mi. to Webster Lane. Turn right on Webster Lane and the trailhead, marked by a small sign, is 0.1 mi. on the right.

Description: The trail parallels the Huntington River to its confluence with the Winooski River. At the first unmarked junction, it turns right toward the river. At the second unmarked junction, it turns left along the Winooski. The path straight ahead leads to the shoreline and the one on the right doubles back toward the trailhead. From the junction, the trail continues downstream, eventually bearing left along the edge of a field back to the road, 0.5 mi. west of Webster Lane. A sign at this trailhead indicates that the trail continues 900 ft. to the right.

MARY LOU RECOR

Trailhead at the Warren and Ruth Beeken Rivershore Preserve, Richmond.

Safford Preserve

The Richmond Land Trust's Stewardship Committee manages the Safford Preserve, which was donated by George Safford, Jr. The short loop trail is best walked in a clockwise direction because the turn-off to complete the loop is easily missed from the other direction. Hunting is permitted in season.

Distance: 0.6 mi.

To the Trail: Since there is no parking at the trailhead, the closest parking area is across U.S. 2 from the post office in Jonesville. From the post office (0.0 mi.), follow Cochran Road 0.4 mi. to Dugway Road and turn left, then right on Orchard Lane (0.5 mi.) and follow it to the end of the public road (0.8 mi.) where signs indicate private property. The entrance to the Safford Preserve is on the right and marked with a Richmond Land Trust sign.

Description: From the trailhead (0.0 mi.), the left-hand side of the loop follows an old road bed, paralleling a driveway and fence line on a gently uphill grade. At 0.1 mi., it turns away from the driveway and climbs more steeply to intersect with a more obvious trail at a T-junction (0.3 mi.). The trail left leads to the end of the preserve (signed) and private property.

Turning right, the loop trail descends gently at first, then more steeply. As it levels (0.5 mi.), it swings right, passes an old apple orchard on the left, then curves right back to the trailhead (0.6 mi.).

⑮ Preston Pond Trails

The Preston Pond Trails follow old woods roads, a snowmobile corridor and narrower woodland paths. They are well-marked with blue disks and signs at the junctions. Although the elevation gains and losses are not great, there are many of them, making this walk more challenging than the distance would indicate. The cliffs near the trail are peregrine falcon nesting sites, closed from March 15 to August 1. The trails are a collaboration between the National Park Service, the Vermont Land Trust and The Nature Conservancy.

To the Trail: From the post office on U.S. 2 in Jonesville (0.0 mi.), follow U.S. 2 east 1.0 mi. to Bolton Notch Road. Turn left on Bolton Notch Road and follow it 3.6 mi. to the trailhead and a small parking area on the left (4.6 mi.).

Description: From the trailhead (0.0 mi.), an arrow trail sign pointing right indicates the route follows a wide woods road, part of the V.A.S.T. corridor, down a slight hill to a gate. The route continues around the gate, below the ledges, and passes a small pond on the left. After a short, steep drop, it reaches a signed junction at an old cellar hole on the right (0.3 mi.) where the loop begins.

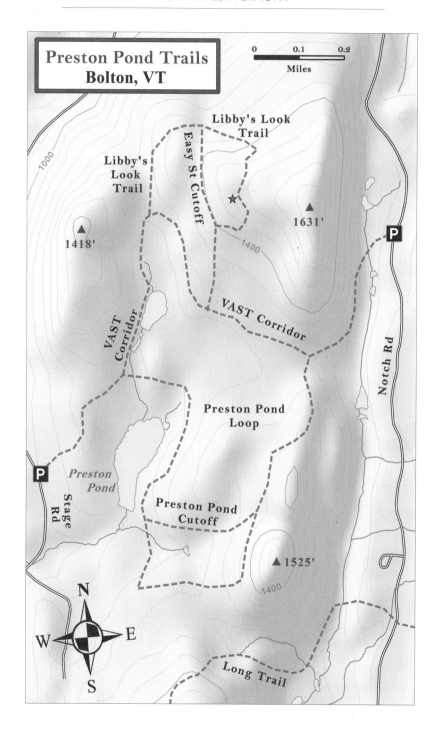

Preston Pond Trails
Bolton, VT

0   0.1   0.2
Miles

Libby's Look
Trail

Easy St Cutoff

Libby's
Look
Trail

1000

★

▲ 1631'

1418'

1400

VAST Corridor

VAST Corridor

Notch Rd

P

Preston Pond
Loop

P

Preston
Pond

Stage
Rd

Preston Pond
Cutoff

▲ 1525'

1400

N
W   E
S

Long Trail

Turning right, the trail follows the V.A.S.T. trail 0.4 mi. to the signed junction with the trail to Libby's Look.

Junction: The narrower Libby's Look Trail, marked with blue disks, leaves right and climbs steadily, steepening the higher it goes. Below some ledges, it bears right. The unmarked Easy Street Cutoff bears left to bypass the lookout and rejoin the Libby's Look Trail. At 0.4 mi. the Libby's Look Trail reaches a short spur left to a rocky outcrop where there is a view down to two ponds and across to the ridge.

From the spur, the Libby's Look Trail (still marked with blue disks) bears right and climbs more gently to a wooded high point. It descends steadily to cross a stream (0.9 mi.), then climbs briefly to a wider old woods road and turns right. It leaves the woods road left on a narrower path, which passes the remains of a school bus on the right. At 1.2 mi., it rejoins the Preston Pond Loop Trail, 0.3 mi. from where it began.

The Preston Pond Loop Trail continues straight and passes the western end of Libby's Look at a signed junction (1.0 mi.). It merges with a wider, rutted woods road and passes two beaver ponds—tributes to animal engineering and intelligence—on the left. At a signed junction, the loop trail turns left onto a narrow path. The V.A.S.T. trail continues straight 0.3 mi. to Stage Road where there is parking space for one or two cars. From the junction, the trail ascends and descends several times before finally dropping to the south end of Preston Pond. A short spur right leads down to the shoreline.

As the trail climbs away from the pond, it passes another beaver dam, then bears right at an unmarked junction with the Preston Pond Cutoff, which rejoins the loop trail closer to the beginning. The loop trail continues to follow blue-disk blazing, turning sharply left at a Vermont Land Trust sign and reaching the other end of the cutoff at a signed junction. At the end of the loop, it rejoins the V.A.S.T. trail and continues straight, retracing the route to the parking area.

🔟 Shelburne

Shelburne Bay Park

Distance: 2.5 mi. loop

To the Trail: From the intersection of U.S. 7 (Shelburne Road) and Bay Road in Shelburne, turn west on Bay Road and follow it 1.1 mi. to the Shelburne Bay boat and fishing access. The next parking lot is Shelburne Bay Park. Park at the farther of the two lots.

Description: A map is located at the entrance to the first parking lot. Following a counter-clockwise route, the trail skirts the shoreline of Shelburne Bay through a pine and hemlock forest with beautiful views of the bay. There are a few spots that are accessible to the water. After a short distance, the trail steeply ascends Mount Allen (200 vertical ft.) and gradually descends, finally turning left to the parking lot, about 50 yds. before the Shelburne Recreation Path.

Ti-Haul Trail

This community path approximates the route that the steamboat Ticonderoga took when it was moved overland from Lake Champlain to its final resting place at Shelburne Museum. The mostly flat, wide gravel path, which runs along the edge of a marsh, provides a link between Shelburne Village and Shelburne Bay.

Distance: 1.25 mi.

To the Trail: From the intersection of U.S. 7 (Shelburne Road) and Bay Road, follow Bay Road 1.2 mi. southwest to the parking area for Shelburne Bay Park on the right. The Ti-Haul Trail begins on the opposite side of Bay Road.

Description: From the trailhead, the path heads south with the marsh on its east side and private property on its west. It passes a bench on the right (0.25 mi.), then a second bench. At 1.1 mi., it veers right before a VELCO substation and ends at Harbor Road, 0.6 mi. from U.S. 7 in Shelburne Village.

LaPlatte River Marsh Natural Area

This trail, which is maintained by The Nature Conservancy, follows the LaPlatte River upstream from its delta with Lake Champlain and is ideal for wetland bird watching. Along with sandy delta, the natural area's 211 acres include marsh, floodplain and upland forest. The root-strewn, but mostly flat, trail is well marked with green and yellow Nature Conservancy markers. The natural area also offers quiet water for canoes and kayaks. Pets are not allowed. Hunting is prohibited.

Distance: 1.25 mi. loop

To the Trail: From the intersection of U. S. 7 (Shelburne Rd.) and Bay Road in Shelburne, turn west on Bay Road and follow it 1.1 mi. to the Shelburne Bay boat and fishing access on the right. The trailhead is directly across Bay Road at a break in the wire fence.

Description: Leaving Bay Road, the trail passes a large signboard and map on the left. It meanders through pine forest along the river's course to a junction and the beginning of a loop (0.5 mi.). Bearing right, the trail continues away from the river, then swings back to the shoreline, where several unmarked spur paths lead down to the marsh. It again turns away from the water, crosses a wide wooden bridge and completes the loop (0.75 mi.). The route bears right to retrace the path to the trailhead (1.25 mi.).

LaPlatte River Trail

Two trails leave from the parking lot for the Shelburne Community Gardens; one leads down to the bank of the LaPlatte River and Shelburne Falls and the other circles open fields between the river and Falls Road. The loop trail may also be accessed behind the post office on Falls Road; parking is limited to postal service customers.

To the Trail: From the intersection of U.S. 7 and Marsett Road in Shelburne (0.0 mi.), turn east on Marsett Road and follow it 0.3 mi. to a four-way stop. Turn left on Falls Road, then right on LaPlatte Circle (0.4 mi.). The parking area for the trail and Shelburne Community Gardens is 0.1 mi. on the left.

Description: For the trail along the LaPlatte River, the route circles right along the edge of the gardens and enters the woods at a break in the trees. It follows a narrow ridge downhill to the river where it bears right as it levels (0.2 mi.) to follow the river upstream. At 0.4 mi., the trail emerges into the open, passes a granite bench on the left and ends at a driveway (0.6 mi.), 0.2 mi. from the bridge on Falls Road.

Shelburne Pond before the spring thaw.

The second loop trail leaves the north side of the parking lot, drops downhill and follows the treeline to an opening where it passes into an open field (0.1 mi.). The mowed path, right or left, loops the perimeter of the field (0.9 mi.).

Shelburne Farms

Shelburne Farms was established in 1886 as the model agricultural estate of William Seward and Lila Vanderbilt Webb. The non-profit environmental education center and 1,400-acre working farm is open to the public for walking and skiing. The many historic farm buildings, footpaths and unobstructed views of Lake Champlain make it an interesting destination any time of year. The grounds and welcome center are open year-round. From mid-May to mid-October, a fee is charged for admission to the grounds and buildings. There is no fee from mid-October to mid-May and the trails are open from 10:00 a.m. to 5:00 p.m. Tickets, information and a map of the grounds are available at the welcome center. For more information, contact Shelburne Farms at 802-985-8686 or www.shelburnefarms.org.

To the Trail: From the intersection of Shelburne Road (U.S. 7) and Bay Road north of Shelburne village, turn west on Bay Road and follow it 1.8 mi. to a four-way intersection. The visitor center and parking lot are across the intersection on the right.

Shelburne Pond

Long known for its variety of spring wild flowers, Shelburne Pond is a beautiful refuge at any time of year. The loop trail through the H. Lawrence Achilles Natural Area is owned and maintained by the University of Vermont.

Distance: 0.6 mi. loop

To the Trail: From the intersection of Dorset Street, Irish Hill Road and Pond Road in Shelburne (0.0 mi.), turn east on Pond Road and follow it 0.9 mi. to the pond access road on the left. Turn left on the access road and follow it 0.2 mi. to its end at a parking area and boat launch (1.1 mi.).

Description: The trail enters the woods at a signboard for the Natural Area, climbs some steps and passes through an opening in a fence. It descends gradually to the pond's shore (0.1 mi.), then bears left to climb steadily away from the water. It levels, then passes a spur to the left that follows the top of the ledges overlooking the marsh before returning to the main trail. At a T-junction, the trail along the ledges rejoins the main trail on the left. The loop trail turns right to follow the shoreline above the pond; a spur left leads down to the water. At 0.4 mi. the trail drops to the water's edge, then climbs briefly to close the loop. Bearing left, it returns to the parking area.

⑰ Waterbury

Little River State Park

The Little River area of the Mount Mansfield State Forest includes more than 10,000 acres of mountainous terrain, bounded on the east by Waterbury Reservoir and on the west by Woodward and Ricker Mountains (USGS Bolton Mountain, Waterbury). Little River State Park lies within the state forest and straddles Stevenson Brook on the west shore of the reservoir. Established in 1962, the park offers camping facilities, but is not open for day-use beyond the hiking trails described here. In season, a fee is charged for day-use of the hiking trails. A state-run beach and picnic area are available for day-use off Vt. 100 in Waterbury Center.

The blue-blazed Little River trails generally follow former town roads, some of which are now used for logging roads and snowmobile trails as well as for hiking. Mountain biking is allowed on some trails. The trail system area is accessible from the vicinity of Waterbury Dam on the south side and from Moscow on the north side.

In November 1927, torrential rains caused widespread flooding and destruction in almost every major watershed in Vermont. Waterbury Dam was constructed as a flood control project on the Little River by the Civilian Conservation Corps (CCC) between 1934 and 1938. Below the dam, on the west side of the access road, only a few stone chimneys remain to identify the 80 buildings in the camp, which served as living quarters for the 2,000 men who worked on the dam construction.

Lying west of the reservoir, the Little River area encompasses the drainage basins of Stevenson Brook and Cotton Brook. In the late 1700s, settlers began clearing the area for farms and it was well populated in the nineteenth century. The inhabitants eked out a meager living from subsistence farming and logging, but depletion of the thin soil, the harsh environment and better economic opportunities elsewhere led to gradual depopulation. The settlement was almost totally abandoned when the land was acquired for the construction of the dam. Stonewalls, cellar holes, cemeteries, clearings, apple trees and lilac bushes remain as reminders of the past.

In 2000 the State drew down the Waterbury Reservoir to make critical repairs to the dam.

To the Trail: From I-89, exit 10, (0.0 mi.), follow Vt. 100 south to its junction with U.S. 2 (0.1 mi.). Turn right on U.S. 2, then right on Little River Road (1.5 mi.). Pass under I-89 and continue past the unsigned Woodward Hill Trail on the left (3.0 mi.). Pass a large state parking lot on the left (3.3 mi.) and continue to a parking area near the top of the western dam abutment (4.2 mi.). A formidable gate blocks the access road when the state park is closed (from mid-October to mid-May). The park contact station lies a short distance farther along the access road (4.8 mi.).

Parking is available at two lots within the park. From the contact station, bear left, then turn right at an intersection (5.0 mi.) to cross Stevenson Brook on a highway bridge. The nature trail parking lot is on the right (5.3 mi.), shortly before another parking lot on the right signed for History Hike parking (5.5 mi.).

Stevenson Brook Nature Trail

This short trail was developed by the Vermont Department of Forests, Parks and Recreation to showcase the cultural and natural history of Little River State Park. *Stevenson Brook Nature Trail*, a trail guide describing the botanical, geological and cultural features of the circuit, is available from the park office. Numbered posts along the trail correspond with the guide; the trail is marked with blue markers.

Distance: 0.75 mi. loop

To the Trail: From the contact station, follow the park road toward Camping Area B. After crossing Stevenson Brook on a bridge, park in the parking lot on the right.

Description: The trail follows signs and numbered posts and is an out and back hike with a short loop at its far end.

History Hike Loop via Hedgehog Hill Trail and Dalley Loop Trail
Distance: 3.8 mi. loop

The historic sites along this loop are numbered and described in "History Hike," a pamphlet available at the Little River State Park contact station or from the Barre district office of the Department of Forests, Parks and Recreation. The hike makes a loop following two trails, the Hedgehog Hill Trail and the Dalley Loop Trail.

To the Trail: The trail starts opposite the History Hike parking lot, which accommodates a half-dozen cars.

Description: Passing through a gate, the trail shortly reaches a signed junction where it follows the Hedgehog Hill Trail to the right to traverse the loop in a counterclockwise direction. The trail ascends steadily with a generally moderate grade to reach a parallel detour (0.3 mi.) on the left.

Junction: The parallel detour (from 0.3 mi. to 0.6 mi.) begins with a very steep grade to avoid an eroded portion of the original road. The detour rejoins the Hedgehog Hill Trail at an unmarked intersection with a road departing right.

Junction: This road leads to the Ezra Fuller farm site. While unblazed and unmaintained, the road follows the northerly side of a stonewall to a junction with the presently maintained north side of the Ricker Lot Trail. This trail loops back to the park access road near Camping Area B, campsite number 59.

Continuing northwesterly, the Hedgehog Hill Trail soon reaches the Ricker Family Cemetery (0.7 mi.) on the left. (For an instance of nineteenth century longevity, note Phoebe Ricker's tombstone.) The trail then comes to an intersection (0.8 mi.) where a trail to the Ricker sugarhouse site branches right at a sign for the Ezra Fuller Farm and eventually connects with the Ricker Lot Trail.

Continuing to ascend on a northerly and northwesterly course, the Hedgehog Hill Trail climbs to a height of land (1.1 mi.) at an elevation of 1,500 ft., then takes a short detour right necessitated by beaver activity and reaches an intersection (1.5 mi.) where a right turn leads to Kelty Corners and Moscow. A schoolhouse was once located at this intersection.

Junction: To the right, the Little River Trail ascends to cross over the ridge between the Stevenson Brook and Cotton Brook drainage basins (0.3 mi.), passes an obscure intersection on the left with the Patterson Trail (0.5 mi.) and reaches Kelty Corners (0.6 mi.).

Junction: The Patterson Trail starts opposite two signs pointing in opposite directions to Ricker Corners and Kelty Corners. It goes westerly along the northerly flank of the ridge, then turns left, passing over the ridge and descending to the Patterson farm site. It then follows a discernible road to Ricker Corners where there is a sign for the Patterson Trail to Kelty Corners. The trail is about 1.0 mi. long.

From the schoolhouse intersection, the Hedgehog Hill Trail continues straight ahead, descending gradually to Ricker Corners (1.8 mi.) where the upper cemetery is located on the westerly side of the intersection. Here the trail turns left onto the Dalley Loop Trail, descending southwesterly to a corner (2.2 mi.) and the intersection with the western end of the Stevenson Brook Trail at a sign for the Sawmill Trail. Turning left, the Dalley Loop Trail goes southeasterly, shortly passing another intersection (2.3 mi.) for the Sawmill Loop Trail and another sign for the Sawmill Trail.

Junction: The Sawmill Loop Trail makes a fairly direct descent to Stevenson Brook opposite the site of the sawmill for the Waterbury Last Block Company. Since there is no bridge across Stevenson Brook, use of the trail is not recommended. The trail is about 0.5 mi. long.

The Dalley Loop Trail continues southeasterly, passing the Bert Goodell farmhouse, the only original building still standing in the Little River area, and returns to the History Hike parking lot (3.8 mi.).

Cotton Brook Trail

None of this trail is blazed and there are few signs; however, it follows the wide Cotton Brook Road and snowmobile trails. Although the trail eventually links into the trail network at the southern access to the state park, it also offers shorter "out and back" walks. From the gate, the gravel road parallels Cotton Brook upstream, crosses it on a bridge, then parallels it downstream toward Waterbury Reservoir. A V.A.S.T. trail completes an 11.0 mi. loop. The trail is open for walking, bicycling, skiing and snowmobiling.

To the Trail: From I-89, exit 10 (0.0 mi.), follow Vt. 100 north 7.3 mi. to Moscow Road and turn left. Follow Moscow Road 2.1 mi. to Cotton Brook Road (9.4 mi.) and bear left onto the gravel road, which ends at two parking areas before a gate (10.1 mi.). In winter, the last 0.5 mi. is not plowed.

The Short Trail

The Short Trail is a half-mile interpretive nature trail at GMC headquarters on Vt. 100 in Waterbury Center. It traces the natural history of the Vermont landscape from glaciers to farms. The GMC publishes a guide, available at its hiker center, highlighting the significance of each of eight stations marked along the route. The trail is open during daylight hours year-round. For more information, stop by or contact the Green Mountain Club.

⑱ Lamoille County Nature Center

Located in Morristown, this 40-acre nature center is owned by the non-profit Lamoille County Natural Resources Conservation District. A self-guided nature trail examines the characteristics of the northern spruce-fir forest and related management practices and land stewardship principles. For more information: Lamoille County Natural Resources Conservation District, 109 Professional Drive, Suite 2, Morrisville VT 05661, 802-888-9218, www.lcnrcd.com.

To the Trail: From Vt. 100 about 1.0 mi. south of Vt. 15A in Morrisville, turn west on the Morristown Corners Road (0.0 mi.). Staying on Morristown Corners Road, bear left at the first intersection (0.1 mi.) and continue straight through the village of Morristown at a four corners (0.7 mi.). Bear left at the next intersection (1.0 mi.) on Walton Road and left again on Cole Hill Road (1.3 mi.). Continue past the Mud City Loop Road to the nature center parking area on the right (about 3.7 mi.).

Description: The main nature loop starts to the left of the signposts and proceeds about 100 yds. to the first station on the trail, where pamphlets are available. A short trail to the right of the signposts leads to a wildflower garden, which attracts many types of butterflies in season. The area is open from dawn to dusk.

⑲ Stowe

Bingham Falls

Until the land surrounding 40-ft. Bingham Falls was sold to a developer in 2000, it had been owned by the same family since 1880. With much public support, the Stowe Land Trust bought the property in 2001, thereby guaranteeing public access for generations. Like most waterfalls, Bingham Falls is most spectacular in spring when the water level is high. Although the distance from the parking area to the bottom of the falls is short, the steep trail down is slippery when wet.

To the Trail: From the intersection of Vt. 100 and Vt. 108 (Mountain Road) in Stowe village, follow Vt. 108 northwest 6.4 mi. to a parking area on the left, just beyond a sign for Smugglers' Notch State Park. The trailhead is across the road.

Description: The trail leaves Vt. 108 and drops gently on a wide path 0.1 mi. to a spur trail left leading to the top of the falls. It then drops more steeply over roots and on rock steps to a view near the base of the falls (0.25 mi.).

Weissner Woods

This 80-acre parcel of woodland was donated to the Stowe Land Trust in 1993 in memory of Fritz Weissner by his family. The trust has established walking trails designed to minimize impact to the site. A map and guide is available from the Stowe Land Trust describing the site and the guidelines for its use; visitors should take care to abide by these rules. For more information, contact Stowe Land Trust, P.O. Box 284, Stowe VT 05672, 802-253-7221, www.stowelandtrust.org.

To the Trail: From Vt. 100 in Stowe village (0.0 mi.), follow Vt. 108 north and turn right on Edson Hill Road (3.5 mi.). Continue past the entrance to the Stowehof Inn and take the next drive on the right (3.9 mi.). Parking is off this private road in a lot on the left.

Description: Two trail loops emanate from a four-corners found 0.2 mi. from the parking area. To the left, the Meadow Trail, 1.1 mi. long, offers views of Mount Mansfield and points south along the main range of the Green Mountains. To the right, the Hardwood Ridge Trail and Sugar House Loop make a 1.6-mi. loop.

Moss Glen Falls

This attractive waterfall, owned by the state of Vermont, is in the northeast corner of the town of Stowe. It should not be confused with the spectacular falls of the same name in Granville Gulf in Granville, Vermont. Note: use caution when viewing the falls from the adjacent ledges.

Distance: 0.4 mi.

To the Trail: From Vt. 100, 3.1 mi. north of the intersection of Vt. 100 and Vt. 108 in Stowe village, turn right on Randolph Road (0.0 mi.). At the next fork, turn right again (0.4 mi.) on the gravel Moss Glen Falls Road and continue to a parking area on the left (0.9 mi.) at a bend in the road before crossing Moss Glen Brook.

Description: From the parking lot, the trail proceeds generally southeast through forest dominated by hemlock trees, then turns to follow the stream. It makes a short, steep ascent to the first of several viewpoints into the bowl of the falls before continuing to climb to its terminus on an old woods road (0.4 mi.).

Moss Glen Falls

Stowe Recreation Path

An internationally recognized 5.5-mi. greenway, this scenic, paved, non-motorized recreation path follows the West Branch of the Waterbury River from the village of Stowe to the field at Topnotch Resort and Spa. Along the way, there are gorgeous views of Mount Mansfield, Vermont's highest peak. With seven access points and four designated parking lots, the path is easily accessible for walking, cycling, inline skating and cross-country skiing. Bikes, skates and skis may be rented at nearby stores. For more information, call 800-24STOWE or 802-253-7321.

㉒ Montpelier

Long home to beloved Hubbard Park, the city of Montpelier and nearby East Montpelier now have an extensive trail network. Walkers and cross-country skiers can enjoy trails connecting Hubbard Park, the North Branch River Park and East Montpelier.

Hubbard Park

In 1899 John E. Hubbard donated 125 acres to the city of Montpelier. Today the park contains 185 acres and nearly 7.0 mi. of hiking and skiing trails, as well as picnic areas, a soccer and softball field, a sledding hill and a 54-ft. observation tower with spectacular views of the Montpelier area and the surrounding mountain ranges. A map of the Hubbard Park Trails is published by the Montpelier Parks Commission and is available at the city clerk's office in City Hall or at www.montpelier-vt.org-parks-index.cfm. A self-guided nature trail booklet is sometimes available at the beginning of the trail. Bikes are not permitted on the trail system, but are allowed on park roads. For more information, contact the Montpelier Parks Department at 802-223-7335.

A range of habitats is found in the park, including meadows, softwood and hardwood stands, swamps and thickets. Hubbard Park has several impressive stands of white pine, red pine and hemlock. The center area is a designated natural area. Near the tower are majestic red oaks, which are at the northern end of their range.

To the Trail: There are several entrances to Hubbard Park and it is easily reached by foot from town or by vehicle from access roads with parking. A road also passes through the park leading to many trails as well as a short hike to the tower. The new Statehouse Trail begins on Court Street, 70 yds. east of the statehouse and leads 3,000 ft. to the tower.

Other entrances to the park are at the end of Winter Street and at the end of Hubbard Park Drive. To reach the Winter Street access, from the intersection of Main and State Streets in downtown Montpelier, turn north on Vt. 12. Travel three-quarters of the way through the roundabout to take a left. At the stop sign, turn right, staying on Vt. 12. Turn left on Winter Street and proceed uphill a short distance to the park entrance and parking.

North Branch River Park

With lands protected by the Montpelier Conservation Commission, the North Branch River Park added 179 acres to Montpelier's parks. Approximately 4.0 mi. of trails are available for walking and skiing. A trail and new bridge connect Hubbard Park trails with the Vermont Institute of Natural Science's North Branch Nature Center. The nature center has additional trails including a self-guided nature trail. A trail also leads from the nature center to conserved lands at Sparrow Farm; this trail is open to snowmobiling. A mountain bike trail will be added through North Branch River Park to connect the Elm Street trailhead to the East Montpelier trail systems above Sparrow Farm.

To the Trail: To access the North Branch trails, park at the city pool parking lot on Elm Street and cross the bridge near the tennis courts. Other access points are at the end of Cumming's Street or at the nature center.

㉑ East Montpelier

East Montpelier Trails

A nice addition to the Montpelier area trails, the East Montpelier Trails are a proposed 17-mile loop that will give a glimpse into the working landscape of Vermont as it passes through sugar stands, cornfields and logged areas. The trails are open for walking, skiing, snowshoeing and access to and from hunting areas. Biking, horseback riding and snowmobile use are also permitted on some sections. The trail system is gradually expanding and includes a link with the North Branch River Park in Montpelier and the VINS nature center. For access points or a map: http://emsignpost.com/emtrails.html

East Montpelier Town Forest

The forest includes a small network of signed trails named after animals, so although the numerous trails are loopy, they are easy to follow. The trail surface is smooth and the trails run on gently rolling hills through a varied forest with one excellent blackberry patch in season.

To the Trail: From Montpelier, follow Main Street north out of town; it becomes County Road. Turn right on Hagget Road (5.8 mi.). The small parking area (6.4 mi.) is on the right at a sign for the town forest.

Mallory Brook

To the Trail: From the rotary on Main Street in Montpelier (0.0 mi.), follow Main Street uphill and bear right on Center Road (1.6 mi.). Bear right on Dodge Road (3.6 mi.), then turn right on Johnson Road (4.6 mi.). There is limited trailhead parking at the end of Johnson Road (4.9 mi.). Please do not block either the unpaved lane that leads to the trail or any private driveways.

Description: From the end of Johnson Road, the Mallory Brook Trail follows plastic East Montpelier Trails markers through a variety of environments. It first traverses an open grassy clearing, then winds down to Mallory Brook, crossed on a bridge. The trail climbs gently through the woods to an open field near Minister Road. This walk is usually done as an out-and-back from the Johnson Road end.

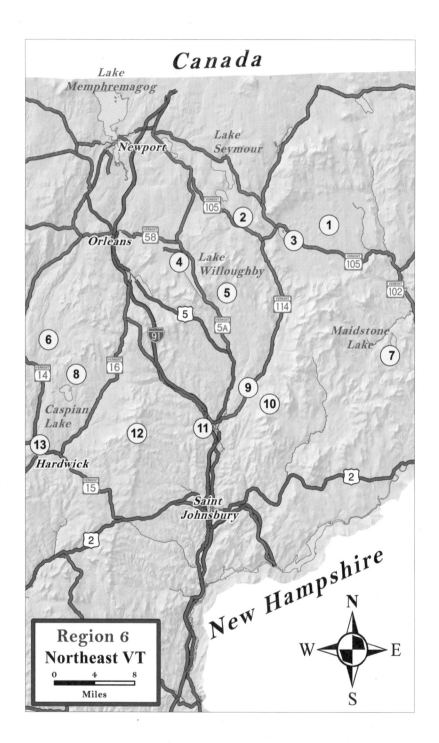

Canada

Lake Memphremagog

Lake Seymour

Newport

VERMONT 105

2

1

VERMONT 58

3

VERMONT 105

Orleans

4

Lake Willoughby

5

VERMONT 102

VERMONT 114

5

VERMONT 5A

Maidstone Lake

91

7

6

VERMONT 14

8

VERMONT 16

9

10

Caspian Lake

12

11

13

Hardwick

VERMONT 15

2

Saint Johnsbury

2

New Hampshire

N
W E
S

Region 6
Northeast VT

0   4   8
Miles

Region 6
Northeast Vermont

① Silvio O. Conte National Fish and Wildlife Refuge

This division of the Conte Refuge is highlighted by three short paths, which are fully wheelchair-accessible. One of these sites includes a boardwalk that provides access to the Mollie Beattie Bog. The other paths offer two very different perspectives on the Nulhegan Basin. While the remote Lewis Pond Overlook provides an impressive bird's-eye view of the region, the Basin Overlook offers a less dramatic, but much easier to reach, worm's-eye view of the same area.

Mollie Beattie Bog

This short, interpretive path is dedicated to the memory of the late Mollie Beattie, who in 1993 became the first woman to serve as director of the U.S. Fish and Wildlife Service (USFWS). This site was made wheelchair accessible in 2004.

Because access points to the refuge are limited, reaching this location involves driving more than seven miles on unpaved roads. Passenger vehicles must yield the right-of-way to logging trucks when traveling through this area.

Distance: 220 ft.

To the Trail: From the village of Island Pond, the shortest approach begins on Henshaw Road, which leaves Vt. 105 (East Brighton Road) nearly one mile east of its junction with Vt. 114. After turning left off Vt. 105 (0.0 mi.), follow the unpaved Henshaw Road as it climbs gradually to some open fields and passes between a white house and an old barn (1.4 mi.). As it swings right, stay on Henshaw while it passes an unidentified road on the left (1.6 mi.). After another three miles, turn right at a junction marked by a vertical signpost for the USFWS (4.7 mi.) as directed by an arrow at the bottom of the post. Follow this road (which is later identified as Four Mile Road) as it descends to a clearing and passes a prominent kiosk for the Refuge on the left (5.0 mi.). After crossing a bridge, turn sharply right (5.2 mi.) and continue an additional two miles to the trailhead on the left (7.3 mi.), opposite a large parking area on the right.

Description: This path begins as a wide, hard-packed gravel surface, passing through the wooded perimeter of the bog before reaching the boardwalk. Extending 100 ft. into the black spruce bog, the boardwalk includes a 12 by 8 foot viewing platform with built-in benches on either side. Illustrated placards, attached to the side-rails of the boardwalk, help visitors identify some of the unique plants that grow in this environment.

Lewis Pond Overlook

Visitors to this short, wheelchair-accessible path will be rewarded with a spectacular view of the Nulhegan Basin from a remote hillside clearing. Because of the driving distance and the circuitous access roads, this can be a challenging destination to reach. While most of these unpaved roads are well maintained, the last stretch on Overlook Road can be rocky and may not be suitable for vehicles with low ground clearance. For information regarding seasonal road closures or conditions, call the Visitor Contact Station at 877-811-5222.

Distance: 200 ft.

To the Trail: Follow the preceding directions to Mollie Beattie Bog (7.3 mi.), then continue southeast on Four Mile Road. After passing a side road on the right (8.4 mi.), turn left on Lewis Pond Road (8.6 mi.). Continue on Lewis Pond Road as it passes Eagles Nest Road on the right (9.4 mi.). After nearly four more miles, Lewis Pond Road bears right at a junction with Carroll Brook Road on the left (13.2 mi.). Continue on Lewis Pond Road as it passes by the pond access on the left (14.1 mi.). Turn left on Overlook Road (15.1 mi.), then bear right at a fork (16.3 mi.). Continue a short distance uphill to the overlook parking area (16.5 mi.).

Description: This gently graded path (consisting of a hard-packed gravel surface) leads from the edge of the parking lot to a viewing area, which is lined by an array of large granite barriers. From this open vantage point there is an extensive view of the Nulhegan Basin, with Lewis Pond in the foreground and the White Mountains of New Hampshire in the distance.

KEVIN WILLIAMSON

Boardwalk along the Mollie Beattie Bog.

Basin Overlook
Distance: 350 ft.

To the Trail: This path leaves from the Visitor Contact Station for the Conte Refuge on Vt. 105 in Brunswick, Vermont. To reach this facility from Island Pond, follow Vt. 105 east 10.6 mi. from its junction with Vt. 114. West from Vt. 102 in Bloomfield, the distance is 5.2 mi.

Description: Visitor parking at the Contact Station is near the left side of the building. Follow the front walkway 250 ft. to the right side of the building where it joins a hard-packed gravel pathway, which leads an additional 100 ft. to the Basin Overlook. The ridge line that can be seen from this location forms the extensive watershed of the Nulhegan Basin.

Nulhegan River Nature Trail

In addition to the Basin Overlook, there is a newly constructed nature trail at the Refuge Contact Station, which forms a loop that descends to the Nulhegan River. It was built in 2008 with help from the NorthWoods Conservation Corps.

Distance: 1.5 mi.

To the Trail: Follow the directions to the Basin Overlook.

Description: The nature trail continues past the Overlook (0.0 mi.) and begins a gradual descent. After nearly 0.1 mi., it turns left to descend more steeply toward the Nulhegan River, which it then parallels for about a half mile. As the trail bears away from the river, it reaches a three-way junction (0.7 mi.) where a spur path leads right and the main loop turns left. The spur path, which is 0.2 mi. long, follows the river to the water's edge (0.9 mi.). From the junction (1.1 mi.), the main trail begins climbing back toward the Visitor Contact Station and ends at the rear corner of the parking lot (1.5 mi.).

② NorthWoods Trails

Founded in 1989, the NorthWoods Stewardship Center serves the Northern Forest with land management, conservation science, environmental education, outdoor recreation and conservation service programs. By combining education and action in all of these programs, it seeks to foster long-term stewardship of the region's human and natural communities.

At its complex in East Charleston, the Center maintains an extensive network of Nordic ski trails, which can also be explored on foot during the summer. Since most of these trails are only maintained for winter use, they tend to be muddier and brushier than the average hiking trail. A detailed map is available at the center or online at www.northwoodscenter.org. A copy of this map

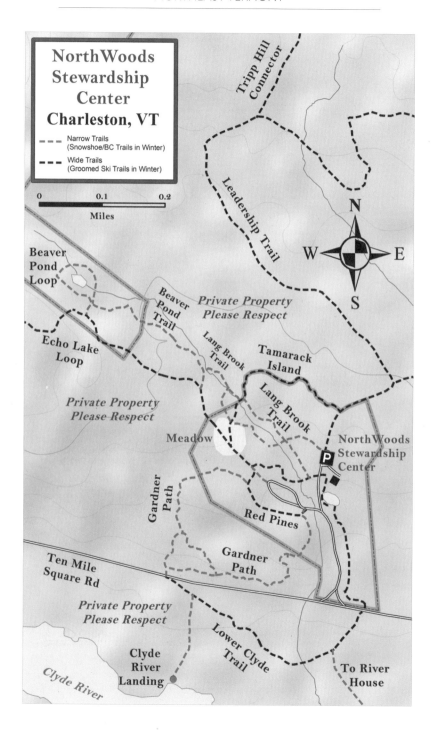

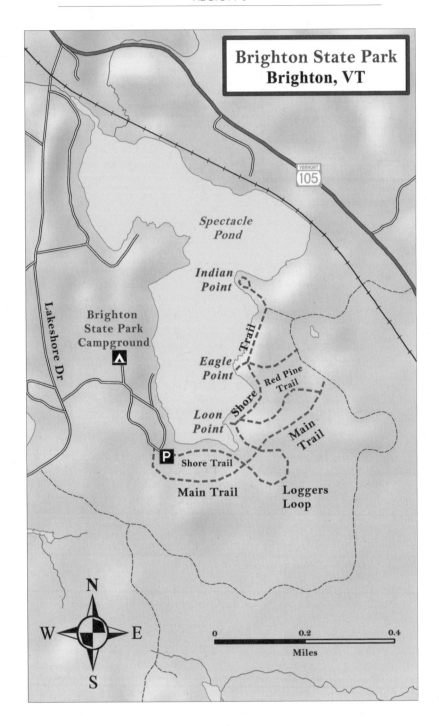

Brighton State Park
Brighton, VT

Spectacle
Pond

Indian
Point

Brighton
State Park
Campground

Lakeshore Dr

Trail

Eagle
Point

Shore

Red Pine
Trail

Loon
Point

Main
Trail

Shore Trail

Main Trail

Loggers
Loop

VERMONT
105

N
W   E
S

0   0.2   0.4
Miles

is recommended when using these trails. The walk described here is a good place to start.

To the Trails: From the junction of Vt. 114 and Vt. 105 south of Island Pond (0.0 mi.), take Vt. 105 west to Ten Mile Square Road on the right (4.0 mi.). Follow this unpaved road to the turn for NorthWoods on the left (5.3 mi.). This road, which is also known as Leadership Drive, leads uphill to the main parking area on the right (5.5 mi.).

Beaver Pond Loop via Charleston Connector
Distance: 0.7 mi.

Description: There are many ways to reach the beaver pond on Lang Brook, but the easiest path is an old roadbed that serves as a ski trail called the Charleston Connector. This route begins on a yellow-blazed trail, which is located about 100 ft. below the parking area and directly across from the Center's main building (0.0 mi.). After crossing a footbridge, this trail passes behind some cabins and enters a wooded area on the right. When it reaches a nearby roadbed (0.1 mi.), it turns right on this wider pathway and follows it uphill. This road soon leads to an otherwise open field where it passes a group of large pines growing around a boulder (0.2 mi.).

As the trail enters the woods at the other end of this clearing, a sign identifies it as the Charleston Connector. There are many side trails along this route, with the main junctions identified by numbers keyed to the Center's trail map.

Shortly after passing the Olympic Trail on the left (0.4 mi.), the route turns right at the junction for the Beaver Pond Trail (0.5 mi.). This path quickly leads to the Beaver Pond Loop, which tends to be soggy.

The short Beaver Pond Loop starts at a four-way junction. Directly ahead, a 50-ft. spur leads to the edge of the pond. The loop turns left at this junction and follows the blue blazes around the beaver pond until it reconnects with the starting point (0.7 mi.).

Another interesting trail at the center is the Gardner Path, which leads to the foundation of an old round barn.

③ Brighton State Park

This state park has a variety of campsites located on the west side of Spectacle Pond, as well as a day-use beach on the nearby south shore of Island Pond. It also features over two miles of interconnected footpaths located near the south and east shores of Spectacle Pond. In spite of the absence of any blazing, these well-worn trails are easy to follow as they travel over mostly gentle terrain. While nearly all the trail junctions are marked with directional signs, pranksters have been known to tamper with this signage. When in doubt, please refer to this guide. A day-use fee is charged from Memorial Day weekend through Columbus Day weekend.

To the Trails: From the junction of Vt. 105 and Vt. 114 in the village of Island Pond (0.0 mi.), head east on Vt. 105 (East Brighton Road) to the turn for Lakeshore Drive on the right (1.6 mi.). Follow this road to the park entrance on the left (2.5 mi.). If the park is open, continue through the gate to the contact station on the right. A short distance past the ranger station, turn right at a junction. At a second junction, turn left (one-way) as directed by a sign (2.6 mi.). Follow this road, which initially swings to the right, until it reaches a final junction (opposite a trailhead sign). Turn left toward the nearby parking area for Campers' Beach (2.7 mi.).

Northeast Kingdom Nature Trail

Distance: 0.6 mi.

Description: This trail combines the Logger's Loop with portions of the Main Trail and Shore Trail to form two short, interconnected loops. A brochure, available at the contact station, describes many points of interest along this self-guided nature walk.

The first leg of this circuit follows the Main Trail to a four-way junction, with the Shore Trail on the left and the Logger's Loop on the right (0.25 mi.). Follow the Logger's Loop to a second four-way junction with the Main Trail and Shore Trail (0.4 mi.). Turn left on the Main Trail and follow it back about 220 ft. to the first four-way junction. Turn right to follow the Shore Trail back to Campers' Beach. Continue past the beach to the parking area (0.6 mi.).

Main Trail

Distance: 0.5 mi.

Description: This trail begins, as does the Nature Trail, at a sign near the last junction on the road to Campers' Beach. From the parking lot, the route follows the access road 140 ft. back to the trailhead (0.0 mi.) on the left. Shortly after entering the woods, the trail turns left (opposite a small outdoor amphitheater), then quickly right at a directional sign. The path continues on easy grades until it reaches the first of two four-way junctions with the Logger's Loop (on the right) and the Shore Trail (on the left). Continuing straight, the Main Trail quickly reaches the second four-way junction (0.3 mi.). It passes straight through this junction as well and begins a gradual climb. After leveling, it comes to a junction with the Red Pine Trail on the left. About 220 ft. beyond this junction, the Main Trail ends at a three-way intersection with a long woods road (0.5 mi.). To reach Indian Point turn left onto this road and follow it west for an additional 0.3 mi., passing two more trails on the left and another (shorter) woods road on the right (see following description).

The Long Woods Road

Distance: 1.7 mi.

Description: From the north end of the Main Trail (0.0 mi.), a right turn onto this roadbed will eventually lead to Lakeshore Drive near the park entrance. While this stretch of road is nearly flat for its entire length, it is seldom used because of the overall distance involved and the relative lack of scenery.

Gradually the road swings south as it travels through dense boreal forest. The first notable landmark is a small swamp on the right (1.0 mi.). Soon, the road reaches a second and much larger swamp (1.1 mi.). After passing another woods road on the left (1.25 mi.), the route finally ends at a gate on Lakeshore Drive (1.5 mi.). The right-hand paved roadway leads to the park's entrance (1.7 mi.).

The Short Woods Road

Distance: 0.3 mi.

Description: This road leads north from its intersection with the long woods road (0.0 mi.). After crossing the tracks of the Canadian National Railroad (0.2 mi.), it ends at a junction with Vt. 105 (0.3 mi.), nearly 1.0 mi. east of Lakeshore Drive.

Red Pine Trail

Distance: 0.25 mi.

Description: This trail connects the Shore Trail at Loon Point with the Main Trail near its northern terminus. It passes through a mature stand of red pines. This path is narrower and the terrain slightly hillier than most of the other trails described here.

Connector to Eagle Point

Distance: 700 ft.

Description: This unnamed trail connects the Shore Trail near Eagle Point to the long woods road at a point about midway between its junctions with the Main Trail and the short woods road.

Logger's Loop

Distance: 850 ft.

Description: This path forms a short loop in a densely wooded area on the east side of the Main Trail, opposite its junction with the Shore Trail.

Shore Trail

Distance: 0.8 mi.

Description: The Shore Trail connects Campers' Beach to Indian Point, passing Loon Point and Eagle Point along the way. While this is arguably the most scenic trail in the park, the terrain that it crosses is also hillier than anything else described here. The trailhead is located near a kiosk at Campers' Beach (0.0 mi.), which is about 250 ft. from the beach's parking area.

After entering the woods that surround the undeveloped east side of Spectacle Pond, the Shore Trail soon passes a short spur path on the left, which leads to a bench near the water's edge. Continuing on easy grades, this trail soon reaches a four-way junction with the Main Trail and the Logger's Loop. From here, the Shore Trail turns left, and follows the Main Trail for about 220 ft. to a second four-way junction. After turning left, the Shore Trail gradually makes its way toward Loon Point (0.3 mi.), where there are two trail junctions near a picnic table. At the first junction, a 60-ft. spur path (on the left) descends to the shoreline. Nearby, the Red Pine Trail departs right. Leaving Loon Point, the Shore Trail continues straight through this second junction and begins to descend.

After passing through a low area, the Shore Trail climbs to an old campsite above Eagle Point (0.5 mi.), where there are two more trail junctions. At the first junction, an unnamed connector trail comes in from the right. Bearing left at this junction, the Shore Trail quickly reaches a nearby spur path on the left. This 140-ft. spur leads past the foundation of a cabin, before it descends to the rock outcrop known as Eagle Point. A plaque at the foundation describes the site's history.

From the campsite, the Shore Trail climbs briefly before turning left at an arrow. Eventually it enters a stand of red pines, where a bench can be found about 30 ft. from the trail on the left. Soon the trail reaches a final junction, where the Shore Trail turns left and follows an old roadbed to Indian Point. As it enters this small peninsula, the trail passes through a clearing with an opening to the water's edge on the left. Continuing straight through this clearing, the trail soon reaches its terminus at another scenic rock outcrop (0.8 mi.).

Westmore Town Forest

This property, which is managed by the Westmore Association and carries an easement held by The Nature Conservancy, was a gift from the Lester Bill family. Two blue-blazed trails provide access to an area that features several beaver ponds, as well as a cedar swamp and bog. Anyone who enters the town forest does so at their own risk. Caution should be used when crossing bridges and boardwalks, as they can be slippery.

An informative guide to the town forest is available at no charge from the Westmore Town Clerk at the intersection of Vt. 5A and Hinton Hill Road,

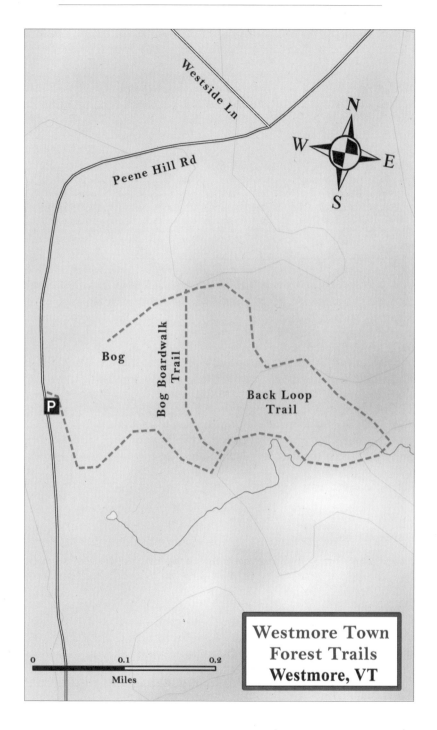

Westside Ln

N

W E

S

Peene Hill Rd

Bog

Bog Boardwalk Trail

Back Loop Trail

P

0   0.1   0.2

Miles

**Westmore Town
Forest Trails
Westmore, VT**

one mile south of Vt. 16 (North Beach Road) on the east side of Lake Willoughby. The office hours are Monday through Thursday from 8:30 a.m. to 4:00 p.m.

To the Trail: From the junction of Vt. 5A and Vt. 16 at the north end of Lake Willoughby (0.0 mi.), follow Vt. 16 (North Beach Road) west, past the north end of the lake, then turn left on Peene Hill Road (0.2 mi.). The sign for this road is hidden at the back of a triangular intersection. Continue to a small parking area on the left, just past a large sign for the town forest (1.3 mi.). When parking, leave room for other vehicles. The trail is located 50 ft. to the left of the parking area.

Bog Boardwalk Trail

Distance: 0.5 mi. to boardwalk

Description: The Bog Boardwalk Trail offers the easiest access to the bog. Over most of its length it travels through a predominantly softwood forest with only minor changes in elevation. As it descends from the roadside (0.0 mi.), the trail enters the forest and quickly crosses a potentially wet area on some bog bridges. It soon passes a small informational kiosk on the left and reaches a junction with a short spur path (also on the left), which leads 50 ft. to the edge of a beaver pond.

Back at the junction, the main trail turns right and crosses a wet area on steppingstones as it works its way around the pond. After crossing a brook on an old log bridge, the trail quickly reaches its first junction with the Back Loop Trail on the right (0.3 mi.). Staying straight at this junction, the Bog Boardwalk Trail meanders pleasantly for its remaining length. Shortly before reaching the boardwalk (0.5 mi.), it passes a second junction with the Back Loop Trail, which comes in sharply from the right. The boardwalk winds narrowly through some trees for 100 ft., then turns onto a wider section that extends 200 ft. onto the floating sphagnum mat.

Back Loop Trail

Distance: 0.6 mi.

Description: This pathway travels through a mostly hardwood forest before it rejoins the Bog Boardwalk Trail. Following this route back to the trailhead adds 0.4 mi. to the return trip. While this route is hillier than the bog trail, the terrain is not difficult.

From the bog, the Back Loop Trail bears left at a junction (0.0 mi.) about 40 ft. from the entrance to the boardwalk. After climbing over a small bank, this blue-blazed trail makes a sharp turn right (any unmarked side trails on the left lead to private property). The trail soon enters a wet area, which is partially traversed on bog bridges and log corduroy. It then makes a relatively steep descent to a brook crossing spanned by a bridge with a handrail (0.3 mi.).

After making a U-turn, the trail begins climbing gradually at first, then more steeply. As it starts to descend again, it reaches a short set of stairs, where there is a view of another beaver pond. Turning left at the bottom step, the trail quickly reaches a second bridge. After crossing a third, and final, bridge, the trail begins climbing again, until it reaches the Bog Boardwalk Trail (0.6 mi.). Turning left at this junction leads back to the trailhead parking area (0.9 mi.).

 Newark Pond Natural Area

The Newark Pond Natural Area is a 44-acre parcel of land owned and managed by The Nature Conservancy of Vermont. The trail forms a one-mile loop on the undeveloped west side of Newark Pond and also provides access to a small section of the pond's shoreline, where it is possible to view (with the aid of binoculars) a tiny island that serves as a nesting site for loons.

Distance: 1.0 mi.

To the Trail: From the junction of U.S. 5 and Vt. 5A in West Burke (0.0 mi.), take Vt. 5A north to Newark Pond Road on the right (3.5 mi.) and follow Newark Pond Road to a small trailhead parking area on the right (5.6 mi.). Some additional roadside parking is available just beyond a small lily pond on the right.

Description: From the trailhead (0.0 mi.), the route follows an overgrown roadbed between the lily pond and an embankment. Soon, the trail swings sharply right as it begins a short, gentle climb to the loop junction where there is a bench and a locator map. Bearing right at this junction, the trail soon passes a register box on the left as it climbs, on easy grades, through a hardwood forest. Before long, the trail ascends to the crest of a small ledge (0.3 mi.) where it begins a gradual and circuitous descent, passing through some wet areas, before reaching another bench and locator map near its southernmost point (0.5 mi.). Continuing mostly downhill, the trail begins to approach the pond's shoreline. Eventually it follows the water's edge until it reaches the loon viewing area (0.8 mi.). After leading away from the shoreline, the trail passes through another potentially wet area before returning to the loop junction. The right-hand path leads back to the trailhead (1.0 mi.).

⑥ Craftsbury Academy Woodlot

This 0.25-mile loop, which winds through a mature pine forest, is wheelchair-accessible. It consists of a wide, hard-packed gravel surface on a raised trail bed. A great deal of work went into building this trail, and while the loop is gently graded and smooth enough, the transition between the path and the parking area may be difficult for some wheelchairs.

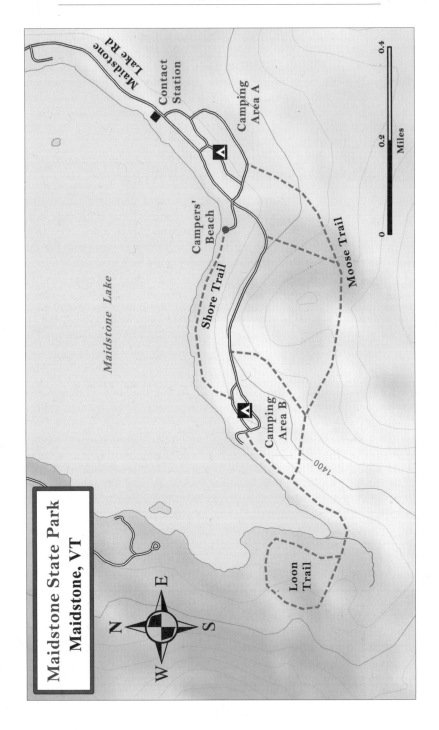

Maidstone State Park
Maidstone, VT

Maidstone Lake Rd

Contact Station

Camping Area A

Campers' Beach

Shore Trail

Moose Trail

Maidstone Lake

Camping Area B

1400

Loon Trail

0   0.2   0.4

Miles

N
W   E
S

Distance: 0.25 mi.

To the Trail: From the junction of Vt. 14 and Vt. 15 in Hardwick, follow Vt. 14 north 7.0 mi. to S. Craftsbury Road on the right (0.0 mi.). This road leads to Craftsbury Village where it becomes N. Craftsbury Road (1.7 mi.). Continue straight on Wylie Hill Road at its junction with N. Craftsbury Road (3.9 mi.) and follow this unpaved road to the signed parking area for the Craftsbury Academy Woodlot on the right (5.7 mi.).

Description: From the main parking area, the easiest approach to this trail is at the upper end of the loop on the right. The lower approach involves a much rougher transition and may prevent wheelchair users from traveling its full length without having to double back.

⑦ Maidstone State Park

Maidstone Lake sits in a remote part of Vermont's Northeast Kingdom. Two facilities operated by the Vermont Department of Forests, Parks and Recreation are located along the shoreline of this 796-acre lake. The first of these has a day-use beach and picnic area, while further south, a larger facility includes overnight campsites, another beach and a small network of trails, totaling about 2.5 mi. A brochure is available at the contact station and a day-use fee is charged in-season, which runs from Memorial Day Weekend through Labor Day Weekend.

To the Trails: From the junction of Vt. 102 and Vt. 105 in Bloomfield, follow Vt. 102 south 5.1 mi. and turn right on the unpaved Maidstone Lake Road at a sign for the park (0.0 mi.). This road passes the day-use area (4.8 mi.) before it reaches the contact station for the camping area (5.8 mi.). Please inquire here about parking at this location. When the facility is not open, parking should be available next to this building. Do not block the gated entrance.

Starting at Campers' Beach, three interconnected trails form an extended loop that encircles many of the campsites. To reach the first of these trails, follow the access road past the contact station about 0.25 mi. to an intersection, then bear right toward the beach, as directed by a sign. Campers' Beach is about 0.1 mi. from the intersection.

Shore Trail
Distance: 0.7 mi.

Description: This trail follows the shoreline at the south end of Maidstone Lake, passing many viewpoints along the edge of the water. While the terrain is relatively flat, the footing is poor due to an abundance of exposed roots. Beginning at the far end of Campers' Beach (0.0 mi.), the trail parallels the shore closely at first, then more distantly. At a junction with a spur path on the right (0.4 mi.), which leads 60 ft. to the water's edge, the main trail bears left. Soon after, it reaches a fork and bears right. The left fork climbs to the access road, about 200 ft. away.

Returning to the shoreline, the trail reaches the first of two small beaches (0.5 mi.) where New Hampshire's Mount Cabot may be seen. After passing straight through this area, the Shore Trail bears left away from the shoreline before reaching its apparent terminus at an unmarked junction (0.7 mi.). The Loon Trail comes in sharply from the left and continues from the Shore Trail. A left turn at this junction, leads to the Moose Trail, which provides a shortcut to the access road in Camping Area B.

Loon Trail
Distance: 1.2 mi.

Description: Heading west from its unmarked junction with the Shore Trail (0.0 mi.), the Loon Trail leads past another shoreline viewpoint, then between two halves of a large boulder and into a wet area that is traversed on puncheon. After crossing a brook, the trail reaches a signed junction (0.3 mi.), where a half-mile loop begins.

Turning right, the Loon Trail approaches, then follows the shoreline. It soon reaches a junction with a 70 ft. spur path on the right (0.5 mi.), which descends steeply to a final viewpoint at the water's edge. The main loop now travels away from the lake and passes through a more secluded part of the forest on easy terrain. After completing the loop (0.8 mi.), it turns right to exit this area. At the next junction (1.1 mi.), the route bears right to join the Moose Trail near its western terminus in Camping Area B (1.2 mi.).

Moose Trail
Distance: 0.8 mi.

Description: From its three-way junction with the Loon Trail, a short leg of the Moose Trail descends 230 ft. to its western terminus in Camping Area B. Heading east from this junction, the Moose Trail crosses two brooks before beginning a moderate climb. After turning left onto a logging road, which it follows 25 ft., the trail quickly diverges to the right. At its next junction, a side trail descends 600 ft. to the access road, while the Moose Trail turns right and continues to climb past three large glacial boulders (0.3 mi.).

After reaching a height-of-land, the Moose Trail begins a sustained descent to a junction (0.7 mi.), where it again turns right. The side trail left provides a final shortcut to the main access road, about 200 ft. away. After crossing a brook near this last junction, the Moose Trail reaches its eastern terminus (0.8 mi.) on the access road in Camping Area A. The route turns left to follow this road back to the intersection near Campers' Beach, then turns right to exit the park.

⑧ Barr Hill Nature Preserve

In 1972, the Philip Gray family donated the 256-acre Barr Hill Nature Preserve to the Nature Conservancy. In 1983, students and staff of Sterling College built a nature trail, which is described in a comprehensive guide usually available at the trailhead. The trail, which forms two interconnected loops, is nearly one mile long.

At 2,120 ft. above sea level, Barr Hill is the highest point in Greensboro. While its summit is heavily wooded, several worthwhile vantage points are scattered about the hilltop. Panoramic viewing guides have been installed at three locations to help visitors identify the more prominent features on the horizon. Please note that hunting, overnight camping and dogs are not allowed.

Distance: 0.9 mi.

To the Trail: From Vt. 16 in Greensboro Bend, follow the Bend Road northwest 2.5 mi. to a junction beside the Greensboro Post Office. Turn left on East Street, then right on Wilson Street (0.0 mi.) at the main intersection in town. At the next junction (0.1 mi.), bear right on Lauredon Avenue (also known as Hinman Settler Road) and follow it uphill. After leaving the paved portion, descend to a final junction (0.7 mi.) and bear left on Barr Hill Road. Eventually this road climbs to a wintertime (and mud season) parking area on the left (1.8 mi.), near a sign for the preserve on the right. Continue uphill on this narrower and slightly rougher section of the road to the trailhead parking area on the left (2.4 mi.). Do not drive beyond this point.

Description: From the parking area (0.0 mi.), the trail passes a registration box on the left and reaches a four-way junction where the loop begins and ends. Heading straight through the junction, the trail soon comes to a viewing guide in an open area with views south and west. After bearing left at an unmarked junction below the picnic area, a view of Caspian Lake opens up on the left (0.1 mi.). The trail passes through a stone wall and descends on some steps, climbing to a junction with a spur path on the left. At the end of this 90-ft. spur is a view of Woodbury Mountain, Caspian Lake and the Worcester Range.

After passing another view of Caspian Lake on the left (0.2 mi.), the trail soon reaches the brass summit marker, which is embedded in some bare ledge on the right. Continuing past a glacial erratic and through a spruce grove, the path reaches another vista with a second viewing guide at its northernmost point. From here the trail makes a U-turn right and begins a winding return, passing a small opening with a view toward the northeast (0.5 mi.). It then comes to a junction with a trail on the right (0.6 mi.), which leads 400 ft. to the picnic area.

Staying on the outer loop, the main trail quickly reaches another (more expansive) view to the northeast, with a third panoramic viewing guide. After passing another small view of Bald Mountain, the loop bears right at a junction, while the path on the left follows a slightly shorter course to the parking lot. As it exits the forest, the main trail returns to a four-way junction and, turning left, descends to the trailhead (0.9 mi.).

⑨ Burke Interpretive Trail

This community nature trail is connected to an extensive network of multiple-use trails maintained for non-motorized recreation by the Kingdom Trails Association (KTA) in East Burke. The trails are shared by both mountain bikers and walkers. This short pathway through a wooded area adjacent to the Henry G. Darling Memorial Recreation Area interconnects with other trails both inside and outside the loop described here. *(See map on p. 228.)*

Distance: 0.5 mi.

To the Trail: From the "business district" in East Burke Village (0.0 mi.), follow Vt. 114 north to the recreation area on the left (0.4 mi.), opposite a cemetery on the right. Park on the gravel surface of the parking lot.

Description: The trailhead kiosk is at the wooded edge of a picnic area 200 ft. north of the parking lot. From the kiosk (0.0 mi.), the trail (identified here as the Park Loop) enters the woods and quickly crosses the KTA's Church Path, which follows a power transmission line. Continuing straight through this intersection, the Park Loop climbs slightly to an unmarked junction with a shorter side trail on the right. Turning left at this junction, it heads south skirting the edge of a high bank with views of the Passumpsic River below.

At a three-way junction (0.1 mi.), the right-hand trail leads to a steeper section of this loop known as the Ridge Run. (Note: to avoid the steepest part of the ridge, turn left at this junction, then take the next trail on the right to return to the loop.) As it begins climbing to the highest part of this small ridge, the main trail passes an unmarked side trail on the right called the River Run.

> **Junction:** The River Run is a steep path with poor footing. To gain access to the water's edge, follow the nearby Dog Trail, which is somewhat longer but offers a much easier approach to the river.

After quickly reaching its highest point, the Ridge Run makes a short descent to the second junction with the aforementioned bypass. Bearing right at this junction, the trail continues on flat terrain to another unmarked junction (0.2 mi.) with the Dog Trail.

> **Junction:** The Dog Trail turns sharply right and descends on easy grades for 300 ft., where it joins the half-mile long Xmas Tree Loop. This KTA bike path follows the perimeter of a flat, open field that is bordered on one side by the Passumpsic River.

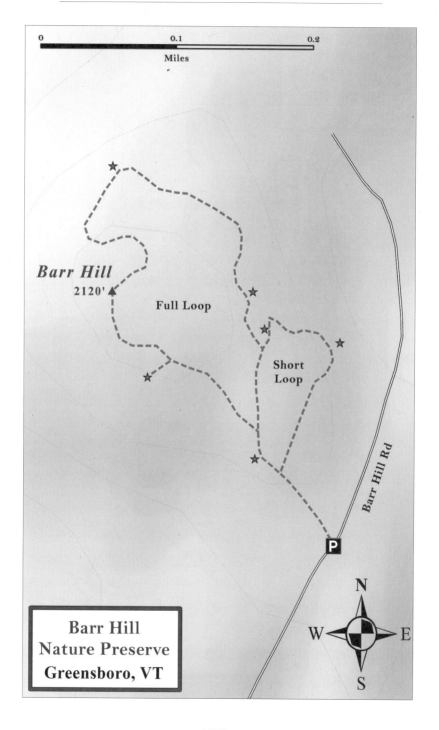

0

0.1

0.2

Miles

Barr Hill

2120'

Full Loop

Short
Loop

Barr Hill Rd

P

N

W E

S

Barr Hill
Nature Preserve
Greensboro, VT

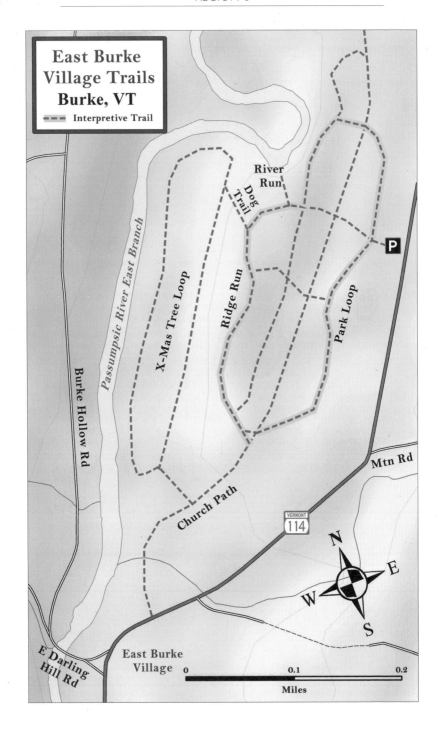

East Burke
Village Trails
Burke, VT
Interpretive Trail

River Run

Dog Trail

Passumpsic River East Branch

X-Mas Tree Loop

Ridge Run

Park Loop

P

Burke Hollow Rd

Mtn Rd

Church Path

VERMONT 114

N
E
W
S

E Darling Hill Rd

East Burke Village

0   0.1   0.2

Miles

The Ridge Run meanders to another intersection with the Church Path. After crossing back over this bike path, the trail quickly reaches a final junction where an arrow indicates a left-hand turn. Continuing on easy terrain, the trail soon reaches a grassy knoll at the edge of the recreation area (0.5 mi.).

⑩ Burke Mountain Summit Trails

The 2.4-mile Toll Road on Burke Mountain provides big mountain views for little or no effort. A small fee is charged per vehicle to use this paved roadway, which is open from 8:00 a.m. until a half-hour after sunset, beginning on May 1st and continuing until late October (weather permitting). If the Toll Road is closed, there is also a view from the Mid-Burke Lodge parking lot at the end of Mountain Road, which is a half mile past its junction with the Toll Road.

The summit of Burke Mountain (3,267 ft.) provides a 360-degree view from its historic fire tower. There are also several vantage points scattered around the top and nearby West Peak (3,150 ft.), which are connected by a small network of hiking trails.

To the Trails: Marked by a large sign for Burke Mountain Ski Area, follow Mountain Road from its junction with Vt. 114 (0.0 mi.) in East Burke village as it travels past the Sherburne Base Lodge Road on the right (1.1 mi.). Continue to the Toll Road junction (2.1 mi.) and bear left. After paying the toll (2.3 mi.), follow this winding road up the mountainside, passing a picnic area on the left (3.5 mi.), before reaching a large parking lot near the summit (4.5 mi.).

From the far end of this parking area, you will find a spectacular view without even leaving your car. To reach the fire tower, follow a short path at the end of a paved cul-de-sac, near the entrance to the parking area.

Summit Trail

Distance: 0.2 mi.

Description: The Summit Trail leaves the left corner of the summit parking area at the far end of the lot. About 70 ft. into the woods it comes to a four-way junction. On the right, a shorter segment of the Summit Trail bypasses the parking lot on its way toward West Peak. Directly ahead, a spur path leads 120 ft. to a vista. On the left, the Summit Trail continues to a nearby junction, then bears right.

At a junction with the Profile Trail, which forms a 0.3-mi. loop with the Summit Trail, (the Profile Trail is easier to follow when starting from this location.), the Summit Trail takes a much shorter route to its second junction with the Profile Trail and the nearby fire tower.

Profile Trail (a.k.a. Under Profile Trail)

Distance: 0.25 mi.

Description: From its first junction with the Summit Trail, the Profile Trail makes a noticeably longer and more circuitous approach to the lookout tower. Along the way, it descends to, and passes under, the rock formation that gives this trail its name. It then leads to a few more viewpoints before reconnecting with the Summit Trail.

West Peak Trail

Distance: 0.3 mi.

Description: Two hiking trails leave the far right corner of the summit parking area along with a ski trail. The path that veers left and skirts around the parking area is part of the Summit Trail. The other path bears right (0.0 mi) and enters the woods at the upper edge of the ski trail. After descending along the shallow ridge between Burke Mountain's main summit and the nearby West Peak, this trail reaches a five-way intersection (0.2 mi.). On the right, an obscure path provides a shortcut to the ski trail. Straight ahead, the Red Trail descends to the base of the mountain. The two trails on the left both lead to the summit of West Peak. The first of these is a shortcut, while the second (a hard left turn) takes a longer, but more scenic approach.

About 300 ft. west of the summit shelter, the West Peak Trail, which eventually rejoins the Red Trail about halfway down the mountain, descends to a small open ledge on the right, which is easy to miss. The view of the Passumpsic River Valley from this final vantage point is unsurpassed (0.3 mi.).

⑪ Lyndon Institute Nature Trail

This trail is located in a wooded area on the grounds of Lyndon Institute, an independent school for students in grades 9 through 12. The Nature Trail forms a short, easy loop connected to some additional pathways on an adjacent hillside. A guide to this site is available at the trailhead kiosk or at the school.

Distance: 0.8 mi.

To the Trail: From I-91, exit 23 in Lyndonville, head north on U.S. 5 (Memorial Drive) to the first set of traffic lights just east of the interstate (0.0 mi.). Turn left on Back Center Road and follow it to a stop sign at its junction with Center Street (1.3 mi.). Continue straight on Center Street for a short distance, then turn left on College Road (1.4 mi.). Follow College Road to the large parking lot behind Lyndon Institute, which is on the right (1.6 mi.). The trailhead kiosk is at the back edge of this lot (1.7 mi.). To exit, continue around the school building on Institute Circle, a one-way road.

LUKE O'BRIEN

Stannard Pond

Description: The main part of this nature trail follows a small loop over flat terrain for 0.3 mi. It enters the woods on a wide lane just left of the trailhead kiosk. After passing three side trails on the right, this path makes a gentle U-turn left on its way to Blue Pond. The footing on the latter part of this trail can be difficult as it follows the shoreline back to the parking lot.

In the hilly area next to this loop, a small network of interconnected trails, which total about a half mile in overall length, are worth exploring. One of these paths leads to an open area at the back of a nearby cemetery, with a nice view of Burke Mountain. Another trail follows a more circuitous route to the far end of the parking lot. All the paths are connected to different points on the main loop, except for one aimless path blocked by a large log at the only four-way intersection in this system.

⑫ Stannard Lookout Trail

Located mostly within the Mill Steam Brook Wildlife Management Area, the route described here is a V.A.S.T. snowmobile trail that follows an old logging road and is not built, marked or maintained to the same standards as a hiking trail. While this trail is easy enough to follow, it is often muddy and some areas never completely dry out. If dry weather prevails during the latter part of the summer season, this trail makes for a pleasant outing. Otherwise, wet feet are inevitable.

Distance: 1.7 mi.

To the Trail: The trail begins at a turnout on the south side of Stannard Mountain Road, 0.25 mi. east of a height-of-land. The distance to this roadside parking area, when traveling east from Vt. 16 in Greensboro Bend (opposite The Bend Road), is 5.8 mi. From Lyndonville, the distance is 9.3 mi. west from the junction of U.S. 5 and South Wheelock Road, which leads into Stannard Mountain Road.

Description: From the turnout, the trail descends to a small brook crossing and climbs to a junction, where it turns left onto a wide grassy lane. Continuing south, the route passes a snowmobile trail on the left (0.1 mi.). (Keep in mind that you will want to bear left at this junction on the return.) After crossing a snowmobile bridge (0.3 mi.), the trail continues on easy terrain to an unmistakable side trail on the right (0.7 mi.).

> **Junction:** This pathway makes a long, extremely wet descent to Stannard Pond. A less conspicuous, but shorter and much drier route to the shoreline continues past this first, more obvious, side trail 140 ft. to a smaller opening in the woods, with a log lying across its threshold. This spur path leads 180 ft. to the water's edge. Shorter trails further on also lead to the pond, but they tend to be wet.

Just beyond this point, the main trail climbs over a small ridge, before making its closest approach to Stannard Pond, which is visible through the trees. At 1.0 mi. the trail reaches a perpetually muddy section, then continues uneventfully until it reaches the bottom of a short, but steep, pitch (1.5 mi.). Near the end of this climb, the trail turns left at a three-way junction (1.6 mi.) and continues straight through a final intersection before reaching Stannard Lookout on the right (1.7 mi.). The view from the lookout includes Burke Mountain in Vermont and New Hampshire's Franconia Ridge and Presidential Range.

⓫ Hardwick Trails

Most of these trails follow an extensive network of logging roads in a wooded area behind the Hazen Union School in Hardwick. Much of the terrain is hilly with several steep pitches. While the views are limited, the opportunities for outdoor recreation are plentiful on these multi-purpose trails, which are maintained for year-round, non-motorized use. Trail blazing is color-coded and most of the major junctions are identified by a letter designation on an accompanying locator map. A detailed map is usually available at the trailhead kiosk as well. For more information: www.hardwicktrails.org.

To the Trails: From the junction of Vt. 14 and Vt. 15 in downtown Hardwick (0.0 mi.), follow Vt. 15 (South Main Street) east, then turn left at the next junction on North Main Street (0.1 mi.). Follow North Main Street

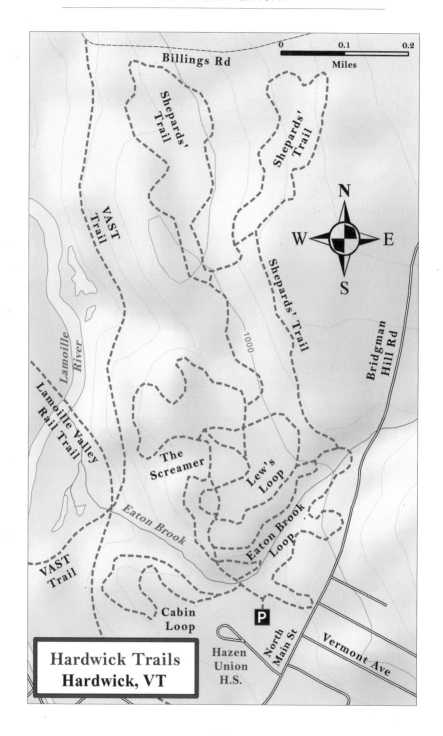

Hardwick Trails
Hardwick, VT

to the entrance for Hazen Union School on the left (0.3 mi.) Turn into the parking area on the right (0.4 mi.). The trailhead kiosk is located at the rear of this lot.

Eaton Brook Loop (a.k.a. Poetry Loop)
Distance: 1.1 mi.

Description: This path is the first of several interconnected trails within this network. It is also one of the easiest to travel. Twelve poetry placards, including several that were written by Hazen Union students, are placed along this route.

Beginning on a dirt road to the left of the kiosk, the Eaton Brook Loop turns right as it climbs uphill and passes the tennis courts. After making a U-turn left, the trail works its way around the Green Mountain Tech Center before entering the woods (0.2 mi.). Gradually, it climbs to a bridge that crosses Eaton Brook. Just beyond this midway point, it passes a junction with the Shepard's Loop on the right. From here it descends back toward the school in a roundabout way before returning to the trailhead (1.1 mi.).

Shepard's Trail
Distance: 2.5 mi.

Description: This blue-blazed trail covers more ground and climbs higher than any other trail in this system. Fortunately, it is also divided into three smaller segments that allow for shorter options. The lower portion is over 0.8 mi. long, the northeast loop adds over 0.7 mi., and the northwest loop adds more than 0.9 mi., for a total distance of 2.5 mi. There are some steep sections and the eastern half of the northwest loop has some long stretches that tend to be wet, but most of the northeast loop stays dry.

The Screamer
Distance: 0.8 mi.

Description: This red-blazed trail connects the lower section of the Eaton Brook Loop with two points on the lower section of the Shepard's Trail. The path is usually dry, but the terrain is steep in a few places. The upper portion trail passes through a grove of maples, part of an active, on-site sugaring operation.

Inner Loop (including Lew's Loop)
Distance: 0.8 mi.

Description: These yellow-blazed trails, which pass over mostly easy terrain, form the center of this sprawling network. Portions tend to be wet, but most of the soggy sections can be avoided by using one of the many alternate routes available.

Cabin Loop
Distance: 0.4 mi.

Description: This indistinct trail begins on an unpaved road behind the school building. After passing a sugarhouse and a log cabin, it diverges from the roadbed and crosses an open area before entering the woods on the right. A short distance later, it emerges from the woods and rejoins the road before returning to the parking lot.

The Farm Barn at Shelburne Farms, Shelburne.

Useful Addresses

Ascutney Trails Association, P.O. Box 147, Windsor VT 05089

Cross Vermont Trail Association, c/o Central Vermont Regional Planning Commission, 29 Main Street, Suite 4, Montpelier VT 05602-2952, 802-498-0079, www.crossvermont.org

Equinox Preservation Trust, P.O. Box 46, Historic Route 7A, Manchester VT 05254, 802-362-4700, www.equinoxpreservationtrust.org

Friends of the West River Trail, P.O. Box 2086, South Londonderry VT 05155, www.westrivertrail.org

Green Mountain National Forest, Forest Supervisor, 231 North Main Street, Rutland VT 05701, 802-747-6700, www.fs.fed.us.

Middlebury District Ranger, 1007 Route 7 South, Middlebury VT 05753, 802-388-4362

Jericho Underhill Park District, P.O. Box 164, Underhill VT 05489, 802-899-2693, www.jerichovt.gov

Kingdom Trails Association, P.O. Box 204, East Burke VT 05832, 802-626-0737, www.kingdomtrails.org

Local Motion, 1 Steele Street, Burlington VT 05401, 802-652-BIKE, www.localmotionvt.org

Middlebury Area Land Trust (MALT), P.O. Box 804, Middlebury VT 05753, 802-388-1007, www.maltvt.org

Millstone Trails Association, 422 Websterville Road, Websterville VT 05678, 802-479-1000, www.millstonetrails.com

Moosalamoo Association, P.O. Box 108, Forest Dale VT 05745-0108, 802-747-7900, www.moosalamoo.org

The Nature Conservancy of Vermont, 27 State Street, Suite 4, Montpelier VT 05602, 802-229-4425, www.nature.org

NorthWoods Stewardship Center, 154 Leadership Drive, P.O. Box 220, East Charleston VT 05833, 802-723-6551, www.northwoodscenter.org

Otter Creek Audubon, P.O. Box 938, Middlebury VT 05753

Putney Mountain Association, P.O. Box 953, Putney VT 05346, 802-387-6635, www.putneymountain.org

Richmond Land Trust, P.O. Box 605, Richmond VT 05477, www.richmondlandtrust.org

Rivendell Trails Association, P.O. Box 202, Fairlee VT 05045, 603-353-4321 x 108, www.crossrivendelltrail.org

Rutland Area Physical Activity Coalition (RAPAC), 67 Merchants Row, Rutland VT 05701, 802-353-0037, www.rapac.info

Rutland County Audubon, P.O. Box 31, Pittsford VT 05763, www.rutlandcountyaudubon.org

Spirit in Nature, P.O. Box 255, East Middlebury VT 05740, 802-388-3694, www.spiritinnature.com

Upper Valley Land Trust, 19 Buck Road, Hanover NH 03755, 603-643-6626, www.uvlt.org

Vermont Department of Fish and Wildlife, 103 Main Street, 10 South, Waterbury VT, 05671-0501, 802-241-3700, www.vtfishandwildlife.com

Vermont Department of Forests, Parks and Recreation, 103 South Main Street, 10 South, Waterbury VT 05671-0601, 802-241-3655, www.vtstateparks.com

Vermont Land Trust, 8 Bailey Avenue, Montpelier VT 05602, 802-223-5234, www.vlt.org

Westmore Association, c/o Paul Moffat, RD 2, Orleans VT 05860, www.westmoreonline.org

The Windham Foundation, 225 Townshend Road, P.O. Box 70, Grafton VT 05146, 802-843-2211, www.windham-foundation.org

Windmill Hill-Pinnacle Association, 35 Sleepy Valley Road, Athens VT 05143, www.windmillhillpinnacle.org

Winooski Valley Park District, Ethan Allen Homestead, Burlington VT 05401, 802-863-5744, www.wvpd.org

Index

Grafton Village Park Trails, 47–49
Grand Isle State Park, 152
Gray, Philip, 225
Greendale Trail, 4, **5**
Green Mountain Audubon Nature Center, 78–79
Green Mountain Audubon Society, 78
Green Mountain Boys, 98
Green Mountain Club, vii; guide, 111; Short
  Trail, 203
Green Mountain National Forest, 6, 17, 18, 90
Green Mountain Trail, 6
Greensboro, 225, **227**
Green Trail (Pittsford Recreation Area), 96
Green Trail (Springweather Nature Area), 36, 39
Griffith Lake, 7
Griffith Lake Trail, 7
Griggs Mountain Loop, 134–35
Groton, 117, **118**
Groton Nature Center, 117
Groton State Forest, 117, **118**, 119–21, 121–22;
  Kettle Pond Hiking Loop, 120–21; Osmore
  Pond Hiking Loop, 119; Owl's Head Moun-
  tain, 119–20
"Groton State Forest Guide" (pamphlet), 117
"Groton State Forest History Guide" (pamphlet),
  117
Grout Pond, 13
Grout Pond Recreation Area, 13–14, **15**
Grout Pond Trails, **15**

H
Half Moon Pond Trail, 104
Half Moon State Park, 103
Hapgood Pond Recreation Area, 11
Hard'ack and Aldis Hill, 146
Hard'ack Inc., 146
Hardwick, 232, **233**
Hardwick Trails, 232, **233**, 234–35; Cabin
  Loop, 235; Eaton Brook Loop, 234; Inner
  Loop, 235; Screamer, the, 234; Shepard's Trail,
  234
Hardwood Ridge Trail, 204
Hardwoods Trail, 149, 150
Harris Hill ski jump, 62, 66
Hartford, 22, 24, **136**
Hartford Parks and Recreation Department, 22
Hartland, 25
Hartness, James, 39
Hartness Park, 39–42; Sidehill Loop, 41–42;
  Wood Thrush Loop, 40–41
Hartness Park Trails, **38**
Hawk Hill, 95
Hawkins Mountain, 127
Hazen Trail, **136**, 137
Healing Springs Nature Trail, 14
Hedgehog Hill Trail, 201, 202

Helen W. Buckner Memorial Preserve, 112–13;
  Susan Bacher Memorial Trail, 113; Tim's Trail,
  112–13
Hemlock Hill Road Trail, 128
Hemlock Island, 14
Henry G. Darling Memorial Recreation Area, 226
Heron Loop, 175
Herschkowitz Extension Loop, 190
High Pond, 94–95
High Swamp Trail, 71
Hilltop Loop Trail (Old Mill Park), 184, 185
Hilltop Trail (Macrae Farm), 160
Hilltop Trail (Old Mill Park), 184
Hinesburg, 76–78; Geprags Park, 76–77; Hines-
  burg Town Forest, 78; Russell Family Trails, 77
Hinesburg Town Forest, 78
"History Hike" (pamphlet), 201
History Hike via Hedgehog Hill Trail and Dalley
  Loop Trail, 201–2
Hitchcock Trail, 98
H. Laurence Achilles Natural Area, 199
Holden Trail, 59, 60
Homestead Loop, 164
Hopkins, John Henry, 164
Hosmer Brook Trail, 119
Howe Truss bridge, 25
Hubbard, John E., 206
Hubbard Park, 206
Hubbard Park Trails, 206
Hubbardton, 103
Hubbardton Battlefield, 98–99
Huntington, 78–80; Green Mountain Audubon
  Nature Center, 78–79; Huntington River Path,
  79–80
Huntington Historical and Community Trust, 79
Huntington River Path, 79–80
Hurricane Brook/Waterbar Loop Trail, 128
Hurricane Forest Wildlife Refuge Park, 22–24;
  Beacon Hill Loop, 23–24; Creek and Monu-
  ment Loop, 23; Pond Loop, 22–23

I
Ice Beds, 3
Ice Beds Road, 3–4
Ice Beds Trail, 3
Ice Pond, 62; from Cedar Street, 66; from Solar
  Hill, 66, 68; from Upper Dummerston Road,
  68; from Retreat Farm, 68
Ice Pond Trail, 66, 68
Independence, Mount, 93–94
Indian Brook Reservoir Park, 156, 170; Circum-
  ferential Trail 170; Overlook Trail, 170–71
Indian Point, 216, 218
Ingalls 4-H Camp, 150
Inner Loop (including Lew's Loop), 235
Island Center for Arts and Recreation, 151